Mobile Learning

Mobile learning is a new way of learning. Mobile devices including handheld computers, mobile phones and smartphones make learning portable, spontaneous, personal and exciting. This book explains the technologies involved, their applications and the multiple effects on pedagogical and social practice.

Emphasising the issues of usability, accessibility, evaluation and effectiveness, and illustrated by case studies drawn from contemporary projects from around the world, this book considers:

- the fundamentals of mobile technologies and devices
- the educational foundations of modern networked learning
- the issues that underpin mobile learning and make it accessible for all users
- the challenges of making mobile learning a substantial and sustainable component in colleges, universities and corporations
- implications and issues for the future.

Mobile Learning provides useful, authoritative and comprehensive guidance for professionals in higher and further education, and trainers in the business sector wanting to find out about the opportunities offered by new technologies to deliver, support and enhance teaching, learning and training.

Agnes Kukulska-Hulme is a Senior Lecturer in Educational Technology in the Open University's Institute of Educational Technology, UK.
John Traxler is a Research Fellow in the Centre for Learning and Teaching and School of Computing and IT at the University of Wolverhampton, UK.

Open and flexible learning series

Series Editors: Fred Lockwood, A.W. (Tony) Bates and Som Naidu

Mobile Learning

A handbook for educators and trainers

Edited by
Agnes Kukulska-Hulme and
John Traxler

Routledge
Taylor & Francis Group

LONDON AND NEW YORK

First published 2005
by Routledge
2 Park Square, Milton Park, Abingdon, Oxon OX14 4RN

Simultaneously published in the USA and Canada
by Taylor & Francis Inc
270 Madison Ave, New York, NY 10016

Routledge is an imprint of the Taylor & Francis Group

© 2005 Agnes Kukulska-Hulme and John Traxler, and contributors

Typeset in Times by
HWA Text and Data Management, Tunbridge Wells
Printed and bound in Great Britain by
The Cromwell Press, Trowbridge, Wiltshire

British Library Cataloguing-in-Publication Data
A catalogue record for this book is available from the British
Library

Library of Congress Cataloging-in-Publication Data
A catalog record for this book has been requested

ISBN 0–415–35739–X (hbk)
ISBN 0–415–35740–3 (pbk)

Contents

Figures

Tables

Contributors

Benedict du Boulay is Dean of the School of Science and Technology at the University of Sussex. His main research interest lies in the application of AI techniques to education, particularly intelligent tutoring systems and the development of tools to support that learning. He is a member of the IDEAs lab which is part of the Human Centred Technology Group (b.du-boulay@ sussex.ac.uk).

Harry Brenton is Departmental Learning Technologist in the Department of Surgical Oncology and Technology St Mary's Hospital, Imperial College, London (h.brenton@imperial.ac.uk).

Diane Brewster is an IDEAs lab (Human Centred Technology Group) researcher at the University of Sussex who is interested in the impact of providing HE students with digital rather than physical learning resources. She is particularly interested in the relationship between 'ownership of learning' and plagiarism (dianeb@sussex.ac.uk).

Susan Bull received her PhD from the University of Edinburgh in 1997. She is now a lecturer at the University of Birmingham. Her research has focused mainly on methods of promoting learner reflection by showing students representations of their understanding using open learner models. More recently she has applied this interest to mobile learning. (s.bull@bham.ac.uk)

Tony Chan is currently a member of staff responsible for the development of the JISC funded Interactive Logbook project (http://www.il.bham.ac.uk). Previously, he had conducted research in the field of mobile learning technology and will imminently complete his PhD. His research interests include: mobile computing, user interface and interaction and data exchanges via web services. (t.k.chan@bham.ac.uk)

Kin Choong Yow is an Assistant Professor and Sub Dean of the School of Computer Engineering, Nanyang Technological University (NTU), Singapore. He leads the MANET group in the Centre for Multimedia and Network Technologies (CeMNeT). His current research interests include multimedia communications, wireless communication technologies, and Mobile Ad-hoc Networking.

Dan Corlett manages a range of innovative learning technology projects at CETADL. Since 2000 he has been researching and developing appropriate systems and tools for distributed mobile learners in Higher Education, with an emphasis on collaboration and learning portfolios. Before that, he led a team developing HandLeR, a mobile computing environment for school field trips. (d.j.corlett@bham.ac.uk)

Judith Gregory is Associate Professor in Information Systems, Department of Informatics, University of Oslo, Norway. Her research interests include social theory approaches to design and use of information systems, design research, understanding design practices and processes, health Informatics and development of qualitative research methods. (judithg@ifi.uio.no)

Kurt Hackemer is Associate Professor of History and Associate Dean of the College of Arts and Sciences at the University of South Dakota (khackeme@ usd.edu, www.usd.edu/~khackeme). He co-chaired the Palm Academic Committee at the University of South Dakota 2002–4 with Doug Peterson.

Claire Kennedy teaches Italian language and contemporary history at Griffith University in Brisbane, Australia. One of her principal research interests is the application of information and communications technologies to language learning. (C.Kennedy@griffith.edu.au)

Roger Kneebone (PhD, FRCS, FRCSEd, MRCGP, ILTM) is Senior Lecturer in Surgical Education, Department of Surgical Oncology and Technology, Imperial College London. His current research focuses on the contextualization of clinical learning. He has developed an innovative approach to learning invasive clinical procedures, where models are attached to simulated patients to create a safe yet realistic learning environment. Initial work with simple procedures is now being extended to a range of more complex tasks. (r.kneebone@imperial.ac.uk)

Chris von Koschembahr is Worldwide m(obile)-Learning Executive with IBM at IBM Southbury, Southbury, CT, USA. (vonkosch@us.ibm.com)

Agnes Kukulska-Hulme's background is in language teaching and linguistics. She is a Senior Lecturer in Educational Technology, Deputy Director of the Open University's Institute of Educational Technology, Chair of one of the Institute's global online Masters courses, and Head of the TeleLearning Research Group. Her research focus is on usability and communication in online and mobile learning environments. (a.m.kukulska-hulme@open.ac.uk)

Mike Levy is Associate Professor of Languages and Linguistics at Griffith University, Australia. His recent books include, *Computer-Assisted Language Learning: Context and Conceptualization* (Oxford University Press, UK, 1997) and *WorldCALL: Global Perspectives on Computer-Assisted Language Learning* (Swets & Zeitlinger, the Netherlands, 1999). He is Associate Editor of the CALL and CALL-EJ online journals and on the editorial boards of the CALICO and ReCALL journals. (michael.levy@griffith.edu.au)

Rosemary Luckin is a Pro-Vice-Chancellor at the University of Sussex and Director of the Human Centred Technology group and IDEAs lab. She is interested in the use of learner centred design and socio-cultural approaches to develop technology that offers learners motivating and adaptive educational experiences. (rosel@sussex.ac.uk)

Jane Magill (BSc, PhD, GRSC) is the Director of the Robert Clark Centre for Technological Education at the University of Glasgow and a Lecturer in the Faculty of Education. She has been researching the use of novel learning and assessment methods for many years and has received several awards for work in this area. (j.magill@elec.gla.ac.uk)

Darren Pearce is an IDEAs lab researcher as part of the Human Centred Technology Group at the University of Sussex. He is interested in natural language processing and the use of technology to support collaborative learning. He is part of the team that has developed the SCOSS (separate control of a shared space) design framework. (darrenp@sussex.ac.uk)

Doug Peterson is Associate Professor of Psychology at the University of South Dakota. In addition he has implemented handheld course review materials into his general psychology course (doupeter@usd.edu). He co-chaired the Palm Academic Committee at the University of South Dakota 2002–4 with Kurt Hackemer.

Mark Polishook is a composer, a jazz pianist, and a new media artist. He is currently an associate professor in the Music Department at Central Washington University where he directs the Music Composition program. From July 2003 to July 2004, he was a visiting professor at Aarhus University in Denmark where he completed Robots-in-Residence (http://robots.music.cwu.edu), an installation that featured robots, sound, video, and incoming e-mail from the audience. (http://www.cwu.edu/~polishoo)

Simon Rae is in the Institute of Educational Technology at The Open University where his recent activities have included participation on various e-learning projects and evaluations of the uses of new technology and of networked learning. He has an MA in Open and Distance Education and research interests in assessment, the acquisition of ICT skills and the use of ICT in the Arts and Humanities. (simon.rae@gmail.com)

Peter Rainger was formerly the Research Officer at the JISC TechDis Service, while based at the University of Sussex as a member of the research faculty in the School of Education. Peter now runs Key2Access Ltd – an Accessibility and Assistive Technology Consultancy. He has interests in e-learning, inclusive learning design, metadata and innovative uses of assistive technology. (peter.rainger@key2access.co.uk)

Andy Ramsden is Learning Technology Adviser with the Learning Technology Support Service at the University of Bristol. (andy.ramsden@bristol.ac.uk)

Paul Rudman has a PhD in Educational Technology from the University of Birmingham. His research interests include the effects of probably-useful ambient information on existing human activities. He has recently completed a two year research fellowship at the University of Glasgow on the Equator project, which investigates the joining of physical and digital information into one unified experience. (rudmanp@dcs.gla.ac.uk)

Scott Roy (BSc, PhD) is a Lecturer in the Department of Electronics and Electrical Engineering at the University of Glasgow. He manages the Microelectronics Process and Device Simulation Centre, a facility dedicated to the use of computer simulation software in the teaching of semiconductor device, technology and integration concepts at undergraduate and postgraduate level and provision of distance learning material in these subjects. Research interests include the effect of the user interface on learning outcomes. (s.roy@elec.gla.ac.uk)

Steve Sagrott has worked for IBM for 25 years in many roles. He is currently a project leader with the IBM Learning Technologies group, specialising in providing an online learning development and delivery service within IBM.

Mike Sharples is Professor of Educational Technology at the University of Birmingham, UK, and Director of the University's Centre for Educational Technology and Distance Learning (CETADL). He is the author of seven books and over 150 other publications in the theory and design of learning technology, artificial intelligence and human–computer interaction.

Richard Siddons-Corby is an experienced teacher and is the technical guru who keeps the IDEAs lab running as part of the Human Centred Technology Group at Sussex University. (rsc@sussex.ac.uk)

Ole Smørdal is Associate Professor at InterMedia, University of Oslo, Norway. His research interests are social theory approaches to understanding and design of ICT-based infrastructure and computer artefact mediation, Health Informatics, Object Oriented Media, Mobility and mobile use, Interaction and Communication Design, Research Mediation and Digital Narratives. (ole.smordal@intermedia.uio.no)

Boon-Hee Soong is currently an Associate Professor with the School of Electrical and Electronic Engineering, Nanyang Technological University (NTU), Singapore. His research interests include ad-hoc networking, wireless networks, seamless mobility and handover strategies, dynamic channel assignment, network modelling for flow control, and economic modelling.

John Traxler's background is in software engineering. He is Learning and Teaching Research Fellow working with the Centre for Learning and Teaching and with the School of Computing and IT at the University of Wolverhampton. His recent work has concentrated on evaluation and development across a range of innovative learning technologies including PDAs, interactive digital TV and large-scale SMS. (John.Traxler@wlv.ac.uk)

Jon Trinder (MSc, IEng) is a part-time PhD student in the Robert Clark Centre for Technological Education at the University of Glasgow. He has been a PDA user and developer for over five years and founded pda-edu@jiscmail.ac.uk to provide a meeting place for anyone interested in using PDAs in education to exchange information and advice. He works in the Department of Electrical Engineering as part of the computing support team. (j.trinder@elec.gla.ac.uk / jont@ninelocks.com)

Ian Weber is an Assistant Professor in the Department of Communication, Texas A&M University, Texas, USA. His research focuses on digital broadcasting, Chinese media and globalization, and media citizenship. He has researched and published extensively on diffusion of new media technologies into Chinese socio-cultural settings in Asia. (iweber@tamu.edu)

Series editor's foreword

Just over a generation ago the opening of the United Kingdom Open University (UKOU) marked the start of a revolution in learning and teaching as it incorporated different media into its distance education programme and focused upon the quality of the learning experience. The combination of print and broadcast media, Home Experiment Kits and tutorials provided learning opportunities for hundreds of thousands of students; 330,000 students have graduated to date. These distance learning methodologies have been refined and adopted worldwide. Indeed, the UKOU is now dwarfed by other mega-universities with distance and open learning methods rapidly becoming mainstream activities.

Mobile Learning, edited by Agnes Kukulska-Hulme and John Traxler, marks the start of another revolution. A revolution that involves access to, usability of, and the pedagogic application of hand-held devices that exploit the power of modern computing, wireless communication and which bring different media and resources to the fingertips of learners at almost any spot on the planet – at a cost substantially less than a conventional desktop machine. This is not an exaggeration, since the World Bank estimates that 77 per cent of the world's population is within reach of a mobile phone network.

Agnes and John have drawn upon their unique international network to assemble a group of colleagues who are not only respected practitioners but also visionaries in the field. The balance they strike between the technical and pedagogic aspects of mobile learning, the case studies and illustrations they provide will be inspirational. Hopefully, it will stimulate a range of initiatives such as the Washington-based World-Link that is providing training for teachers in developing countries in the new technologies. Similarly, Schoolnets around the world are exposing children to the power of the Internet whilst national projects, such as the mobile van that takes the battery-powered technology to villages in Cambodia and the solar-powered technology taken by river to communities in Bangladesh, will be replicated.

Ten years ago Tony Bates, in his book *Technology, Open Learning and Distance Education* (1995), predicted that 'The countries that embrace the new technologies and exploit them in teaching and training will be the economic power houses of the next century'. This prediction, coupled with the potential of mobile learning, is even more valid today. I believe that this book, particularly its contribution to teaching and learning, will contribute to millions of learners achieving their potential and contributing to the development of their country.

I recommend the book to you and your future students.

Fred Lockwood
Manchester, June 2005

Acknowledgements

The editors and authors would like to extend their thanks to: Doug Clow, Martyn Cooper, Adrian Kirkwood, Patrick McAndrew, John Pettit and Josie Taylor from the Open University; Jon Bernardes, Martin Cartwright, Astrid Klaar, Megan Lawton, John O'Donoghue and Brendan Riordan from the University of Wolverhampton; and Alice Mitchell from Ultralab at Anglia Polytechnic University, Jane Seale from Southampton University, and Tony Hulme at IBM. We would also like to thank all those case study contributors who generously gave their time to help us with critical reading of draft chapters.

Chapter 1

Introduction

Agnes Kukulska-Hulme

What is mobile learning?

'Mobile learning' is both a new concept and one that has some familiar connotations. It is certainly concerned with learner mobility, in the sense that learners should be able to engage in educational activities without the constraints of having to do so in a tightly delimited physical location. To a certain extent, learning outside a classroom or in various locations requires nothing more than the motivation to do so wherever the opportunity arises – from books, electronic resources, places and people. What is new in 'mobile learning' comes from the possibilities opened up by portable, lightweight devices that are sometimes small enough to fit in a pocket or in the palm of one's hand. Typical examples are mobile phones (also called cellphones or handphones), smartphones, palmtops and handheld computers (Personal Digital Assistants or PDAs); Tablet PCs, laptop computers and personal media players can also fall within its scope. These devices can be carried around with relative ease and used for communication and collaboration, and for teaching and learning activities that are different from what is possible with other media.

We are beginning to see significant adoption of these technologies in further and higher education, in schools and the community, and in training and updating. They are having an impact on teaching, learning, and on the connections between formal and informal learning, work and leisure. They are extremely interesting for educators due to the low cost of many of these devices relative to desktop computers and the spontaneous and personal access they give to the vast educational resources of the Internet. When combined with wireless connectivity, learning activities can be monitored and coordinated between locations. However, the task of designing such activities and appropriate learner support is complex and challenging. The impacts of the new mobile technologies need to be appraised and evaluated. The purpose of this book is to promote and develop our collective understanding of these new possibilities. We will see how they have begun to be put into practice in education and training, and we will assess their impacts to date.

O'Malley *et al.* (2003) have defined mobile learning as taking place when the learner is not at a fixed, predetermined location, or when the learner 'takes advantage of the learning opportunities offered by mobile technologies' (2003: 6). Mobile learning has a range of attributes that might contribute to its definition:

it can be spontaneous, personal, informal, contextual, portable, ubiquitous (available everywhere) and pervasive (so integrated with daily activities that it is hardly noticed). With these attributes, it has much in common with other types of e-learning on desktop computers, but with the advantages and drawbacks of more varied and changing locations, more immediate ('anytime') interaction, and smaller, often wireless devices. Just as e-learning wrestles with a dual identity – is it just learning, or is the 'electronic' aspect still important? – so mobile learning is partly about learning and partly about the breakthroughs of mobile computing and global marketing of mobile devices. It is rapidly becoming a credible and cost-effective component of on-line and distance learning and anyone developing courses in companies, universities and colleges must consider carefully what it has to offer.

Mobile devices everywhere

To read about mobile learning in the research literature is to enter a world of daunting technical terms and futuristic concepts. However, even for a non-technical person, some computing-related jargon is worth knowing. This includes: 'ubiquitous', 'pervasive' and 'ambient'. These concepts introduce a certain perspective that should be understood in order to get an idea of the direction in which mobile learning is taking us.

'Ubiquitous' began to be used in computer science in the late 1980s, when questions were raised about how computers were embedded within the social framework of daily activity and how they related to the physical environment. Researchers were looking for a radical answer to what they perceived was wrong with the personal desktop computer. Recounting their story, Weiser *et al.* remember that the personal computer was considered to be:

> ... too complex and hard to use; too demanding of attention; too isolating from other people and activities; and too dominating as it colonized our desktops and our lives. We wanted to put computing back in its place, to reposition it into the environmental background, to concentrate on *human-to-human* interfaces and less on *human-to-computer* ones.
>
> (Weiser *et al.* 1999: 693)

If computers were 'ubiquitous', that is, available everywhere and part of our environment, it could be easier to concentrate on learning activities instead of computing hardware being the learner's focus. The next logical step would be for the computing devices to become so small and so easily available in many locations that in a sense they would become invisible and intrude even less on the task in hand. What is more, once all devices were networked, information would only have to be entered once and would then be available whenever and wherever it was needed. 'Pervasive' computing aspires to this ideal:

> We think of pervasive computing as a move from an interaction between an individual and a single device to an abundance of networked mobile and

embedded computing devices that individuals and groups use across a variety of tasks and places.

(Dryer *et al.* 1999: 652)

Taking this even further, 'ambient' technology would be something like ambient temperature or sound – surrounding us completely and perhaps as natural as the air we breathe. For ambient learning to take place, buildings and public spaces would have to be 'learning enhanced': they would have to have devices or systems ready to respond to what is in the learner's field of view, giving information about specific places or objects and enabling on-the-spot interactions. This kind of ambient technology, which is said to 'augment' the environment for learning, is being trialled in urban and natural environments (e.g. Weal *et al.* 2003; Fritz *et al.* 2004).

Mobile devices, whether embedded in the environment or carried around by their users, are redefining the nature of public and private spaces. Learning is becoming more personal, yet at the same time more connected to the surroundings and with more potential for connected, collaborative activity. There is a tension here that comes from the fact that most mobile devices in current use are not designed specifically for education or training but rather for personal (even individual) information management or personal communication largely within work contexts or home and one-to-one social use. The idea of making connections to the environment, to resources and communities or groups of people comes more from educational technology research and practice (e.g. Collis 1996; Preece 2000) and educational research on mobile communities (e.g. Frohberg 2002). It may also be seen in those projects that have the financial resources to design technology and learning spaces that meet specific target user requirements.

Practical mobile learning now and in the future

Although many examples of mobile learning come from computing research that aims to push the boundaries of knowledge and technical capability, there are also plenty of very interesting initiatives and trials resulting from the need to find solutions to practical needs or from seizing opportunities as they arise. Some technologies have already reached very high levels of availability and acceptance – this is the case for mobile phones in many parts of the world. Other devices will follow suit when they become cheaper, lighter, and perhaps when they are able to combine several communication and storage facilities in a single portable device. Educators and trainers can respond to this situation by exploring how these devices may be used for teaching and learning, while bearing in mind the various educational, personal, social and cost implications of such a move. We can also work toward the realization of a long-term vision for the development of institutions and training departments to take account of new staff and student development needs.

Mobile learning is now moving beyond short-term, small-scale pilot projects and is ready to tackle issues of scale, sustainability, accessibility, evaluation, cost-effectiveness and quality in the mainstream of education and training, blending with other forms of delivery and support. This book reflects on existing systems, technologies and pedagogies, addressing key issues such as accessibility and usability. It provides the conceptual framework to understand and evaluate the book's broad range of case studies that show best practice from around the world. These case studies illustrate projects that use mobile devices to enhance and extend individual academic subjects, to provide students with general course support, as well as institution-wide initiatives forming part of a total integrated learning technology provision. The aim of including the case studies is to support teachers, lecturers, trainers, managers and staff developers in thinking through mobile learning in their own institutions, planning for both the present and the future. Throughout the book, we draw on examples and scenarios of how mobile technologies being developed now are starting to be used and may be used in the future.

Keeping up with developments

Mobile learning is an extremely fast-moving field that is both specialized and interwoven with daily life and work. Every day there are new developments and new facts and figures about device ownership and patterns of use that require us to stop and think about the implications. For example, according to one source, Hong Kong mobile users send an average of 23 text messages a month compared with 124 in China, 219 in Singapore and 466 in the Philippines (Textually.org 2004). What are the reasons for such differences – are they technical, economic, social or cultural? Many such questions remain unanswered.

To keep up with developments in this field, there is a growing pool of dedicated conferences, seminars and workshops. MLEARN began in 2002 and has become an annual event. Another regular dedicated event is the International Workshop on Mobile and Wireless Technologies in Education (WMTE). Other events have included The National Workshops and Tutorials on Handheld Computers in Universities and Colleges, held in the United Kingdom; The Social Science of Mobile Learning, held in Hungary; and the ICML (International Conference on Mobile Learning): New Frontiers and Challenges, held in Malaysia.

There have also been a rising number of references to mobile learning at generalist conferences such as Online Educa Berlin, the world's largest international e-learning conference, and ED-MEDIA, the world conference on educational multimedia, hypermedia and telecommunications. Issues of usability and interaction with mobile devices are the focus of events such as the annual International Symposium on Human–Computer Interaction with Mobile Devices and Services. As academic learning becomes more integrated with workplace learning, we are also seeing a growing emphasis on collaborative ways of working and learning, including collaboration using mobile devices. Mobile technology can be used as a bridge between formal and informal learning. In the United States, mobile learning has been one of the key themes of the EDUCAUSE National Learning Infrastructure Initiative.

Aims, structure and target readers

We want to introduce mobile learning to a wide readership by making the topic accessible in spite of its associated technical jargon, and by giving it a certain structure. We offer in-depth treatments of mobile technologies, pedagogical approaches, usability and accessibility. A rich array of case studies illustrates how mobile technologies are being used and evaluated in a number of different learning situations. We then address the place of mobile learning strategies and projects within the wider institutional context, and finally we draw out some overall conclusions about the current aims and state of mobile learning and possible future developments.

This book is intended for lecturers, tutors, trainers, developers, managers and researchers in universities and colleges and in commercial training. Some may be tasked with showing others how to use mobile technologies for teaching and learning, or explaining key benefits and concepts. Many are increasingly aware of the educational potential of handheld computers and mobile communications devices and may know of the growing number of studies, trials and pilots that are currently exploring this potential across a range of settings and subjects. This book draws on the most illuminating and imaginative of these in order to provide a comprehensive examination of mobile learning in further and higher education and training. We aim to provide interested professionals in education and training ('teachers', for short) with both a well-informed grasp of the principles and concepts and a familiarity with the breadth of current experience and practice. The book does not assume any technical knowledge of mobile devices. A glossary of terms is provided for convenience.

Readers will probably position themselves differently in their own definitions of mobile learning, as indeed do the various contributors to this book: there are many ways to conceptualize, theorize about and experiment with mobile learning. We hope that this book addresses key aspects of mobile learning that need to be understood, as well as offering a range of 'entry points' to this topic according to readers' preferences, interests and needs.

Bibliography

Collis, B. (1996) *Tele-learning in a Digital World: The Future of Distance Learning*, London: International Thomson Computer Press.
Dryer, D.C., Eisbach, C. and Ark, W.S. (1999) At what cost pervasive? A social computing view of mobile computing systems, *IBM Systems Journal – Pervasive Computing*, 38(4): 652–76.
Fritz, G., Seifert, C., Luley, P., Paletta, L. and Almer, A. (2004) Mobile Vision for Ambient Learning in Urban Environments, MOBILEARN 2004 – Learning Anytime Everywhere, Rome, 5–6 July 2004. On-line. Available HTTP http://www.mobilearn.org/download/events/mlearn_2004/presentations/Paletta.pdf (accessed 14 October 2004).
Frohberg, D. (2002) Communities – the MOBIlearn perspective. Workshop on Ubiquitous and Mobile Computing for Educational Communities: Enriching and Enlarging Community Spaces, International Conference on Communities and Technologies,

Amsterdam, 19 September 2003. On-line. Available HTTP http://www.idi.ntnu.no/~divitini/umocec2003/Final/frohberg.pdf (accessed 14 October 2004).

National Statistics, UK (2004) Oftel Residential Survey. On-line. Available HTTP http://www.statistics.gov.uk/STATBASE/ssdataset.asp?vlnk=7202 (accessed 14 October 2004).

O'Malley, C., Vavoula, G., Glew, J.P., Taylor, J., Sharples, M. and Lefrere, P. (2003) MOBIlearn WP4 – Guidelines for Learning/Teaching/Tutoring in a Mobile Environment. On-line. Available HTTP http://www.mobilearn.org/download/results/guidelines.pdf (accessed 19 November 2004).

Preece, J. (2000) *Online Communities: Designing Usability, Supporting Sociability*, Chichester: Wiley.

Textually.org (2004) Hong Kong children top mobile phone ownership in Asia. On-line. Available HTTP http://www.textually.org/textually/archives/004862.htm (accessed 14 October 2004).

Weal, M.J., Michaelides, D.T., Thompson, M.K. and De Roure, D.C. (2003) The Ambient Wood Journals – Replaying the Experience, Proceedings of ACM Hypertext '03, 14th Conference on Hypertext and Hypermedia 2003, Nottingham, UK. On-line. Available HTTP http://www.equator.ac.uk/PublicationStore/p307–weal.pdf (accessed 14 October 2004).

Weiser, M., Gold, R. and Brown, J.S. (1999) The origins of ubiquitous computing research in the late 1980s, *IBM Systems Journal – Pervasive Computing*, 38(4): 693–6.

Chapter 2

Mobile technologies and systems

Jon Trinder

This chapter will provide the basic context and framework for understanding the technical environment and systems within which mobile learning operates. It will look at emerging and established systems, especially their technical characteristics, performance and connectivity. There is a glossary at the back of the book that provides additional simple explanations of many of the relevant concepts and more technical explanations are also available (Sharples and Beale 2003; Burkhardt *et al.* 2002).

We are primarily concerned with Personal Digital Assistants (PDAs) and mobile phones or smartphones, but there are many other handheld device types that share their characteristics in size, form or function. These range from simple single-purpose devices, such as audio players, to multipurpose devices that typically combine a PDA or phone with other functionalities such as cameras and MP3 players. Figure 2.1 shows there are many different functions that may be combined into a mobile device.

We will start by examining these two popular handheld devices – the mobile phone and the PDA.

Mobile phones

Probably the most popular and widely owned handheld device is the mobile phone. Even the most basic phones provide simple Personal Information Management (PIM) tools, such as address books and calendars. More advanced phones incorporate cameras and infrared or Bluetooth connectivity enabling information, for instance address book entries, to be 'beamed' to other similar devices. Many phones contain modems. This means they can be used to connect other devices, e.g. laptops and PDAs, to the Internet. In addition to voice communication, most phones provide at least some of the following facilities:

* Short Messaging Service (SMS) – Text-based service that allows messages of up to 160 characters to be sent to other phone users. Some manufacturers have extended the SMS capability to enable sending simple picture messages. These pictures are small bitmap images, not photographs, and may be chosen from a built-in library or sent to the phone from another suitable device.

Figure 2.1 Types and functionality of mobile devices

- Multimedia Messaging Service (MMS) – An extension to SMS that enables other types of media, such as photographs, movies and sound files to be sent.

Personal digital assistants

A PDA is a computer-based handheld device that incorporates personal organizer tools. It also has the ability to exchange information easily with a desktop PC. PDAs were originally designed to act as electronic equivalents of diaries and personal organizers, but most can now perform a variety of additional functions. On many models, you can display documents, write notes, do word searches, play games, record your voice, listen to sound files, view pictures and video clips, and take photographs.

Computing power that, in the past, was only available on a desktop machine is now available in these pocket-sized devices. It is even possible to obtain a PDA-sized personal computer that runs the same version of Windows as a desktop machine. So if we can carry a mini PC in our pocket that can 'do everything', why do we still need PDAs, MP3 players and a variety of other mobile and handheld devices?

Although a PDA is a computer-based appliance, it should not be considered a computer in the same way as a laptop or desktop PC (and in fact, we make the analogous case for mobile learning, it should not be considered in the same way as desktop learning). The PDA's purpose is to provide adequate performance and functionality for specific tasks. Many computer-based mobile devices, such as MP3 players and digital cameras, hide their internal complexity behind simple task-oriented interfaces that enable a user to focus on the task the device is designed to perform and not on the device itself. The computer inside has become invisible.

A PC is a versatile general-purpose tool, but it is often better to use a simple, specialized tool optimized for a specific task. This is the domain of 'Information Appliances'. The psychologist Norman (1998) defines an Information Appliance as

> An appliance specialising in information: knowledge, facts, graphics, images, video or sound. An information appliance is designed to perform a specific activity, such as music, photography, or writing. A distinguishing feature of information appliances is the ability to share information among themselves.
>
> (Norman 1998: 53)

A basic PDA provides the functionality of a personal organizer. It has built-in PIM facilities including: diary or calendar; tasks or to-do lists; notepad or memo; contacts or address book; but, like a personal computer or the more advanced mobile phones, it can also provide a rich variety of additional functions depending on its configuration.

A handheld device such as a PDA is a combination of hardware, operating system and application programs. There are many manufacturers of PDA hardware, whilst Palm, Microsoft and Symbian produce the most popular operating systems. Application programs are available from a wide variety of developers and sources.

A PDA though should be considered as operating within a different domain to a PC. It is a different type of device for use in different ways. PDAs '… should not be viewed as replacements for laptops or desktops, rather as useful, lightweight portable adjuncts to these systems' (Smith 2003: 2). The size of the display on the device forces a PDA to be different. What works well on a large screen does not necessarily work well on a small screen (Malliou et al. 2002).

People use their PDAs very differently from how they use their PCs. A desktop system is usually only switched on once per day, therefore a long 'boot-up' time is acceptable. Applications are typically used for long periods and, again, users accept waiting for an application to start up. The typical use for a PDA, however, is to use it to quickly look up or jot down a piece of information, so the device must respond quickly. Most PDAs are instantly ready at switch on and have no latency or 'boot-up' time. Any delays, however small, will detract from how useful the device is and become a barrier to its use. The designer of the PalmOS interface uses the analogy of how annoying a wristwatch would be if, to check the time, you had to 'boot up' your watch and wait for several seconds for the time to appear (Bergman 2000).

Figure 2.2 A 'typical' PDA

An important factor in the versatility of a PDA is how easy it is to exchange and synchronize data with other devices. One of the Palm designers, Jeff Hawkins, described the Palm as being '... a tentacle reaching back to your desktop' (Rhodes and McKeehan 1999: 7). It enables you to carry with you a view of data that may be stored on your PC. This is done either via a cable or wireless connection, a process known as 'Synching' (the term used by Palm is 'HotSynching' and Microsoft use the term 'ActiveSync').

Most PDAs can easily synchronize data with popular desktop PIM applications such as Microsoft Outlook, and exchange data with other applications, such as word processors and spreadsheets, using third party applications. Beaming is usually used to exchange information, such as address book entries, between other handheld devices like mobile phones or another PDA.

The anatomy of a PDA

There are various physical designs of PDA, but a 'typical' device is illustrated in Figure 2.2.

Some other common form factors are illustrated in Figure 2.3. An unusual variation is the Alphasmart Dana, a PalmOS based machine with a full size integrated QWERTY keyboard.

Screens

Most PDA screens are touch-sensitive and a stylus is used to draw or tap on the screen for data entry or navigation. The PDA screen is one of the largest, expensive and most vulnerable components of the device, and one of the most important. For a phone or PDA to be truly mobile it must be lightweight and compact enough

Smartphone   Clamshell

Figure 2.3 Differing shapes and layouts of PDAs

to be carried in a pocket and this places a constraint on the maximum physical size of screen that can be integrated into the device (Malliou *et al.* 2002).

Screen size should not be confused with screen resolution. The screen resolution refers to the dimension of the screen in pixels rather than the physical size of the screen. Most current PDAs have colour screens, but there are still a few with monochrome screens that can usually display 16-level greyscale. Monochrome screens do have some advantages – they are easily viewable in bright sunlight and as they do not require a backlight (except at night!), devices using monochrome screens have better battery life.

Current colour screens are normally lit from either the back or the front, dependent on the display type. The backlight is an extra drain on the battery, but some displays are usable in bright light without needing a backlight.

There are three main types of display screen currently in use:

- Transmissive – the pixels are lit internally from the back
- Reflective – light from the front of the screen reflects back
- Transflective – a combination of transmissive and reflective.

Organic Light Emitting Diode (OLED) displays are gaining popularity. These emit light directly and do not require a backlight. OLED displays are much brighter, have lower power requirements and better viewing angles than the above display technologies.

Navigation buttons

The number of buttons and their purpose is dependent on the type and manufacturer of the device. A phone usually has a numeric keypad and some extra multipurpose buttons to navigate menus, whereas PDAs traditionally have a minimal number of physical buttons to provide rapid access to the most important functions. Most

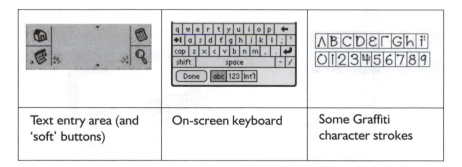

| Text entry area (and 'soft' buttons) | On-screen keyboard | Some Graffiti character strokes |

Figure 2.4 Screen text and data entry options

PDAs have at least four buttons dedicated to launching frequently used applications. By default, these are Diary, To-Do List, Notepad and Address book. The application launched by each button is usually reconfigurable by the user.

Until recently most buttons on PDAs were simple pushbuttons but the influence of mobile phone technology can now be seen with the inclusion of jog dials, roller wheels and other controls. Jog dials and roller wheels can be used to navigate through menus or scroll the screen and are positioned to facilitate the use of the PDA with one hand. A recent innovation has been the inclusion of five way navigation pads (also known as DPads). These usually appear as one large button or small joystick and are effectively five buttons disguised as one.

Text and data entry

Most PDAs do not have a physical keyboard and instead use some form of handwriting recognition. Handwriting recognition can be broadly divided into those that recognize cursive handwriting, and those notational systems that require each letter to be input in isolation. Notational systems require the user to learn special strokes to represent each character. The most widely used is the Graffiti system found on PalmOS PDAs. PDAs using Graffiti have a special screen area for entering the strokes, divided into two input areas: one for entering numbers, the other for entering letters and punctuation. Utilising separate areas simplifies the recognition of similar number and letter shapes, e.g. S and 5. Graffiti is quite easy to learn, as most of the shapes are very similar to the character they represent. The majority of devices also provide a 'pop-up' on-screen keyboard that can be tapped on with a stylus (see Figure 2.4), and there are a number of portable keyboards available.

Some PDAs and smartphones incorporate a physical keyboard, though its size, key spacing and usability depend on the size and form factor of the device. Most are only adequate for the entry of small amounts of text; however, with the addition of an external keyboard (advisable when large amounts of text are to be entered) the PDA can provide a convenient alternative to a laptop. External add-on keyboards are available in various formats:

- Rollup flexible full-size keyboards
- Mini keyboards
- Thumb keyboards
- Projection keyboards.

Projection keyboards are an emerging technology. They project an image of a keyboard onto any solid surface. The system uses optical recognition to sense where the user is typing on the virtual keyboard.

Speech and alternative means of input and output

Although most PDAs use a touch-sensitive display screen for the display and entry of information, there are other user interface methods. Because of the increased computing power incorporated into current mobile devices, speech recognition has become more practical.

Speech recognition converts speech into text allowing information to be spoken into a PDA. Text-to-speech conversion enables a device to speak the contents of the display screen or file, e.g. a PDA could read an e-book to you. Many entry-level PDAs can be used as simple voice recorders or Dictaphones but do not have adequate processing power to provide speech recognition. Some of these are capable of text-to-speech conversion.

Such speech functionality can make PDAs more accessible to users with visual disabilities. There are also special Braille PDAs, (www.pulsedata.com/Products/Notetakers/braillenotepk.asp).

CPU and memory

To provide basic PDA functionality only requires a modest amount of memory or processing power: in 2002, a basic Palm PDA had 16MB of RAM and a 16MHz processor. However, the trend is for faster CPUs and more memory – this is the result of the integration of multimedia applications, such as video players and MP3 players, etc. For current PDAs processor speeds range from 105–400MHz with 21–64MB of RAM. When looking at the specifications of PDAs it should be noted that not all the RAM is available to the user and variable amounts are reserved for operating system use.

On a typical desktop PC, data and programs are stored on a disk drive. When a program is run, it is first copied automatically into the system's RAM, where it is then executed. Most PDAs do not incorporate a disk drive and instead use the PDA's RAM to store data and programs. As the program is already in the main memory it does not have to be moved in order for it to be executed and can be 'executed in place' (XIP). PDAs may also store programs (as well as data) on removable 'flash' memory cards. The use of a flash memory card is analogous to a disk drive on a desktop system.

Flash memory is 'non-volatile' and retains its contents when power is turned off. Flash memory cards are available in a number of different types and sizes, ranging in size from 16MB (approx. £15) to 6GB (£1,000+). The most common types are:

- CompactFlash – The oldest of the currently used Flash card formats and used in a wide variety of devices. 12GB cards are available but, at time of writing (October 2004), extremely expensive.
- MultiMediaCards (MMC) and SecureDigital (SD) cards are the same shape and size and so are interchangeable in many applications. SD cards incorporate encryption functions and are faster than MMC as they have a 4-bit interface compared to the single bit MMC interface.
- MiniSD is less than half the size of a normal SD card. Special adapters are available to allow them to be used in normal SD card slots.
- Memory Stick – Invented by Sony and used mainly in their cameras, PDAs and music players. Limited to a maximum size of 128MB.
- Memory Stick Pro – As above but available in sizes above 128MB, the currently largest available card is 2GB.

Currently the most widely used card types used in PDAs are MMC/SD cards. CompactFlash is still popular for use in high-end digital cameras.

It is possible to store programs on one of the above types of memory card but in order to run the program it must first be copied into the device's main memory (when a program is run it is automatically copied into the device's memory). This is the same as running a program on a desktop system; the program is first loaded from the storage device (normally your hard drive) into RAM, where it is then executed.

Memory cards are used by many devices so can provide a simple means of transferring data between other devices, for example images could be transferred from a digital camera and then viewed or e-mailed using the PDA.

Communications

PDAs now use various methods for exchanging information. These include direct connection to the PDA by cables, usually Universal Serial Bus (USB), and various wireless connection technologies mainly:

Infrared: Most PDAs incorporate an infrared port that is used for 'beaming' items such as memos and business cards to other IrDA (Infrared Data Association) enabled devices such as PDAs, phones or desktop systems. Selection of the device to communicate with is by simply pointing at it. It is a short distance (a couple of metres) 'line of sight' system.

Bluetooth: A short distance radio system with a range of around ten metres. Selecting which device to exchange data with is more complicated than using IrDA but the devices do not have to be 'in line of sight' with each other.

Bluetooth and infrared are complementary technologies, each with its own advantages in different situations. Infrared has some advantages over other radio based wireless technologies, as it is less likely to be intercepted by other users and is line of sight. In addition, it does not 'leak' through walls. For beaming a business card, it is easy to select who you are beaming the card to by pointing at their machine. With Bluetooth, however, the selection is much more time consuming as the sending device has to first locate and pair with the intended receiving device. This may not take long if there are only a few other Bluetooth devices in the vicinity, but if there are many (such as at a conference or classroom) it can.

Wireless Fidelity (Wi-Fi): A radio system usually used for connection to corporate LANs (Local Area Networks) to provide Internet connectivity. The two main variations are known as 802.11b (with a speed of approx 11MB/sec) and 802.11g (with a speed of 54MB/sec). New variations are emerging all the time and more public spaces, for example hotels, cafés and stations, are becoming wireless-enabled.

Battery

Most current PDAs use built-in rechargeable batteries based on Lithium Ion or Lithium Polymer technology. Recharging a PDA usually takes 2–4 hours. Portable battery-powered 'travel' chargers, powered by easily obtainable disposable alkaline batteries, are available. Lithium Ion and Lithium Polymer batteries do not need to be fully discharged prior to charging and will benefit from frequent top-up charging (Buchmann 2001).

Manufacturers claim a fully charged battery in a PDA is sufficient for 5–15 days of normal use. It should be noted that many manufacturers' definition of typical use is often rather unrealistic, e.g. 30 minutes use per day, not including the date book application and with the backlight switched off, which considering that most screens now require a backlight to be readable, is not really typical use.

When a PDA is switched off, it is not actually completely turned off; instead the system is put into a low-power 'sleep' mode, with most of the electronics switched off. During sleep mode, power is still supplied to the memory so that data and programs in the memory are not lost. It is important that batteries are not allowed to run out as any data stored in the PDA memory, e.g. diary entries, is likely to then be lost (removable storage cards are *not* affected). Some systems include auxiliary internal batteries specifically to maintain the memory in the event that the main batteries fail, but this may not last long. Most systems will give a warning when the battery level is getting low and refuse to power on before the batteries are totally exhausted, thus conserving the data in memory for a short while.

Some devices (mainly portable audio/video players) still use disposable batteries that have a greater capacity than rechargeable batteries. When they run low, replacements can be easily obtained.

PDA designers have employed various strategies to maximize battery life. Earlier systems conserved battery power by using various 'sleep' modes. For instance, whilst using a calendar application that is displaying static information the processor and many peripherals can be turned off. Current systems now employ more intelligent and adaptive mechanisms to reduce power consumption. By varying the supply voltage of the CPU and optimizing the speed the processor is running at, considerable power saving may be made with a consequent increase in battery life.

The operating system

The main operating systems in use on PDAs and smartphones are:

- Palm Operating System, used for PDAs and smartphones
- Microsoft Pocket PC ('Windows') operating system, also used for PDAs and smartphones
- Symbian, used for some smartphones.

There are also a number of devices that use a version of Linux.

The operating system is responsible for managing the resources of any computer. Resources include:

- Memory
- Input/output ports
- Scheduling of internal system tasks
- Managing data storage.

The operating system also provides an Application Programmers Interface (API). An API is a set of functions that is used by application programs. The API provides basic building blocks that a programmer combines with other functions to create a program. The API also provides an abstraction away from the real underlying hardware, such as input and output ports, sometimes called I/O ports. The programmer interacts with hardware through the API – this is important as it allows some parts of the underlying hardware to change without the need for new versions of a program. If changes need to be made to the operating system, these are often minor and are achieved by loading 'system patches' or new drivers.

Synchronization and back-up

Synchronization or 'synching' checks and updates data, such as appointments, contact details, and documents, on the handheld and another device, such as a desktop:

- If one version has not been changed since the previous 'synch' and the other has, the most recent version will be written to both devices
- If neither has been altered, no changes are needed
- If both are changed, the necessary action is decided by the desired automatic setting, such as 'handheld overwrites desktop', or each contentious case can be flagged for individual decision.

Synching between one desktop or laptop and one handheld is straightforward. It is also easy to synch one handheld to two or more desktops or laptops. Synching a group of handhelds, such as with a class of students, to a single desktop or laptop, is problematic – for example, where some data is public and some is personal, the computers must be specifically instructed to avoid accidentally deleting or distributing the personal data. It is a technical issue (Hansmann *et al.* 2002) and it might be best to use proprietary software for synching between multiple devices.

'Back-up' or copying information to another computer or device for safekeeping and archiving, usually happens as part of the synching process.

Software and content

Although the PDA was originally intended to act as an electronic replacement for personal organizers, developers have produced a rich variety of other innovative solutions. A big shock for the new PDA user is that when looking for a particular type of application, they are faced with having to choose one from a large number on offer!

PDA software is relatively inexpensive compared to desktop applications and most costs from $5 to $30. There are a large number of high-quality free applications available and many are supplied with source code enabling them to be modified by a user with programming knowledge. There is plenty of choice in the field of PDA software and for almost every type of application there are a number of competing products. As an example, a search at a software website for database applications listed 100+ applications for PalmOS-based PDAs, 50+ for Pocket PC-based PDAs, and 30+ for Symbian-based smartphones.

Many companies produce different versions of an application to suit each of the most popular PDA platforms and may also have a version that will operate on a PC. An application program is written for a specific operating system running on a specific set of hardware. This has an important and often overlooked consequence: a program written to run on Windows XP on a desktop computer will *not* run on a Pocket PC, nor will a program intended for a PalmOS PDA work on a Pocket PC, and vice versa. A separate version of each must be used depending on the device (there is some interoperability with applications written for mobile versions of JAVA).

Shareware: The majority of PDA software is 'shareware'. Shareware software allows you to 'try before you buy'. An evaluation version is normally available for no cost and can be used on a trial basis for a specified period (typically 7–30 days). If you wish to continue to use the software after the trial period, you are required to buy and register the software. During the demo period, some shareware programs will display 'nag screens' to encourage registration and, after the demo period has expired, most either refuse to run or run with limited functionality. There are a number of download sites where shareware software can be downloaded and registered. Once an application is registered, the author sends a registration key to unlock the software and remove any nag screens or limitations. Registration keys are often linked to the user's PDA 'hotsync' name, and so cannot be used on the device of another user.

Office applications: If you have a requirement to view or modify documents from Microsoft Office, it does not mean you need to use a Pocket PC-based PDA. Many PDAs including PalmOS PDAs are supplied with applications that enable documents from programs such as Microsoft Word to be viewed on a PDA. Some applications also allow 'Office' documents to be created and edited on the PDA and transferred to a desktop computer. In some cases, the document is automatically converted to a different format for use on the PDA and then back to Office format when transferred back to the desktop (the files that are converted are considerably smaller); in other cases it is edited still within the appropriate 'Office' format, the so-called 'native' mode.

Internet Applications: With the improvement in Internet connectivity of PDAs there has been an increase in the number of Internet applications, including web browsers, e-mail and SMS clients, and File Transfer Protocol (FTP) clients. Google, the search engine, has a PalmOS-specific version (www.google.com/palm).

In addition to applications, there is also a large amount of 'content' readily available for use on PDAs in the form of e-books, newspapers and reference databases, much of which is readily downloadable from the web.

E-books: There are a number of different formats for e-books, some of the more popular being:

- Mobipocket (available for PalmOS/Pocket PC)
- Microsoft eBook (Pocket PC)
- Palm Reader (PalmOS and Pocket PC).

It is easy to produce your own e-book and programs to convert existing documents into the various e-book formats are available for a modest cost. Some types of e-books enable content to be copy protected. Programs such as Mobipocket allow you to save web pages on your PC then to load them into the PDA as an e-book.

News Readers: daily news channels can be downloaded for off-line reading via popular applications such as AvantGo and Mobipocket.

Reference: There are a large number of database applications for PDAs reflecting one of the PDA's most popular uses – to keep lists and reference information. There are on-line resources providing databases of specialized reference inform-ation for the most popular handheld database formats. Many of these are free.

Software development

If one of the many PDA applications does not quite provide the functionality that you require then you may want to write your own. PDA users from many professions have written their own software to provide specialized applications.

Writing a customized application does not have to be daunting depending on the type of application you require – for data collection many database applications can be customized to provide the required data entry forms.

There are variations of Visual Basic RAD (Rapid Application Development) environments for most PDA operating systems. For programmers wishing to write low-level code, the main choices are C, C++ or JAVA.

There are limitations that must be taken into consideration when designing an application for use on a PDA. Apart from the limitations enforced by the size of the display, many devices do not have a keyboard, and rely on handwriting recognition. Even on machines with a miniature keyboard entering large amounts of text is time-consuming. It is better to provide choices for a user to select from, using interface devices such as lists and check boxes (Palm 2003).

JAVA

Ideally, it should be possible to develop a platform-independent application that could be used on any of the currently available systems and easily adaptable to future devices. One way of providing platform independence is through the use of 'virtual machines'. Rather than a program being written to run on a specific platform it is instead written for a virtual machine. Thus a program written for the virtual machine may run on any platform for which there is a virtual machine interpreter program available.

This concept is the basis for the JAVA programming language. Programs written in JAVA are compiled into virtual machine instructions. There are implementations of JAVA Virtual Machines for many types of system, from small, embedded devices to large mainframe systems. Obviously the capabilities in speed and storage vary widely between that of a small, embedded processor used in a consumer device such as a phone and the capabilities of a multiprocessor workstation or server.

To support these variations of system capabilities there are a number of subsets of the full JAVA implementation. There are an increasing number of mobile phones and PDAs that support JAVA. Manufacturers have attempted to create a generic portable device platform with the standardization of the JAVA Connected Limited Device Configuration (CLDC) specification (Sun 2004a) and Mobile Information Device Profile (MIDP) (Sun 2004b).

The evolution of PDAs

Design approaches

There are now wide varieties of PDA type devices and to understand the differences between apparently similar devices we need to look at how PDAs have evolved. A major factor in this evolution is the operating system. Palm and Microsoft, for example, approached the design of the PDA and its operating system in different ways. The Microsoft strategy was to produce a cut-down version of its Windows desktop operating system. Their reasoning was that by maintaining the same interface 'look-and-feel' users would be familiar with how to use it. Microsoft produced the operating system with other companies such as Hewlett Packard designing the hardware. The first devices running Windows CE, as it is known, were of clamshell design.

As Palm designed both the hardware and software, they were able to make quick tradeoffs between the two. Palm designed a new operating system and user interface specifically for use on a small-screen device that was powered by batteries. Palm's philosophy was to first specify what tasks a PDA should be capable of performing and then design a device that used the minimum of technology to perform those tasks adequately.

Palm's designers realized that the design parameters for a small screen device were radically different to design for a desktop PC. Palm did not rely on their user's familiarity with another interface. Instead, they designed the system to be easy to learn and quick to use. A lot of thought went into the user interface and the built in PIM applications to reduce the number of steps required to perform a task. Amongst the documentation for Palm developers is a document called 'The Zen of Palm' that explains their philosophy and illustrates their approach to design; even some of Palm's competitors' developer documentation refers to this document!

The effect on the hardware requirements of the different approaches to design made by Palm and Microsoft can be seen in Table 2.1, which shows the difference in the specification of devices available in 1996.

Convergence

As technology continues to improve it will be possible to integrate even more features into small handheld devices and we are likely to see many different types of hybrid device appearing. Different functions may be combined for convenience or to complement existing features. A danger of combining functionality in one device is that compromises have to be made with the interface and this might reduce the overall usability of the device.

However, there are many applications for which a combined device may not be suitable or desirable. Combinations that appeal to the public may not be suitable for use in business and education environments. For example, many phones now incorporate a camera but some companies and schools ban cameras on their premises and this includes those built into devices such as phones and PDAs.

As we have said above, technologies such as cameras and MP3 players are being integrated into many different types of handheld and mobile device, such as

Table 2.1 The first Palm and Windows CE machine specifications

Operating System	PDA	CPU speed	RAM	Screen size (pixels)	Battery life
Windows CE	Hewlett Packard HP 300LX	44MHz	2MB	640 * 240	20 hours
PalmOS	Palm Pilot 1000	16MHz	128K	160 * 160	6–8 weeks

phones and PDAs, and simplified PIM tools are even integrated into MP3 players. It seems likely we may all own a variety of devices, many of which overlap in their purpose.

Mobile phones have become fashion statements and users frequently change their phones. Phones have also become both 'throw-away' and 'throw-about' items. Many people prefer a phone to be as small as possible: this sets a constraint on the size of the screen. PDAs, however, are not treated in quite the same way. This may be because their screens are more vulnerable to damage as they tend to be larger, or it may be because the devices are perceived differently.

Personal Digital Assistant or merely Portable Digital Assistant?

Whilst many laptop users would consider allowing a colleague to use or even borrow their laptop for a day and many people would lend their mobile phone, albeit briefly, to a friend, a PDA user is unlikely to let someone else borrow their PDA. A PDA is a *personal* device. The personal qualities of the device are reinforced by a combination of customization of the device by the installation of applications and the personal nature of the data stored on the device.

This is worth bearing in mind when looking at handheld devices for learning. A PDA is unlikely to be used to its full potential if it is only loaned to a student and merely becomes a *Portable* rather than *Personal* Digital Assistant.

Security

As confidential and personal data may be stored on a PDA, security is an important consideration – what happens if the device is lost or left on the train? At its simplest level, security may be provided by a password that is issued to restrict access either to the device or particular records on the device. More advanced security measures include the encryption of important files.

The use of passwords can be problematic on PDAs; as data entry is not particularly fast the action of entering a password may be greater than the time the device is being used for! There are a number of alternative security mechanisms available for PDAs that are quicker than entering a password:

*   Biometric mechanisms such as dynamic signature recognition, where you 'sign in' to the PDA using your signature. The software analyses your signature and how you write it.
*   Fingerprint recognition devices.
*   A 'picture password' is an interesting alternative to a written password. A picture is displayed and the user taps a special secret point on the image to unlock the device.

The future

The dividing line between mobile phones, smartphones and PDAs has become less distinct and it is becoming more difficult to differentiate between the available devices (already there are phones with built-in hard disk drives). Advertising tries to convince us that a particular machine is better because it has more features, more storage, or a faster processor. In many respects, it is a pity the improved performance of modern systems is only used to cram more features into a device, rather than making the device easier to use.

Perhaps we would be better having a collection of specialized separate devices that performed their intended tasks well and could communicate with each other, variations of the 'information appliances' mentioned earlier in this chapter. The PDA would be a combination of the devices being carried rather than one device that attempts to do everything.

As we will be carrying more information, the need to keep back-up copies will become more important and it may be advantageous that some of the devices we carry do duplicate some functionality, e.g. keeping a copy of important names and address on both your phone and PDA.

Choosing a PDA

The best PDA for your purpose depends on what you intend to use it for. The main areas of PDA use are shown in Figure 2.5.

When choosing a PDA or other mobile device, remember that what suits one person may not suit another. Approach the task with an open mind and forget the normal PC wisdom of more being better – in this domain less is more! The current trend is for PDAs to use faster CPUs and more memory; this is the result of the inclusion of more multimedia applications, such as movie players, MP3 players, etc. There is a danger that a simple functional device is being made to behave more like a mini-PC. For many applications processor speed is irrelevant and specifications of clock speed misleading. Concentrate on how easy the device is to use and whether it performs the functions that *you* require.

The main choice for PDA type devices is between the Windows Mobile platform and PalmOS-based machines. An organization does not need to standardize on a particular type of PDA as many PDA applications are available for both Windows Mobile and PalmOS and these can readily exchange information.

Pick the device up and try to use it; see how easy it is to perform specific tasks. See how long it takes and how easy it is to access a particular feature (e.g. try adding an appointment to the diary). How many menus do you have to navigate? Do you have to wait for the machine? Initially you may think that a short delay is acceptable or that it is alright to have to start the machine up, then find and launch an application, but every step is an extra barrier to actually using the device quickly and efficiently.

Do not buy a machine just because it has more 'features' than another one, unless you not only need, but also will actually remember how to use these features.

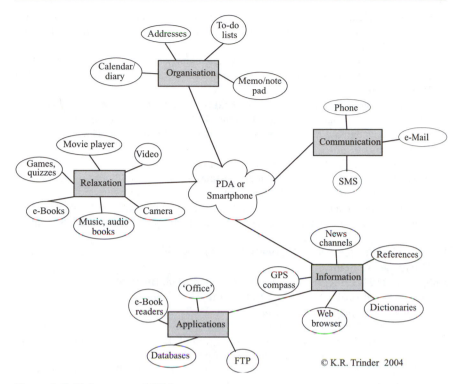

Figure 2.5 Main types of PDA use

To be useful a PDA does not need to be the latest model nor does it need to be complicated, but it does need to be used! What made the early PDAs attractive to non-technical people was the simplicity and ease of use of the device. Because the device was simple it actually got used rather than being left in a desk drawer.

The following was written long before PDAs were invented, but it succinctly expresses the benefits of simple devices:

> Manifestly it is better to use simple tools expertly than to possess a bewildering assortment of complicated gadgets and either neglect or use them incompetently.

(Rolt 1947: 9)

References

Bergman, E. (2000) *Information Appliances and Beyond*, San Francisco: Morgan Kaufmann.

Buchmann, I. (2001) *Batteries in a Portable World*, 2nd edition, Richmond, BC: Cadex Electronics Inc.

Burkhardt, J., Henn, H., Hepper, S., Rintdorff, K. and Schack, T. (2002) *Pervasive Computing – Technology and Architecture of Mobile Internet Applications*, Harlow: Pearson Education.

Hansmann, U., Mettala, R., Purakavastha, A. and Thompson, P. (2002) *SynchML – Synchronising and Managing Your Mobile Data*, Upper Saddle River, NJ: Prentice Hall International.

Malliou, E., Stavros, S., Sotirou, S. A., Miliarakis, A. and Stratakis, M. (2002) The AD-HOC Project: eLearning Anywhere, Anytime: 47–50. In *Proceedings of MLEARN 2002* (eds, S. Anastopolou, M. Sharples and G. Vavoula), Birmingham: The University of Birmingham.

Norman, D. (1998) *The Invisible Computer*, London: MIT Press.

Palm, Palm OS User Interface Guidelines. On-line. Available HTTP http://www.palmos.com/dev/support/docs/uiguidelines.pdf (accessed 6 April 2005).

Palm (2003) Zen of Palm: Designing products for PalmOS. On-line. Available HTTP http://www.palmos.com/dev/support/docs/zenofpalm.pdf (accessed 22 November 2004).

Rhodes, N. and McKeehan, J. (1999) *Palm Programming: The Developers Guide*, Cambridge: O'Reilly.

Rolt, L.T.C. (1947) *High Horse Riderless*, reprinted 1988, Bideford: Green Books.

Sharples, M. and Beale, R. (2003) A technical review of mobile computational devices, *Journal of Computer Assisted Learning*, 19(3): 392–5.

Smith, T. (2003) Personal Assistants (PDAs) in Further and Higher Education. On-line. Available HTTP http://www.ts-consulting.co.uk/DownloadDocuments/PDAsinFurther&HigherEducation.doc (accessed 5 April 2005).

Sun (2004a) JAVA CLDC Specification. On-line. Available HTTP http://java.sun.com/products/cldc/ (accessed 22 November 2004).

Sun (2004b) JAVA MIDP Specification. On-line. Available HTTP http://java.sun.com/products/midp/ (accessed 22 November 2004).

Chapter 3

Mobile teaching and learning

Agnes Kukulska-Hulme and John Traxler

Introduction

The growing popularity of the term 'mobile learning' brings with it a shift in focus that may impact on educators and trainers: it is mainly learners who carry the mobile devices and move around with them, whilst the term 'mobile teaching' is hardly used at all. This separation of meanings contrasts sharply with the way that 'web-based teaching' and 'web-based instruction' have generally been used with equanimity alongside 'web-based learning'. So our starting point and our focus is an emphasis on learning, but our take on mobile teaching is to redefine it as facilitation and support of mobile learning.

In the course of researching this book, we have sometimes been approached by people wanting to find out what difference 'mobile learning' might make to their teaching. They have also shared with us their curiosity, scepticism or excitement about what they think mobile devices might offer, from the point of view of interested outsiders. Typical questions have included the following:

- Is it really possible to learn with such small devices?
- What sorts of people use mobile devices for teaching and learning?
- What sorts of subjects and situations are appropriate for mobile learning?
- Are our students already using handheld computers for learning?

Questions like these evoke issues that are familiar to anyone who has used technology in educational contexts: concerns about whether a technology is fit for the purpose of learning, what kinds of learners will benefit from using it, and whether learners are already ahead of the game in comparison with the technology ownership and expertise of their instructors.

In this chapter, we have set ourselves the objective of being relevant both to those who are asking themselves such simple yet important questions, and to those who have experience of using mobile devices in teaching and learning but may have lacked the opportunity to see their own pedagogical approach in the context of other possibilities. We propose to review the overarching conceptual issues, beginning with conceptions of teaching and learning, within the landscape of the prevalent pedagogical approaches in education and training. We draw on the theories and practices of mobile computing and of e-learning, as well as 'blended' learning that may combine face-to-face with virtual components. These will act as the framework for a practical exploration of types of mobile learning and their realisation through various mobile technologies. They should also prove helpful when considering how to evaluate teachers' and learners' experiences with mobile technologies.

Mobile devices open up new opportunities for independent investigations, practical fieldwork, professional updating and on-the-spot access to knowledge. They can also provide the mechanism for improved individual learner support and guidance, and for more efficient course administration and management. However, mobile learning, indeed any learning, must work within a number of constraints. In our present context, the most important of these are the conceptions of teaching held by teachers and trainers and the styles of learning espoused by learners. These will determine the manner in which materials, support and technologies are adopted, developed and used.

Conceptions of teaching and learning

Conceptions of teaching and learning have been extensively explored and documented in educational literature (Richardson 2000; Laurillard 2002), yet they continue to be the subjects of debate and revision (Coffield *et al.* 2004). In this section, we outline the more significant ideas and point to their relevance to the practice of mobile learning. The most pragmatic position for educators and developers to adopt is that mobile content and delivery systems must be robust in the face of contending and conflicting ideas in this area, that any conceptions of learning or teaching are potentially at the mercy of poor usability or accessibility, and to plan wherever possible for redundancy, diversity and inclusiveness amongst their communities of intended users. For example, redundancy might be designed-in by allowing learners a degree of choice about the way in which the same information can be accessed: say, on a handheld device or on a desktop. Diversity would be well served by attending to differences in learners' needs according to their past experience and ability to adapt to mobile learning. Inclusiveness should address varied cognitive, psychological and physical traits as well as the widely accepted issues of accessibility and usability, and the growing issue of personalisation (Kukulska-Hulme and Traxler 2005).

Before considering more complex issues of pedagogical intent and design, a stark yet helpful distinction can be made between didactic and discursive mobile learning. *Didactic* learning can be understood as learning from mobile educational material, including novel formats such as e-books and web caching, in a way that responds to the potential and the limitations of mobile devices. Didactic teaching would be the means to that end. *Discursive* learning, on the other hand, relies on the development and support of interaction and discourse amongst communities of mobile learners who may, in some cases, never meet each other or their tutors face-to-face. Mobile devices can also be used for other generic learning activities, such as gathering information, evaluation by ranking or rating, reflection, problem solving or skills acquisition (for further discussion of generic categories of learning activity, see Fowler and Mayes 2004). Other categorisations of learning specifically derived from analysis of virtual learning have been devised (e.g. Peters 1999).

Conceptions of teaching

It is perhaps easiest to start by looking at teachers' conceptions of teaching since in this area some consensus is now emerging (Kember 1997). This consensus is centred on the notion that teachers and lecturers all have their own individual and perhaps implicit conceptions of what in essence constitutes the act of teaching. They then attempt to enact these conceptions in their work but these individual conceptions of teaching can nevertheless be seen as falling somewhere on a continuum. Some teachers are at one end of this spectrum and will act as if the teacher, the content and its transmission were paramount, whilst others will act as if students and their learning were paramount. The emphasis in the first case is on imparting information, and structuring and transmitting knowledge; the emphasis in the second case is on facilitating understanding, and supporting conceptual change and intellectual development. Most educators and trainers will fall between these two extremes, and there is obviously a relationship – but there need not be a match – between these two extremes and the discursive/didactic dichotomy described above.

There are several concerns that may modify this apparently systematic picture:

- Teachers may not be empowered to enact their particular conception of teaching due to the constraints of their environment or their institution; by resource constraints or by team teaching.
- Teachers may have professional priorities such as research, management or administration that are higher than enacting their own conception of teaching and they may instead adopt some conception representing least investment of time, effort or imagination.
- Teachers may be inhibited from enacting their particular conception of teaching by views about their students' learning styles and conceptions, or indeed by the views and ethos of their colleagues, departments and institutions.
- Teachers' understanding of learning technologies may suggest, accurately or otherwise, that it is difficult or impossible to enact their particular conception of teaching using the learning technologies at their disposal.
- Teachers' capacity, confidence and enthusiasm to embrace change (for example, to exploit emerging technologies in a fashion consistent with their particular conception of teaching) may be weaker than their allegiance to a particular conception of teaching.

The last points are clearly the relevant issues in our discussion of mobile learning, though the others may still be influential especially in a departmental or institutional context. They are a reflection on teachers' capacity to embrace change and a reflection on their institutions' capacity to stimulate change. Other aspects of this issue are discussed when we look at the institutionalisation of mobile learning.

In their review of theories, frameworks and models in the field of e-learning, Mayes and de Freitas (2004) and Fowler and Mayes (2004) have drawn together the main perspectives: associationist, cognitive and situated. Each of these views implies a set of pedagogical approaches, for example:

- The associationist perspective emphasises behavioural change, expressed through goals, progressive sequences and accurate reproduction or performance.
- The cognitive view has many different pedagogical manifestations, ranging from co-instruction with learners, knowledge construction through active participation, social construction of knowledge through group work, to applied, problem-based learning.
- The situated view encompasses apprenticeship, coaching and learning from real world settings.

The challenge is to find mappings between pedagogical approaches and functionality requirements for tools, such as presentation, dissemination, text and data manipulation, data storage and management, or communication. As educators and trainers, we have to try to understand our own conceptions and approaches to teaching, then check that these are in line with the activities that we expect our learners to undertake, and finally query whether the available technologies can support them.

If we leave aside some basic issues of usability and accessibility, the take-up of mobile technologies may depend on perceptions about the capacity of mobile technologies to support different conceptions of teaching. Handheld devices are increasingly able to carry media-rich content and thus to support a conception of teaching focussed on the teacher and on the content. Increased interaction with educational materials, for example the capacity to bookmark and annotate them, will strengthen this. However, basic handheld computer functionality is currently insufficient to support the level and richness of discussion and interaction amongst students that a more student-centred conception of teaching would envisage. The growth of wireless connectivity and the rise in numbers of smartphones may take us nearer this conception, as will increased appropriation of text messaging by educators and trainers and their companies and institutions.

Conceptions of learning

If we now move on to learning, there is a considerable quantity of research into its processes and characteristics. There are several authoritative accounts of this work (e.g. Richardson 2000) but also ongoing work that questions the rigour and validity of much of what is routinely accepted within higher and further education and training (Coffield *et al.* 2004). It is a complex and evolving subject. To many practitioners within further and higher education it is enormously interesting and underpins developments in their day-to-day teaching. In the context of mobile learning however, it is best to approach it with modest and pragmatic questions that allow informed and trustworthy progress to be made despite the ever-changing theoretical and conceptual formulations. Significant questions are:

- What are the relevant differences between face-to-face learning, learning supported by on-line technology and learning supported by mobile technologies?
- What is the impact of differences between the different mobile technologies?
- What kinds of learning, learners, subjects and situations can mobile learning support most effectively?

At the moment, mobile learning is still too novel for us to provide definitive and comprehensive answers to questions like these and the purpose of this book is to document experiences to date, to provide a technological, pedagogic and environmental framework and perhaps to refine the questions and areas where researchers and developers in mobile learning should focus.

These kinds of questions cannot be addressed without discussion of the wider context, for example:

- The convergence of distance learning and campus-based learning, in terms of both students' characteristics and learning technologies;
- The increasing industrialisation, 'commodification' and 'massification' of further and higher education in much of the developed world (Peters 1998);
- The blurring of divisions between conventional education on the one hand and informal learning, information gathering, 'edutainment', performance support and vocational training on the other;
- The increased participation and widening access agendas; increased diversity and complexity within training and within further and higher education.

All these issues and many more create a very fluid context for trying to understand and exploit the literature about conceptions and styles of learning.

However, to return to learning itself, the idea of conversation, with teachers, with other learners, with ourselves is central as we question our concepts, and with the world as we carry out experiments and explorations and interpret the results (Pask 1976 quoted in Sharples *et al.* 2002).

Sharples (2001) addresses the application of Conversational Theory to mobile devices. He concludes his discussion:

... we can welcome students who bring their own personal communicators and computers, but in the full knowledge that they will disrupt traditional teaching and that this disruption needs to be managed. This is not an argument for technological determinism, for proposing that because students come armed with new technologies then education must adapt to accept them. There is a more defensible case for moving to a more conversational approach to teaching and learning. The skills of *constructing* and exploring knowledge, *conversing* and collaborating with peers, and the ability to *control* one's own learning are fundamental requirements of effective learning.

(Sharples 2001: 7)

He goes on to look at the relationship between the educational theory and the software tools needed to support it, in the context of a mobile learning pilot with school children. The tools that are needed to support such a scenario can be divided into three sets, based on the conversational model: for learning actions, learning descriptions, and learning conversations. A web browser is used for accessing learning resources and a notepad with handwriting recognition and an integral camera can capture annotated objects that result from learning experiences. Learning descriptions are enabled through a timeline to view the learning objects in the order they were created and a topic map to link the objects by conceptual association, with optional links that can be shared with other learners or published on the Web. The conversational tools enable the learner to hold a conversation or to share the topic map with another similar device.

This is one of the few examples where one can see a clear line of argument from the educational theory to the specific technological toolset underpinning a mobile learning project.

One of the objectives of the recent MOBIlearn project (www.mobilearn.org) has been to develop practical and robust high-level guidance for lecturers, developers and managers proposing to work with mobile learning. Some of this work is coming into the public domain (Vavoula *et al.* 2004).

At a more practical level, mobile technologies can support learning that is more situated, experiential and contextualised within specific domains and they support the creation and use of more up-to-date and authentic content (Sariola and Rionka 2003). These are its most significant attributes.

In an era when education is increasingly multicultural, global and widely accessed, we need to remember that much of the research on teaching and learning has been derived from a relatively narrow social, cultural and geographical base. The experience of educators and trainers working with learners from outside this base – perhaps working with non-traditional university entrants, with overseas course participants and working outside Europe, North America and Australasia – will often be radically different.

Personal learning

Early evidence (Plant 2001), especially in relation to handheld computers and mobile phones, suggests learners and users regard handheld devices as far more 'personal' than the equivalent static or desktop devices. This means that mobile learning is also personal learning, which could be remote and individual, or social and collaborative.

Mobile devices offer ways to complement, improve and enhance current face-to-face learning and other technology supported learning and to respond to practical constraints and barriers. They also offer the opportunity to move beyond current ideas of teaching and learning, and to devise new methods, practices and formats that draw on their unique technical characteristics. These characteristics derive from the essential portability of the devices but there is also potentially:

- Connectivity for spontaneous communication and collaboration.
- Beaming of stored information from device to device.
- Location-awareness, giving instant information about objects within sight.
- Portable sound-recording and voice-recording.
- Cameras for taking photos and making video clips.

Much of the current work with mobile technologies, especially in schools, is in fact on personal connected learning. It takes place in the classroom and exploits the synergy between 'active' whiteboards, data projectors, Personal Digital Assistants (PDAs) and networked desktop PCs, so is not strictly mobile learning. It does, however, inform developments in mobile learning.

Personal learning is also at the heart of three scenarios described by de Freitas and Levene (2003) in their report on mobile and wearable devices in further and higher education institutions: web lectures delivered on handheld devices, a campus without walls, and enhanced field trips such as museum visits and wildlife projects.

Mobile learning must exploit the potential of different technologies to support different learning activities differently; from attracting, engaging, attending, delivery, assessment, all the way to revision. Clearly, the usability constraints of most mobile devices play to the 'bite-sized' character of some revision and the spontaneity and informality of mobile devices is useful in the attracting phase. Designers and developers of mobile learning must, however, also exploit the spontaneous and opportunistic nature of learning on the move, alongside the more structured and premeditated approaches to learning the mobile learners may adopt. Many mobile devices, unlike their desktop counterparts, are either 'always-on' or can be turned on instantly and can consequently respond quickly to learners' impulses.

Given the variety and uncertainty of work on learning styles, any learning material needs to be accessible by a number of routes in a number of ways, and possibly for a number of purposes; learning material must be designed redundantly. One of the most overlooked attributes of networked learning content is its capacity to be accessed via hyperlinks. Too much of this content is only accessible on a linear basis that probably betrays its origins as a sequence of chapters or a weekly schedule of lectures. Once the specifics of designing and navigating mobile web pages are better understood, there may be the chance to look at richer ways of accessing content, where perhaps its organisation and navigation could match the diversity of its users.

Having briefly reviewed current ideas relating to conceptions of teaching and learning, we can now proceed to explore the extent to which mobile learning technologies support or constrain these various ideas.

The interplay of technologies with teaching and learning

Didactic content

As we have said earlier, one of the dominant models for what happens in education is that content, for example knowledge, information, facts, procedures and rules, is transmitted from teacher to learner. In face-to-face teaching, this takes place using lectures, books and handouts whilst in technology supported learning it takes place using web pages, computer-assisted learning packages or virtual learning environments. Mobile learning already offers a similar range of choices.

Short Message Service (SMS) texting presents a variety of content delivery possibilities and some of these are mentioned elsewhere in this book. The potential of camera-phones and Multimedia Messaging Service (MMS) is still largely untapped although one company, Impatica (www.impatica.com), is developing a technology that will convert PowerPoint presentations with voice-overs into MMS. This technology is being used by Vodaphone to deliver short instructional sessions to its customers. VoiceXML is another phone technology with largely untapped potential. It is the technology that drives speech-to-text/text-to-speech systems (for example, in the menu systems used by call centres) and was trialled by the EU-funded m-learning project (www.m-learning.org/index.shtml) for delivering small segments of basic skills material. In many respects, this work parallels other 'bite-sized' learning initiatives, most obviously the BBC's Bitesize campaign.

Mobile learning with Wireless Application Protocol (WAP)

An under-exploited technology is WAP. There is, however, some evidence of WAP being used as a delivery mechanism for content. In November and December of 2000, a consortium of INSEAD, NOKIA and ICUS mounted a short pilot to trial mobile teaching and learning with Second Generation (2G) technologies (Gayeski 2002). The pilot was limited to one phone (Nokia 6210) and one telecommunications WAP service provider, in one country, Singapore. INSEAD provided the course content and the 'coaches' (that is, the tutors or moderators), ICUS designed and developed the e-learning and mobile learning course, NOKIA provided the phones and WAP expertise, and Starhub, a Singapore telecommunications company, provided the WAP service.

The pilot involved a course entitled 'eBusiness on the Move'. Its length was approximately 20 learner-hours. There were 22 students on the course, which took place in the Far East, and they were all experienced business managers. The pilot showed that the mobile learning supported by only 2G technologies exceeded learner expectations and that 2G technology could provide a viable learning environment.

The pilot, although short-lived, provided interesting insights into reversioning web-based content for mobile learning and on the necessary 'media-mix' for this particular situation.

About 70 per cent of the course, namely all the text content, quizzes and schedules, was available on both web and WAP. This redundancy gave users the choice of delivery platform. Twenty per cent of the course was on web only, namely digital video clips, bulletin board discussions, PDF files and e-mail exchanges, and 10 per cent was on WAP only, mainly visits to external WAP sites, getting quick reminders and getting alerts from the coach.

Course navigation raised reversioning issues. Compared to the web content, there were different design constraints for the WAP course material, for example: shorter chunks of text, more screen displays and more section titles.

In order to reversion the existing web-based material a Word document was produced to cross-reference the WAP 'chunks' and the web 'topics'. This was a navigational aid when learners were switching back and forth between modes.

By comparison, content delivery for PDA technology is far more stable, mature and varied. In many respects, it mimics existing PC-based technologies. The content may be:

- Notes and presentations, delivered with a PDA-enhanced or PDA-specific document reader such as RepliGo or Adobe Reader for Palm including Flash animations and sound files, or indeed just a PDA-based word-processor.
- eBooks, such as the Mobipocket library, including textbooks and reference books.
- Websites and Virtual Learning Environments (VLEs) perhaps customised for PDA presentation, such as AvantGo, Blackboard-To-Go or FirstClass. These may be cached or connected.

As always with educational material, there is a distinction between 'in-house' material (that is, developed locally by the lecturer or their institution) and 'bought-in' material (that is, commercially published and available on the open market). Website content and VLE content can be either in-house or bought-in, as can notes and presentations. This means that lecturers and trainers are faced with decisions and choices. Bought-in material will usually have high production values and good usability and should be standards-compliant but may lack specificity in terms of coverage and level for a specific course and will of course have to be paid for. In-house material can exactly fit local course requirements and teaching styles but may be poorly designed and presented. Certainly, in its early days, mobile learning will be heavily dependent on pre-existing material originally developed for other formats. In-house material can be reversioned though this may not be done well. The e-book format is almost exclusively bought-in and is a way of accessing conventional literature, textbooks and reference works.

A radical alternative to reversioning existing content is to develop content that complies from the outset with standards that make it portable across platforms and devices. The global standard for educational content is likely to be ADL's Shareable Content Object Reference Model (SCORM). There is already at least one potential mobile learning implementation of the SCORM standard; PocketSCORM aimed at the PDA sector complete with editing tools for the Windows PPC platform (Lin *et al.* 2004).

Adopting such an approach would enable content to track changes in devices and innovations in platforms with no additional effort or cost. It would not, however, guarantee that portable content was equally usable and suitable pedagogically for every platform, merely that it was viewable.

Discursive interactions

The other dominant model for what happens in education is that learners, perhaps facilitated by a teacher or a moderator, come to a greater understanding of their subject by shared exploration and discussion. In face-to-face teaching, this takes place during seminars, discussions and tutorials. In the course of the last ten to fifteen years, the use of technology, especially networked computers used by distance learning students, has provided increasing support and richness for this discursive element of learning. Technical advances have added visual and aural dimensions to the originally textual format of web-based meetings and conferences in synchronous and asynchronous modes. The strategies to support and enhance on-line educational conferences and meetings are now relatively stable and established (Salmon 2000) and depend crucially on the idea of an 'e-moderator'.

The idea of e-moderating naturally leads us to examine the idea of 'm-moderating', that is the idea of moderating for mobile learning. The goals and objectives are comparable but the different technologies may transform the nature of the interactions. Currently, experience of m-moderating is limited. Nevertheless, it can be expected to follow the same trajectory as e-moderating, moving from an early model based on administrative support and reacting to individual content queries to a more mature model of pastoral support and proactively supporting new forms of learning. The peculiarities of the technology will exert an influence. Some mobile technologies, mobile phones and most PDAs, support peer-to-peer communications that are analogous to e-mail and not necessarily visible to any moderator. Some mobile technologies offer a multiplicity of communications channels on one device, for example, e-mail, voice, SMS and MMS, and these will enrich but also complicate the discourse. The implementation of VoiceXML within mobile devices will eventually blur the division between speech and text.

In mobile learning, there is a noticeable difference in content delivery mediated by phone technologies and that mediated by PDA technologies. Discussion has previously been seen as textual, consisting of students' written or spoken contributions, and this may mean that there is less of a distinction between discussion mediated by phone technologies and that mediated by PDA technologies. Many phones support not only voice and SMS but also e-mail, and connected PDAs support e-mail and web-based conferencing. It is anticipated that the various strategies used to support Computer Mediated Conferencing (CMC) will 'cross over' to SMS and other mobile formats. Apart from issues identified elsewhere, such as accessibility, usability and connectivity, one other issue is relevant to the educationally fruitful use of mobile discussion and that is the emergence of norms or mores of acceptable behaviour. Currently forms of 'netiquette' govern CMC whilst texting has its own codes of expression and behaviour. Mobile learning will grow its own culture ('mob-etiquette' perhaps?) from these and other roots.

Mobile learning and social inclusion

At least one project and its technologies have attempted to span both didactic and discursive modes, and to span the full range of delivery technologies from smartphones to desktop PCs with an integrated and specially developed software system. *m-learning* was a three-year pan-European project, which began in October 2001 and finished in September 2004. The project was funded by the European Commission under the Education Area of the Information Society Technologies (IST) Programme and was led by the UK's Learning and Skills Development Agency (LSDA). The consortium was composed of the Centro di Recerca in Matematica Pura ed Applicata (CRMPA) in Italy and Lecando AB in Sweden; project partners in the UK were Cambridge Training and Development Limited (CTAD) and Ultralab, a Learning Technology Research Centre based at Anglia Polytechnic University.

The project addressed three social/educational issues relating to many young adults aged 16–24 in the EU:

- Poor literacy/numeracy.
- Non-participation in conventional education.
- Lack of access creating ICT 'haves'/'have-nots'.

The project was large and some 200 learners were involved in the final trials. There were several different software deliverables, including a range of educational games, a micro-portal and a learner management system. The impact of the project on its target group was positive and rewarding, and provided grounds for exploring the potential of mobile learning across a variety of disadvantaged groups including travellers and the homeless (Attewell and Savill-Smith 2004).

Generic academic support

A more diffuse but increasingly important activity within further and higher education is based around the need to develop the study skills and personal information management skills of students. This activity is important as the foundation for personal transferable academic skills, for subsequent lifelong learning and continued professional development, and for increased individual and institutional efficiency. Developing these skills can be the responsibility of subject lecturers, specialist support lecturers or library staff.

The Personal Information Management (PIM) functionality within most mobile devices can easily be appropriated to support learning, for example by providing course timetables, tutors' contact details, academic regulations and assessment deadlines, and this is the base-line for any mobile learning activity (Traxler and Riordan 2004).

At the next level of functionality, there are currently various software applications that have specifically academic or pedagogic uses. Several of the bibliographic database market leaders (for example EndNote and Biblioscape) have versions for handheld computers or PDAs, and the same is true for the graphical tools that support mind-mapping or cognitive mapping (for example MindManager). Both of these types of application will usually synchronise with a PC version of the software. There are also specialised dictionaries and other reference books but in most cases these do not yet fully exploit all the potential of PDAs and smartphones in terms of multimedia functionality and location-awareness. There is, for example, considerable potential for multimedia location-aware field-guides of the type used by ornithologists and other naturalists. There is currently a large commercial market for this software based on PCs, for example that of Bird Guides (www.birdguides.com). There is, however, still some reluctance to make the move to PDAs owing to memory limitations.

Subject-specific support

Mobile learning technologies provide ways of enhancing the teaching and learning of specific subjects.

Many field-based subjects can clearly benefit from real-time data logging as part of fieldwork activities. There has been some preliminary work in schools (Hine *et al.* 2004) and some in higher education. At the Pennsylvania State University at Delaware County Geoscience students now use PalmOne PDAs to enter field data straight into a spreadsheet for analysis rather than using paper-

and-pencil first, followed by transcription to a PC later. This means that hypotheses can be tested in the field and further evidence gathered immediately to refute or strengthen them (PalmOne 2003).

One constant theme for vocational and professional education is the need for experience in the workplace. The training of teachers, lawyers, doctors and nurses are examples where large numbers of students are involved. It is also the case that large numbers of these students spend a substantial part of their courses off campus in placements gaining practical experience. All these activities present challenges that mobile technologies can meet. Learners need continued access to content, or course material and resources, whilst in the workplace and they may need continued access to other learners within their on-line community. They need to gather data and complete assignments whilst in the workplace and they need support with personal information management in a novel environment. How institutions eventually support these learners will depend partly on the overall mix of media and methods used by the courses, partly on the specifics of the institutions, the subjects and the courses and partly on the technology. Students will need to synch and back up their PDAs and will need to transfer data. The students may or may not own their own networked PCs; they may or may not come onto campus at frequent intervals.

Mobile learning and teacher training

Jocelyn Wishart and Angela McFarlane with Andy Ramsden: University of Bristol, UK

The one-year science teacher training course in the UK, the Postgraduate Certificate of Education (PGCE), is particularly information-heavy. It also requires the students to spend 24 of the 36 weeks of the course in a partner school rather than in the university, so access to conventional information sources relating to the course can be difficult. Initial teacher training (ITT) students need access to the documentation of various statutory requirements including the National Curriculum and Qualifications and Curriculum Authority Schemes of Work as well as subject knowledge. Then there is the documentation associated with being on a PGCE such as timetables, assessment guidance, pupil mark books and lesson observation and lesson plan proformas.

The Graduate School of Education at the University of Bristol, specifically the current authors, believes that mobile devices have a clear potential benefit to trainee professionals such as their PGCE science students. In order to identify where and to what extent these potential benefits can be realised, 14 PGCE science students on the teacher training course have been given handheld computers with mobile phone connectivity and cameras to take with them on teaching practice. They have been given either a Windows Pocket PC or a PalmOS-based handheld and four hours of training, specifically identifying its potential for:

- Accessing the VLE (Blackboard) discussion groups and e-mail.
- Accessing course documentation (on PDA or via Blackboard or via synching).
- Just-in-time acquisition of knowledge from the Web.
- Acquisition of science information from e-books and encyclopaedias.
- Delivering accurate figures for scientific constants and formulae.
- Organising commitments, lesson plans and timetables.
- Recording and analysing lab results.
- Recording pupil attendance and grades.
- Photographing experiments for display and reinforcing pupil knowledge.
- Maintaining a reflective web log (blog).

Though the students are only on their first short (four week) teaching practice there already appear to be three applications on the PDAs that are proving key to managing their learning of how to teach in the field. These are the calendar or diary scheduler for organising yourself, the spreadsheet of attendance or mark book for organising your pupils and the use of a word processor to make notes on information and events immediately they are encountered.

There is still a vast and unexploited potential for using mobile devices in student projects, investigations and fieldwork. Collaborative learning, where students work together on tasks, is another area where mobile learning is unexploited. Many researchers have informally reported that students use beaming to collaborate on shared tasks. As the technologies become more powerful and robust, the potential for collaboration will increase and will enhance distance learning with remote students.

Guidance and support

Mobile learning technologies provide ways of enhancing and extending the non-academic and para-academic support and guidance that institutions can give to their students, as well as providing the means for increased social integration.

Learners need a range of services, irrespective of whether they are on-campus students, part-time students, distance learners, or employees learning in the workplace. These services might include counselling and guidance, mentoring, pastoral care, careers advice, and representation within their institution. There is considerable debate (for example for some years in the UK's Counselling and Psychotherapy Journal) about whether it is indeed possible to provide on-line counselling in the sense that counsellors and psychotherapists would understand the term counselling. There are, however, grounds for a belief that guidance, rather than counselling, can be provided to technology supported learners in general and mobile learners in particular. This is due in part to the increasing richness and timeliness of information that learners can access and in part due to the potential spontaneity and richness of contact with guidance services. In specific forms of guidance, for example careers guidance, mobile technologies can take their place in the blend of learning technologies used to deliver content and support discussion on careers topics. Specific suggestions for careers guidance (Vuorinen and Sampson 2003) include:

- Group career education assignments as fieldwork, supported by e-mail or voice phone.
- Individual assignments investigating specific occupations, using videophone or telephone to interview occupational experts.
- Creating a vocational portfolio using picture messaging and text messaging.
- Job search skills practice using videoconferencing.

Industrial and commercial training

This section specifically addresses mobile industrial, corporate and commercial training but in doing so, it may be overstating a distinction between education based in universities and colleges and training based within corporations and businesses.

Universities and colleges now offer more vocational courses than ever as well as more continued professional updating, and offer courses in a variety of part-time modes for students working in commerce, industry and the public sector. These are sometimes studied at a considerable distance, in relative isolation from tutors and other students. Universities and colleges now accredit students' experiential and professional experience, and work-based learning is a growing component of many courses.

At the same time, the training provided within commercial and industrial organisations has become increasingly ambitious. It may often be more responsive than that offered by universities and colleges; commercial organisations can purchase new technologies quickly and can deliver courses rapidly without the need for the time-consuming validation procedures characteristic of universities and colleges. Corporations and businesses are more aware of the issue of 'return-on-investment' from courses than universities and colleges. Training may in the future be a regular constituent of the work of universities and colleges. This will be both within their core educational business and as part of knowledge transfer and support for local and national industry, often now an explicit part of university and college mission statements and their services to the wider community.

The current modest literature of mobile industrial and commercial training, for example the work of Gayeski (2002), differs only in emphasis from the mainstream of literature of mobile learning. The case for mobile learning is clearly driven by the imperative that it must deliver local efficiency gains and cost savings in short timescales. There is a powerful business case for looking at how mobile technologies can improve both business processes and corporate training (Pasanen 2003) if examined and developed in an integrated fashion.

Mobile learning and corporate training

One major high-technology corporate using mobile devices to support training is CISCO. The company initially introduced PDAs widely for training but this has changed over time. This was because the company felt that a number of issues stood in the way of a wider deployment of PDAs: buying PDAs was an additional cost when employees already had laptops, it was difficult to support various operating systems and models and users' attention span was an issue.

PDAs are now seen as being good for 'knowledge management', i.e. as repositories of reference materials such as glossaries, maps or diagrams and for quick access. They are no longer considered good for what is seen as 'learning'. Some materials are still provided for optional download to individuals' own PDAs.

The company's mobile strategy ('the connected workforce') is now based around laptops, hotspots, home working DSL or cable and Wi-Fi around the office. Materials are developed using templates and they keep to a simple structure. Many diagrams are used in the materials, with emphasis on colour and shape. There is also some video on demand. The company continues to use MP3 material and its own radio stations for newsflashes or tuning in to a debate while driving, but it has been found that staff literally 'switch off' if this is not extremely interesting. Although no formal evaluation of mobile learning was undertaken, staff gave a positive response when asked whether they wanted mobile connectivity.

The corporate curriculum usually has a greater focus on content rather than on discussion. This content tends to be quite factual, perhaps dealing with new product details or updates to working procedures that can be assimilated 'on the fly', as and when needed. It is aimed typically at service engineers and sales representatives and it might use video clips and audio material. It is generally the 'bite-sized' end of the content spectrum, geared to the recognition and recall of facts and information. In general, mobile training is quite closely allied with 'performance support', which is enabling mobile workers to do their jobs better by providing detailed and up-to-date guidance, information and data. There are accounts in the popular and technical press of mobile devices being used by the police and other emergency services in a 'decision-support' capacity.

Mobile learning and performance support

by Diane Evans: The Open University, UK

The MOBIlearn Project (www.mobilearn.org) is an extensive mobile learning project with a range of European partners, one of which is the UK's Open University. The OU has been developing support for the 'Designated First-Aiders' in their departments within the OU. In addition to their normal job role, these people deal with First Aid incidents around the OU. Their training comprises instruction, practice and testing, with refresher courses and further testing at prescribed intervals, provided by organisations such as the St John's Ambulance Brigade.

Discussions revealed that many of the First-Aiders felt insecure in their diagnosis and treatment of casualties and identified the need for support with procedures and treatments and for mutual personal support through collaboration. The MOBIlearn system was designed to supplement the required formal training activities provided by St John's Ambulance and was based on socio-constructivist pedagogy involving learner interaction focussed around defined activities or learning episodes with a clear collaborative focus to each of the activities.

Both mobility of the users and the mobile devices themselves were factors within the system. The First-Aiders have access to a range of facilities including content, communication tools e.g. messages and chat, and collaboration tools e.g. workspaces, brainstorming etc. Access can be via PC, Tablet PC, PDA or mobile phone enabling participation in both individual research and distributed collaborative activities.

A longer account of training in the corporate sector can be found in the case studies.

Finally, particularly in this area rather than mobile learning generally, it is sensible to be aware of potentially negative side effects of learning on the move. Employees, that is mobile learners, may feel under pressure to learn or train anywhere at any time and feel that location-aware technologies can monitor their movements. They may also feel that devices holding personal and professional appointments, tasks and contacts jeopardise their privacy and that encapsulating their professional knowledge on a computer deskills them.

Evaluation of mobile teaching and learning

Taylor (2004) suggests how to evaluate the 'pedagogical soundness' of a mobile learning environment involving users who are new to this technology. Teachers and learners may be fascinated by the new devices but overlook the fact that they produce no lasting valuable impact on their work practices. Taylor advocates an approach to evaluation that is driven by task-centred user requirements, which implies an examination of the learning opportunities presented by mobile technology, its (potential) impact on the way people perform learning tasks as well as on human social processes and interactions, and how these in turn are changed or modified by the technology.

Mobile learning practitioners must address evaluation in a rather different context once mobile learning gradually becomes embedded and institutionalised. In this context, evaluation will be an ongoing part of institutional monitoring and quality assurance procedures. Preliminary work has been done identifying the issues and methods that might be appropriate for this rather utilitarian activity (Traxler 2002).

Conclusions

In reality, mobile technologies will seldom, if ever, be used in isolation to support learning. They will join the range of technologies and methods that deliver and support learning. In small-scale projects, this has already happened and is illustrated in many of the case studies. Finding the factors that determine the most appropriate mixture of methods and technologies in any given circumstances is obviously a high priority issue for the next generation of mobile learning researchers and developers.

Looking further ahead, mobile learning has the capacity to challenge much conventional practice. It challenges the need for buildings and campuses and makes us question the need for education to take place at fixed physical locations; it challenges the need for timetables and makes us question the need for synchrony; it challenges the need for lectures and seminars and makes us question the essence of face-to-face teaching and learning.

Mobile learning can take education back out into the home, the workplace and the community.

Mobile learning can be spontaneous, portable, personal, situated; it can be informal, unobtrusive, ubiquitous and disruptive. It takes us much, much nearer to 'anytime, anywhere' learning but it is still too early to predict how our under-standings of learning and teaching will evolve as a consequence. This chapter and indeed much of this book are intended to not so much provide prescriptions and formulae for delivering mobile learning as an established concept, as provide a set of reflections and experiences being passed from a first generation of researchers, developers and teachers in mobile learning to – hopefully – a second generation!

References

Attewell, J. and Savill-Smith, C. (2004) Mobile learning and social inclusion: focus on learners and learning, 3–11, Proceedings of MLEARN 2003 Conference. London: LSDA.

Coffield, F., Moseley, D., Hall, E. and Ecclestone, K. (2004) *Should We Be Using Learning Styles? What Research Has to Say To Practice*, London: Learning and Skills Research Centre.

de Freitas, S. and Levene, M. (2003) Evaluating the development of wearable devices, personal data assistants and the use of other mobile devices in further and higher education institutions. TechWatch Report. On-line. Available HTTP http://www. jisc.ac.uk/uploaded_documents/tsw_03–05.pdf (accessed 22 November 2004).

Fowler, C. and Mayes, T. (2004) Mapping theory to practice and practice to tool functionality based on the practitioners' perspective. JISC E-Learning Models Desk Study. On-line. Available HTTP http://www.jisc.ac.uk/uploaded_documents/ Stage%202%20Mapping%20(Version%201).pdf (accessed 22 November 2004).

Gayeski, D. (2002) *Learning Unplugged – Using Mobile Technologies for Organisational and Performance Improvement*, New York: AMACON – American Management Association.

Hine, N., Rentoul, R. and Specht, M. (2004) Collaboration and roles in remote field trips, 69–72, Proceedings of MLEARN 2003 Conference, London: LSDA.

Kember, D. (1997) Reconceptualisation of research into university academics' conceptions. *Learning and Instruction*, 7(3): 255–75.

Kukulska-Hulme, A. and Traxler, J. (2005) Making the case for personalisation through mobile learning, CAL'05 Conference, Bristol.

Laurillard, D. (2002) *Rethinking University Teaching – A Conversational Framework for the Effective Use of Learning Technology*, 2nd edition, London: RoutledgeFalmer.

Lin, N.H., Shih, T.K., Hsu, H., Chang, H.-P., Ko, W.C. and Lin, L.J. (2004) Pocket SCORM workshop, Proceedings of the 24th IEEE International Conference on Distributed Computing Systems, pp. 274–9, Hachioji, Tokyo, Japan, 23–24 March.

Mayes, T. and de Freitas, S. (2004) Review of e-learning theories, frameworks and models. JISC E-Learning Models Desk Study. On-line. Available HTTP http://www.jisc.ac.uk/ uploaded_documents/Stage%202%20Learning%20Models%20(Version%201).pdf (accessed 22 November 2004).

PalmOne (2003) On-line. Available HTTP http://www.palmone.com/us/education/studies/ study47.html (accessed 22 November 2004).

Pasanen, J. (2003) Corporate Mobile Learning, in H. Kynaslahti and P. Seppala (eds), *Mobile Learning*, 115–23, Helsinki: IT Press.

Peters, O. (1998) *Learning and Teaching in Distance Education: Analyses and Interpretations from an International Perspective*, London: Kogan Page.

Peters, O. (1999) A pedagogical model for virtual learning space. Articles on flexible learning and distance education. On-line. Available HTTP http://www.tbc.dk/pdf/peters-a_pedagogical_model.pdf (accessed 28 November 2004)

Plant, S. (2001) *On the Mobile – The Effects of Mobile Telephones on Individual and Social Life*, Motorola. On-line. Available HTTP http://www.motorola.com/mot/doc/ 0.234_ MotDoc.pdf (accessed 5 April 2005).

Richardson, J.T.E. (2000) *Researching Student Learning*, Buckingham: Society for Research into Higher Education/Open University Press.

Salmon, G. (2000) *e-Moderating – The Key to Teaching and Learning Online*, London: Kogan Page.

Sariola, J. and Rionka, A. (2003) Mobile Learning in Teacher Education – The LIVE Project, in H. Kynaslahti and P. Seppala (eds), *Mobile Learning*, 79–90, Helsinki: IT Press.

Sharples, M. (2001) Disruptive devices: mobile technology for conversational learning. *International Journal of Continuing Engineering Education and Lifelong Learning*, 12(5/6): 504–20

Sharples, M., Corlett, D. and Westmancott, O. (2002) The design and implementation of a mobile learning resource, *Personal and Ubiquitous Computing*, 6: 220–34.

Taylor, J. (2004) A Task-centred Approach to Evaluating a Mobile Learning Environment for Pedagogical Soundness, in J. Attewell, and C. Savill-Smith (eds) *Learning with Mobile Devices: Research and Development*, 167–72, London: Learning and Skills Development Agency. Also on-line. Available HTTP http://kn.open.ac.uk/public/document.cfm?documentid=3102 (accessed 22 November 2004).

Traxler, J. (2002) Evaluating m-learning. Proceedings of MLEARN 2002, European Workshop on Mobile and Contextual Learning, 63–4, University of Birmingham, 20–21 June 2002.

Traxler, J. and Riordan, B. (2004) Supporting students with mobile devices. Proceedings of International Conference on Innovation, Good Practice and Research in Engineering Education, 7–9 June 2004, Wolverhampton: University of Wolverhampton.

Vavoula, G.N., Lefrere, P., O'Malley, C., Sharples, M. and Taylor, J. (2004) Producing Guidelines for Learning, Teaching and Tutoring in a Mobile Environment, in J. Roschelle, T. Chan, Kinshuk and S.J.H. Yand (eds), *Proceedings of the 2nd IEEE International Workshop on Wireless and Mobile Technologies in Education* (WMTE) 173–6, Los Alamitos, CA: Computer Society Press.

Vuorinen, R. and Sampson, J. (2003) Using Mobile Information Technology to Enhance Counselling and Guidance, in H. Kynaslahti and P. Seppala (eds), *Mobile Learning*, 63–70, Helsinki, Finland: IT Press.

Chapter 4

Mobile usability and user experience

Agnes Kukulska-Hulme

Introduction

We all know when a familiar object is not usable: a pen with no ink cannot be used for writing in a notebook and a scratched photo lens will not produce a good picture. Objects can become unusable because of breakages, missing parts or flat batteries. Alternatively, an object may have been so badly designed that it was never of much use in the first place. In either case, this is 'usability' in its most basic definition: whether something can be used for its intended purpose. However, as this chapter will try to show, in mobile learning this basic level of usability (it works/it doesn't work) cannot be taken for granted. What is more, this basic level is often not enough for understanding complex devices, the demands of educational activities and the needs of hurried lifestyles.

Consequently, it can be helpful to think in terms of levels or degrees of usability. To take an example from common experience, nowadays many people carry with them a card that allows them to enter designated buildings. If it is a swipe card, you may have to pull it through a device to make the doors open. This can be a bit cumbersome, especially when several attempts are needed. An improvement to this is a system that allows one simply to hold the card next to the device that activates the opening of the door, making it easier for authorized people to open it. Sometimes the system can recognize your card while it is still in a bag or pocket, so that you do not even have to take it out in order to enter the building. This adds a welcome degree of ease or comfort for most people. With these improvements, the system becomes more and more usable.

In the human–computer interaction (HCI) literature, *usable* systems and devices are generally regarded as being easy to learn, effective to use, efficient and enjoyable from the user's perspective. To achieve this degree of usability, a broad set of concerns have to be taken into account. Over a decade ago, Preece *et al.* (1994) already discussed usability in the context of 'user experience': it meant creating systems that were helpful, fun, entertaining, aesthetically pleasing, supportive of creativity, satisfying, rewarding or emotionally fulfilling. As can be seen from these descriptors, user experience is highly subjective and dependent on a user's expectations, which in turn are shaped by the user's age, education, cultural background, gender and many other factors. Although in the 1990s there was no literature on user experience in mobile learning, the point is that even then, human–computer interaction researchers recognized that to produce systems with good usability, it was important to understand the psychological, ergonomic, organizational and social factors that determine how people operate. Nielsen (1993) explained usability in terms of a system's overall acceptability, which included its social acceptability and all practical aspects such as reliability, cost, compatibility and usefulness.

Preece (2000) then moved on to analyse on-line communities, concluding that software with good usability supports rapid learning, high skill retention, low error rates and high productivity; it is consistent and predictable, which makes it both pleasant and effective to use. In a subsequent book, Preece *et al.* (2002) explained the related concept of 'interaction design', an area of activity that focuses on how to support people in their everyday and working lives and is concerned with an even broader range of issues than has traditionally been the scope of human–computer interaction. Interaction design entails 'creating user experiences that enhance and extend the way people work, communicate and interact' (Preece *et al.* 2002: v). We have to realize, however, that on the whole, this is still something of an ideal to aspire to rather than a description of current user experience.

Usability is often perceived by educators and trainers to be a technical topic but from a pedagogical perspective, it is about ensuring good educational experiences and enabling successful interactions. It is essential that those who teach have a good grasp of the issues and actively draw attention to usability in discussions with technical experts and others who advise them on the choice of mobile devices, software, applications and services. Usability influences whether learning is an engaging experience and will have an impact on learning effectiveness and efficiency. Put more starkly, potential learners will reject technologies and learning materials that are unusable, drop out of courses and find alternative education and training providers.

Usability of mobile devices

Current mobile devices are designed for specific uses that typically focus on allowing users to enter and access fairly structured data like contacts, lists, dates, financial information and memos, to send and receive messages, to view documents and pictures, or to access the web. Although they can work well for these purposes, mobile devices and services have inherited some of the ongoing problems of usability that most people will recognize from their experience as computer users and they have introduced a number of new issues. In his book on handheld usability, Weiss (2002) remarks on the 'general lack of usability on most handheld devices' (p. xiii). He attributes this largely to inconsistencies in design; for example, the lack of a 'back' button on many internet-enabled handsets makes it difficult to browse the web in ways that people are accustomed to on their desktop or laptop computer. Each manufacturer develops a unique user interface, so there is also little consistency between devices.

Nielsen's verdict on mobile usability in 2003 was that, 'The latest mobile devices are agonizingly close to being practical, but still lack key usability features required for mainstream use' (Nielsen 2003: 1). According to Nielsen, in some parts of the world there are persistent problems with service provision, constraining the ability to use a connected mobile device anywhere, anytime. He goes on to say that on-line services such as e-mail should be 'reconceptualized' for mobile devices through better filtering of messages and summarisation services that highlight urgent messages needing to be read while away from one's desktop computer. Physical aspects of a device, such as a wheel for scrolling, also need to be refined to take account of common user actions such as wanting to 'flick' through pages of text.

These are all very pertinent remarks, showing that now and over the next few years, users may be faced with some difficulties surrounding the use of a mobile device. Any problems encountered will depend on the device itself, users' familiarity with it and its suitability for particular activities or tasks.

How is mobile usability different?

Usability issues in computer systems generally have been researched over several decades now and there are many good practice guidelines, but these relate to desktop systems and they have mostly been developed within the human–computer interaction research community or by practitioner designers. It is not simply a case of taking such guidelines and applying them to mobile devices. The following are some of the new factors that have to be taken into consideration:

- The considerable variety of devices and types of connectivity
- The nature of fragmented, context-dependent use on the move
- Small screens with poor readability, especially in monochrome
- Short battery life and dependency on re-charging
- The new concept of synchronization between PC and mobile device
- The paradox that a 'personal' device may not be owned by its user
- Few educational applications and learning-specific software
- Relatively slow transfer speeds, such as slow access to websites
- Inconvenient means of input to some devices, for some tasks
- A new way of communicating, e.g. Short Message Service (SMS) and endless new acronyms
- Mobile devices form part of a way of working that involves other devices
- Bystanders can feel annoyed when mobile phones are used in public.

To get an idea of what issues might arise when learners are using mobile and wireless devices or services, it is vital for educators and trainers to be able to describe how, where and when learners will be undertaking learning activities. This can be done by thinking in terms of scenarios of use (Evans and Taylor 2004). In turn, Weiss (2002) suggests that mobile device developers should ask themselves questions such as: Why would someone use the application? Under what circumstances would they use it? What are the various things they would want to do? He offers some guidelines for the designers of handheld devices, the top one being, 'Design for users on the go':

> Whether in the back of a taxi or walking down the street, people are likely to need their handhelds to perform in distracting situations. … designs must include context and forgiveness. While desktops accommodate 'surfing'… wireless devices are more about instantaneous search and retrieval …. Wireless users may be using their leisure time to gather information, but they typically have immediate goals.
>
> (Weiss 2002: 66)

The authors mentioned above were not writing specifically about the use of mobile technologies in the context of teaching and learning. It is possible for a mobile device, such as a phone or Personal Digital Assistant (PDA), to be perfectly usable in one context but not usable, or less usable, in another. For example, it may be easy to access a list of contacts, but difficult to read and study a lengthy text. It may be easy to send a simple message, but hard to use the same device to communicate with a tutor about one's understanding of a difficult concept. Educational contexts tend to impose new sets of requirements that may not always be met by existing devices and services.

The first step in any product or application design project is to define the target audience, just as the first step in designing a learning or teaching activity is to understand the participants and their characteristics. A good example of the two going hand-in-hand is provided by the development of the Interactive Logbook on Tablet PCs at the University of Birmingham: target users were consulted and when interface designs were drafted, these were shown to groups of students for them to select and modify (Kiddie *et al.* 2004). Another fine example is a hospital information system developed at the Campus Bio-Medico University of Rome, for students to access on PDAs. The initial interface design was enriched through student feedback that included requests to avoid long web pages, provide drop-down lists and checklists of options and to vary text box sizes for inserting additional information such as observations (Cacace *et al.* 2004).

O'Malley *et al.* (2003) remind us in their guidelines that usability should account for two sets of users: those who create mobile content (in many instances these will be teachers) and those who access the mobile content, namely learners and teachers. Elaborating on this, we can say that it is essential to get to know users' requirements and interface preferences, their new work or study environments and patterns of use, along with new demands placed on them by mobile technologies. Pehkonen and Turunen (2003) endorse the view that in the case of mobile learning, user-centred design means not only planning learning goals and actions but also specifying different contexts of use and the requirements of different 'actors' – which might include teachers, students and even parents. Syvänen and Nokelainen (2004) have identified some special features of mobile learning materials and environments: pedagogical concerns include how personal the learning materials are, the extent of flexibility in collaboration, support for contextual use and the added-value of mobility.

How usability affects teaching and learning

If we look through the case study accounts in this book from a usability perspective, they reveal both positive and negative aspects. When a device has good usability, learning can proceed without obstacles and can be enhanced by the availability of certain device features. For example, the Trinder *et al.* case study in Chapter 9 shows the advantage of the immediate readiness of PDAs – they can be switched on and used straight away with no 'boot up' time. This makes them ideal to grab a few moments' useful working time at times and in locations where even a laptop would not be useful. They also claim that among their learners, the ability to beam items between PDAs encouraged collaboration and communication, illustrating how, at best, a usable facility can support educational goals. The Levy and Kennedy case study in Chapter 7 shows how mobile phones worked successfully alongside conventional paper tools: language students copied into their personal dictionaries foreign language words that they had received in SMS messages while commuting.

Several authors of our case studies have made suggestions about what they see as potential usability improvements or ways in which they are planning to use mobile technologies in the future. Table 4.1 gives some examples.

On the negative side, the Smørdal and Gregory case study in Chapter 10 identifies problems in cutting and pasting material from one application to another, which limited the usefulness of the PDA as a communication device; for Global System for Mobile Communication (GSM) connected PDAs in their study, the slow transmission of web pages also resulted in a negative experience. The Luckin *et al.* case study in Chapter 12 describes the substantial overhead of staff time in terms of technical support, account administration and finding workarounds for features that did not work as required. The Sharples *et al.* case study in Chapter 15 reports that students expressed discontent about the size and weight of their mobile devices, their inadequate memory and short battery life; the memory was considered too small to hold the course resources, additional PDF and media files, added software, games and music files. An additional factor was the lack of device ownership: as the students were required to return their handhelds at the end of the year, they did not want to invest in additional memory modules. The Hackemer and Peterson case study in Chapter 17 notes that whilst students were comfortable with their handheld's built-in functions, additional applications proved problematic, as most of the available software for handheld devices lacks formal usability assessment and documentation; this resulted in very few students being willing to explore applications in order to understand how they could be used. The Polishook case study in Chapter 14 shows that for some individuals, the small, poorly lit low-resolution screens, tiny dialogue boxes and the need to connect extra wires, stood in the way of productive use for music composition. The Weber *et al.* case

Table 4.1 Possible improvements suggested by case study authors

	When internet access presents a problem:
Smørdal and Gregory case study (Chapter 10)	The PDA did not have any direct connection to the internet, but content from the internet could be downloaded during synchronization with desktop PCs.
	Convergence:
Ramsden case study (Chapter 8)	A Bluetooth or an all-in-one unit would be preferable to the infrared connection between the telephone and PDA.
	Integration:
Luckin *et al.* case study (Chapter 12)	Provide learners with simple tools to help them link together the different elements of the course content.
Smørdal and Gregory case study (Chapter 10)	Integrate parts of existing institutional, social and technical resources, and make them available on the PDAs.
	Ownership:
Trinder *et al.* case study (Chapter 9)	If students own the PDA then perhaps they are more likely to buy and install applications and tailor the device to their learning needs.
Kneebone and Brenton case study (Chapter 11)	Unless participants feel a sense of ownership towards their PDA the technology may be regarded as an 'imposed gift'.
	Learning materials:
Ramsden case study (Chapter 8)	Engage the academic in how best to author material to ensure its suitability for small screens and to make sure that they account for small screen devices when recommending websites.
Koschembahr and Sagrott case study (Chapter 18)	Breaking an hour-long web lecture into six 10-minute segments for mobile devices; Providing lecturers with a 'preview mode' where they can see what their presentation would look like on a mobile device and make any necessary changes.
	Assessment:
Ramsden case study (Chapter 8)	In survey/assessment questions, reduce the need for free text entry, since entering a large amount of text in the PDA without a keyboard would take significant time and have a large number of errors.
	User support:
Kneebone and Brenton case study (Chapter 11)	Correct software functioning means nothing without a dedicated member of support staff who can talk about PDAs in plain English.
	Teacher mindset:
Weber *et al.* case study (Chapter 16)	The teaching pace in the classroom will no longer be driven solely by the instructor, who will have to be more adept at maximizing interactivity while meeting more student demands and expectations.

study in Chaper 16 indicates that peer-to-peer interaction on mobile devices could become a distraction in class – perhaps this is a case of good usability facilitating communication to the extent that it becomes 'second nature', but may then be used inappropriately with regard to educational goals.

Elsewhere in published literature and project reports, the ICT Team at Aberdeen City Council (2003) in Scotland describe both positive and negative experiences of schoolchildren and adults using early models of Tablet PCs: one of the most powerful features was the ability to import files into the Windows Journal application and use the digital pen (stylus) to annotate document images. The children experienced no difficulty using the stylus and those children who did not have keyboard skills found that this no longer created a barrier to producing work electronically. There were, however, some issues with the weight of the device and short battery life. In a higher education context, Corlett and Sharples (2004) report that pen input on a Tablet PC was useful but unreliable. Taylor (2004) explains that from an evaluator's point of view, what is important is the effectiveness with which learners are able to achieve their goals and complete learning activities, irrespective of the specific devices they are using. De Freitas and Levene (2003) remark that greater interactivity will be based upon the usability and adaptability of mobile devices. These approaches put the emphasis on successful learning activities and interactions, with the technology playing a supporting or mediating role so that ideally its usability becomes transparent.

To highlight the requirements of teaching and learning, it is in fact insufficient to refer to usability as though it were the same notion irrespective of the context in which technology is used. Muir *et al.* (2003) have addressed this issue with respect to educational websites, describing usability in terms of four levels: technical, general, academic and context-specific. At the *technical* and *general* levels, one is mainly concerned with reliable functioning of software and hardware and with design that is based on good practice. *Academic* usability foregrounds one's pedagogical approach, the place of the website within a course and in relation to other media and expected study behaviour. *Context-specific* usability stresses the needs and intended outcomes of a specific course of study and its subject matter. Kukulska-Hulme and Shield (2004) subsequently proposed 'pedagogical usability' as a way of describing the interplay of technical and pedagogical issues and concluded that technical usability is the basis for other aspects, whilst not being sufficient in itself. Also, some disciplines have quite definite requirements, e.g. multimedia in music education and in language learning, or the availability of symbols for mathematics. Syvänen and Nokelainen (2004) express similar concerns when they distinguish between technical and pedagogical mobile usability: aspects such as accessibility, reliability and consistency come under the *technical* heading, whereas *pedagogical* usability criteria focus on aspects such as learner activity and cooperation, added value for learning (e.g. better adaptation to individual needs) and feedback. This is an area of active research, but the key point to note is that educators and trainers have a crucial role in asking the following question: If a mobile device has been tested for usability, what contexts of use were taken into account?

Human needs and contexts of use

Mobile and wireless technologies require users to develop new habits both in relation to the upkeep of the device, e.g. having to recharge a battery on a regular basis and in relation to new patterns of work or study. In the Smørdal and Gregory case study in Chapter 10, there is emphasis on acquiring new habits of caring for and interacting with a new technology and the realization that use of existing PCs, phones and paging systems may work against adoption of PDAs. In the Ramsden case study in Chapter 8, the author remarks that two learners displayed behaviour that was different to that of others in the group – they constantly transferred information between their Palm Pilot (handheld) and computer – thereby reminding us that emerging patterns of use are likely to be quite diverse and may digress from what was envisaged.

An investigation by Kukulska-Hulme (2002) pointed to a range of cognitive, ergonomic and affective issues associated with the introduction of PDAs for reading course materials in higher education. Table 4.2 shows a range of cognitive and ergonomic issues. Affective issues included the fear of overwriting diary or personal information by mistake, some reluctance to switch over to a new PDA (offered by the institution) from one's own familiar handheld and an emotional attachment to one's device which made it impossible to lend it to someone else. It was also noted that some learners naturally look for fun and games on a PDA – just as they do on desktop computers. Waycott (2004), who undertook several case studies of mobile technologies in learning and workplace contexts, used the concept of 'appropriation' to describe how people adopt a device over time as a useful aspect emerges.

Environmental factors also have an impact on usability, when one considers the range of settings in which mobile devices could be deployed. Outdoor use often brings problems of screen readability and the case studies in this book provide further examples, e.g. hospital regulations prohibiting use of PDAs for internet access or mobile communication within the local hospital, or the difficulties of writing and selecting information while travelling on a bus.

Role and extent of technical support

In the case studies reported in this book, training and technical support for users is frequently mentioned. The Luckin et al. case study in Chapter 12 reports that students were given a training session and technical support was freely available throughout the period of use. The Smørdal and Gregory case study in Chapter 10 confides that there were about as many technical support personnel as medical students in their project; a team of 'super user' medical students in fact provided the IT support to other students. In the Trinder et al. case study in Chapter 9, students were given basic training in the use of the PDA and its applications and the authors note that if PDAs were to be deployed in larger numbers, training could be a significant overhead. In the distance education context described in the Kukulska-Hulme case study in Chapter 13, students were not given training, though a set of instructions was made available for downloading from their course website.

Table 4.2 Examples of cognitive and ergonomic challenges in using PDAs (adapted from Kukulska-Hulme 2002)

Cognitive challenges:

- Using a new PDA invites comparisons with other devices, e.g. battery life or memory on one's PC, laptop, or other handheld device, compared with the PDA.
- Conceptions of paper-based study tools may need to be revisited, e.g. is a PDA just like a paper organizer?
- What one notices in print can differ to what one notices on a screen.
- Skim-reading on a PDA may be slower than skim-reading print materials.
- Users may want to mark text, to underline, highlight, or circle words.
- Taking electronic notes can be difficult, as this disrupts reading.
- PDAs can open up new information gathering strategies that learners have to get used to.

Ergonomic challenges:

- Preference for a good quality colour screen, which may be more expensive.
- When font is enlarged, text can be difficult to scan.
- Possibility of eye ache and visual disturbance.
- Possible preference for a portable keyboard rather than an on-screen keyboard.
- Dislike of clicking noise when selecting a function on a PDA.
- Possible requirement for predictive text (automatic word completion).
- Problems caused by cleaning finger marks off the PDA screen while the device is switched on.
- Screen needing to be re-calibrated from time to time.
- Difficulties with gripping a very thin stylus.
- Leaning heavily on the PDA whilst writing, inadvertently pressing buttons at the bottom of the device.

The Ramsden case study in Chapter 8 also makes several points about training and support. It describes how groups of two or three students underwent initial training on Palm hardware and software, but states that improved training and advice was needed, in particular on the use of preference settings and assistive technologies; the case study recommends a shift towards more self-help documentation and a culture of student peer support. In addition, students required training on the most efficient use of the PDA e-mail client in conjunction with their PC e-mail clients. Students could share memo documents, however for this more sophisticated use of the technology, it is estimated that significant support would be needed. The Hackemer and Peterson case study in Chapter 17 warns that although students suggest that additional training is necessary, there is an initial steep learning curve and few of them attend enough sessions to get to the point where they would understand the use and usefulness of handhelds.

Conclusions

Whilst envisaging a design ideal that is focused on human interactions, we have to recognize, as Schneiderman does (2003), that educators and trainers as consumers have to exert greater pressure on companies to produce more reliable, learnable and usable designs:

There is no magic bullet that will bring widespread use of low-cost devices that are easy to learn, rapid in performing common tasks and low in error rates. The main change that is needed is not a technology breakthrough. The most important breakthrough will be your change in expectations and willingness to ask for higher quality.

(Schneiderman 2003: 26–7)

Unfortunately, educational users are often least able to afford the more expensive technologies that might offer them improved usability, e.g. a lighter device, a better screen, a multifunctional tool. So on a practical level – whilst expecting designs to improve in the longer term – it is also important to reflect on how learning activities can be planned for existing devices so that they take advantage of usable features and avoid, or provide alternatives for, those that are least usable. This should take place at the same time as consideration of accessibility for learners with disabilities and all those requiring special support.

Aspects of usability have surfaced in all the case studies presented in this book. From the perspective of further research into mobile usability, it will be important to work in multidisciplinary teams, since it is impossible for technical experts and software developers to be fully aware of educational possibilities and constraints, just as it is impossible for educators and trainers to have detailed knowledge of technical and design aspects of mobile devices. We need a better theoretical understanding of the mutual interaction of technical and pedagogical usability and continued evaluation of user experiences in education and training.

References

Aberdeen City Council (2003) Sweet result in tablet trials. *Connected Online magazine – ICT in Practice for Scottish Education*. On-line. Available HTTP http://www.ltscotland. org.uk/connected/connected9/ictinpractice/tablettrials.asp (accessed 22 November 2004).

Cacace, F., Cinque, M., Crudele, M., Iannello, G. and Venditti, M. (2004) The impact of innovation in medical and nursing training: a hospital information system for students accessible through mobile devices. MLEARN 2004 Proceedings, The Third Annual MLEARN international conference, Rome, Italy, 5–6 July 2004. On-line. Available HTTP http://www.crudele.it/papers/00269.pdf (accessed 22 November 2004).

Corlett, D. and Sharples, M. (2004) Tablet technology for informal collaboration in higher education. MLEARN 2004 Proceedings, The Third Annual MLEARN international conference, Rome, Italy, 5–6 July 2004. On-line. Available HTTP http://www. mobilearn.org/download/events/mlearn_2004/presentations/Sharples.pdf (accessed 22 November 2004).

de Freitas, S. and Levene, M. (2003) Evaluating the development of wearable devices, personal data assistants and the use of other mobile devices in further and higher education institutions. JISC Technology and Standards Watch Report: Wearable Technology. On-line. Available HTTP http://www.jisc.ac.uk/index.cfm?name= techwatch_report_0305 (accessed 28 November 2004).

Evans, D. and Taylor, J. (2004) The role of user scenarios as the central piece of the development jigsaw puzzle. MLEARN 2004 Proceedings, The Third Annual MLEARN international conference, Rome, Italy, 5–6 July 2004.

Kiddie, P., Marianczak, T., Sandle, N., Bridgefoot, L., Mistry, C., Williams, D., Corlett, D., Sharples, M. and Bull, S. (2004) Interactive logbook: the development of an application to enhance and facilitate collaborative working within groups in higher education. MLEARN 2004 Proceedings, The Third Annual MLEARN international conference, Rome, Italy, 5–6 July 2004.

Kukulska-Hulme, A. (2002) Cognitive, ergonomic and affective aspects of PDA Use for Learning. Proceedings of MLEARN 2002, European Workshop on Mobile and Contextual Learning, University of Birmingham, 20–21 June 2002, 32–3. On-line. Available HTTP http://kn.open.ac.uk/public/document.cfm?docid=2970 (accessed 22 November 2004).

Kukulska-Hulme, A. and Shield, L. (2004) Usability and pedagogical design: are language learning websites special? Proceedings of ED-MEDIA 2004, World Conference on Educational Multimedia, Hypermedia and Telecommunications, Lugano, Switzerland, 23–26 June 2004.

Muir, A., Shield, L. and Kukulska-Hulme, A. (2003) The pyramid of usability: a framework for quality course websites. Proceedings of EDEN, Twelfth Annual Conference of the European Distance Education Network, The Quality Dialogue: Integrating Quality Cultures in Flexible, Distance and e-Learning, Rhodes, Greece, 15–18 June 2003, 188–94.

Nielsen, J. (1993) *Usability Engineering*, Boston, MA: Academic Press.

Nielsen, J. (2003) Mobile devices: one generation from useful. On-line. Available HTTP http://www.useit.com/alertbox/20030818.html (accessed 22 November 2004).

O'Malley, C., Vavoula, G., Glew, J.P., Taylor, J., Sharples, M. and Lefrere, P. (2003) MOBIlearn WP4 – guidelines for learning/teaching/tutoring in a mobile environment. On-line. Available HTTP http://www.mobilearn.org/download/results/guidelines.pdf (accessed 22 November 2004).

Pehkonen, M. and Turunen, H. (2003) Preliminary guidelines for the design of the mobile learning activities and materials. In *EUROPRIX Scholars Conference, Conference Papers and Presentations*. Tampere: European Academy of Digital Media, MindTrek Association. On-line. Available HTTP: http://www.mindtrek.org/liitetiedostot/materiaalit_editori/75.doc (accessed 22 November 2004).

Preece, J. (2000) *On-line Communities: Designing Usability, Supporting Sociability*, Chichester: John Wiley and Sons.

Preece, J., Rogers, Y. and Sharp, H. (2002) *Interaction Design: Beyond Human-Computer Interaction*, New York: John Wiley & Sons.

Preece, J., Rogers, Y., Sharp, H., Benyon, D., Holland, S. and Carey, T. (1994) *Human–Computer Interaction*, Harlow: Addison-Wesley.

Schneiderman, B. (2003) *Leonardo's Laptop: Human Needs and the New Computing Technologies*, Cambridge, MA and London: MIT Press.

Syvänen, A. and Nokelainen, P. (2004) Evaluation of the technical and pedagogical mobile usability. MLEARN 2004 Proceedings, The Third Annual MLEARN international conference, Rome, Italy, 5–6 July 2004.

Taylor, J. (2004) A task-centred approach to evaluating a mobile learning environment for pedagogical soundness. In Attewell, J. and Savill-Smith, C. (eds) *Learning with*

Mobile Devices: Research and Development. London: Learning and Skills Development Agency, 167–72. Also On-line. Available HTTP http://www.mobilearn.org/download/results/Mlearn_paper.pdf (accessed 22 November 2004).

Waycott, J. (2004) The Appropriation of PDAs as Learning and Workplace Tools, Unpublished PhD Thesis, The Open University, Milton Keynes, UK.

Weiss, S. (2002) *Handheld Usability*, Chichester: John Wiley & Sons.

Chapter 5

Accessibility and mobile learning

Peter Rainger

Introduction

Accessibility is an increasingly significant factor in the provision of learning and training and is the key to strategies to support inclusion, participation and diversity within education and training (Phipps *et al.* 2002). There is a range of reasons for supporting improved accessibility. These include:

- The moral case that promoting the inclusion and participation of disabled people through 'inclusive' product design is a moral or ethical activity.
- Social responsibility, in the sense that society defines and constructs notions of disability. This is a social model of disability and puts the case that disabled people do not face disadvantage because of their impairments but experience discrimination in the way society is organized and services are provided.
- Technical efficiency, namely that accessible technology will usually be more interoperable (that is, it will operate with a wider variety of other technologies) and so reduce future development costs.
- Legal requirements, for example, in the UK, the Disability Discrimination Act 1995 (DDA) and Special Educational Needs and Disability Act 2001 (SENDA) prescribe minimum levels of accessibility. (Further details on the legislation can be found on-line at http://www.disability.gov.uk/dda/ and http://www.hmso.gov.uk/acts/acts2001/20010010.htm.)

This chapter draws on a UK research project (http://www.techdis.ac.uk/PDA). It looks at accessibility issues for mobile devices and the technologies that are available to extend or enhance the accessibility of current mobile devices. The features that support or hinder people with specific disabilities, and the use of mobile devices as assistive technology will also be discussed. Recommendations are made for more inclusive mobile learning courses to assist teachers, lecturers and trainers in this emerging field.

Assistive technologies are any items, pieces of equipment or product systems, whether acquired commercially off-the-shelf, modified, or customized, used to increase, maintain or improve functional capabilities of individuals with disabilities in employment, education and at home. Mobile devices have been used for a few years as specialist forms of assistive technology, because:

- market forces and economies of scale are lowering device prices;
- there is increasing awareness of the technology in the student population;
- there are developments in the accessibility of mobile phone technology.

Accessibility issues of mobile devices

Before students can engage in any mobile learning activity, they must first be able to effectively access and interact with the actual mobile device. Therefore, by being aware of any technical barriers that may restrict the use of a mobile device, educators and trainers can provide disabled students with strategies and technical solutions to tackle and overcome these issues.

When investigating the accessibility of mobile learning devices, the principles of Universal Design have been used as tools for discussion of the range of factors involved. These principles of Universal Design are:

- *Equitable Use*: The design must be useful and marketable to people with diverse abilities. For example, the learning content must be such that older students, students with disabilities and students with English as a second language could all use it.
- *Flexibility in Use*: The design must accommodate a wide range of individual preferences and abilities. An example would be content that allows a student to choose different text sizes.
- *Simple and Intuitive Use*: Design must be easy to understand, regardless of the student's experience, knowledge, language skills or current concentration level. An example of this principle would be clear and intuitive control buttons and on-screen icons.
- *Perceptible Information*: The design must communicate necessary information effectively to the student, regardless of ambient conditions or the student's sensory abilities. An example of this principle would be a text-based description provided for all videos or animations.
- *Tolerance for Error*: The design must minimize hazards and the adverse consequences of accidental or unintended actions. An example would be asking the student to confirm all file deletions.
- *Low Physical Effort*: The design must be used efficiently and comfortably, and with a minimum of fatigue. An example would be the control of an application using the hardware or software buttons alone.
- *Size and Space for Approach and Use*: Appropriate size and space must be provided for approach, reach, manipulation, and use regardless of the student's body size, posture, or mobility. An example would be a mobile device that can be operated comfortably with one hand.

Further examples and an explanation of the principles can be found at http://www.design.ncsu.edu/cud/. The following sections discuss the issues of accessibility for particular common device features and the suggestions and recommendations are based on these principles.

Issues of size and portability

Mobile devices should ideally be compact and easy to hold; should be portable and not too heavy. However, the current trend is to design increasingly smaller gadgets, mobile phones and Personal Digital Assistants (PDAs). In terms of portability, this would appear to be a natural development from the chunky oversized gadgets of the past. However, for students who have lost some sensitivity in their fingers or have manual dexterity problems, and indeed those who are visually impaired, the small size can make using the devices extremely difficult. When choosing a mobile device, the priority should be well designed, clearly identifiable buttons and switches with clear visual and tactile markings in ergonomic positions.

Touch screens and displays

The touch screen display is usually the main interface by which students interact with and control mobile devices. As such, the size and clarity of the screen can have a large impact on the accessibility of the devices for the majority of users.

The screen is like a personal computer's monitor; it is used to display the Graphical User Interface (GUI), which in turn allows the user to operate the device. PDAs and smartphones usually have touch (or pressure) sensitive screens, that allow the device to be operated by stylus or touch control.

The screen sizes are around 8–12 cms long and 6–8 cms wide, usually in portrait format. Their resolutions vary and they may or may not be back, front or side lit with or without colour.

The screen should have a high resolution for greater clarity (the more pixels that make up a picture, the better the picture), and a good depth of colour, as the higher the resolution capabilities the clearer and more focused the images will appear.

Switches and buttons

These are used to execute functions such as cursor and focus navigation, quick start buttons for applications, power switches etc. They tend to be at the bottom of the body of the device, small and conspicuously lacking in tactile detail which is often a problem for those with visual impairment. Sadly, very few devices offer the alternative of a Jog Dial at the side of the device that is often easier to use.

The key to ensuring the accessibility of the device's controls and buttons is not to rely on one control mechanism. The hardware (or fixed software screen) buttons should be intuitive and customizable to allow the user to perform all navigational functions and most operational commands without using a stylus. Software support for the hardware buttons' functions should be provided to ensure all the commands or operations are available via keyboard commands (if a peripheral keyboard has been added or connected).

In this context, students with mobility and dexterity difficulties may have problems when they try to access the GUI with a stylus, small button or keyboard owing to difficulties with manipulation. The options for mouse or switch access are limited but remote control, infrared and Bluetooth may be the way forward.

Graphical User Interfaces (GUI)

Ideally, the GUI should be intuitive and have user-friendly navigation and functionality, with a clear, readable, uncluttered visual design that can be re-sized or enlarged. The operating system should support large enough graphics to allow easy viewing and stylus control.

In this context, students with visual impairments may have problems reading the text and graphics on the display as well as identifying the functions of the hardware buttons. They may benefit from the ability to re-size text or magnify graphics and change the colour or contrast of a display. External keyboards with shortcuts for navigation as well as an external magnifying glass may also be necessary.

Students with specific learning difficulties or dyslexia may find the complex GUIs provided on some PDAs confusing – those trying Pocket PCs will come across cramped toolbars and menus with long lists. All small screens tend to result in a lack of 'white space', which can impede reading. It may help to provide options to re-size text or graphics and change the colour or contrast of a display. Students with hearing impairments may not have any difficulties with the GUI interface and operating system. However, those who tend to communicate in sign language or use English as a second language may find the interface language confusing.

Batteries

The longer the battery life, the better! Most students will be at university or college for up to eight hours a day and will have different usage needs. Some older devices use small AA batteries or have additional back-up batteries but most now depend on an AC charger and it can help to choose a model that does not require a cradle for charging.

Expansion slots, ports and connectors

When peripheral add-ons or extras are required to aid the accessibility of a mobile device, it is essential to consider devices that offer:

- the means to add extra memory (useful if you wish to store a large volume of files, or run memory-hungry programs like text-to-speech or voice memos);
- an additional means of backing up data to a desktop PC or other storage device, perhaps by an infrared port or a cable;
- the chance for the PDA to be connected to a network or mobile phone for local file access or/and the internet;
- additional connectors for peripherals, such as a printer, modem, mass storage devices (hard drives), camera etc.

Docking stations and synchronization cradles

The difficulties that tend to arise with this aspect of using a mobile device are related to dexterity and being able to slot it into the fitting. Plugging in cables and setting up the synchronization through the hardware button or software synch program can also be problematic with some models.

User alerts

Students with hearing impairment may benefit from a vibrating alert to accompany an alarm. Ideally, the auditory alarm should have a variable pitch and volume to allow for students with different hearing ranges.

Visual alerts such as a flashing light emitting diode (LED) or flashing display screen may help users with visual and/or hearing difficulties and those who do not wish to disturb others, in a library for instance.

Adapting and modifying devices

Making changes to the user interface

For students with visual difficulties, for example visual impairment or dyslexia, allowing changes to the user interface can make a huge impact on the accessibility of the device due to the reliance on the graphical user interface.

Features of Palm OS 4.0+

The Palm operating system, PalmOS, has only a few options for changing the user interface. In the PalmOS Personal Information Management (PIM) applications (Diary, Address Book, Memo and To Do list), the user has the choice of displaying the main text in three font sizes: standard, bold and large. Later versions of PalmOS provide a range of fixed colour styles for the GUI.

Third party applications are available to:

- modify the interface colours (e.g. Butterfly http://www.ranosoft.net);
- change the fonts (e.g. Font Hack-123 http://www.sergem.net/fonthack123/);
- magnify a static image of the screen (e.g. TealMagnify http://www.teal point.com/softlens.htm).

Features of Pocket PC 2002+

The Pocket PC operating system has few user interface options built-in. In Pocket Word, Notes and Excel the user can specify the zoom level (75 per cent to 300 per cent) for the text as one would with Microsoft Windows desktop versions. Unfortunately, in Tasks, Contacts and Calendar the user has only the choice of a slightly larger font. This may not be sufficient for students with visual impairments.

Third party applications are however available to:

- modify the interface colours (e.g. Pocket Tweak http://tillanosoft.com/ce/ptweak.html);
- change the fonts (e.g. CeTuner http://www.penreader.com/PocketPC/CETuner.html);
- change the screen resolution or orientation (e.g. Nyditot http://www.nyditot.com/).

Speech recognition and text-to-speech

The most promising development of mobile technology for supporting students with disabilities is the advancement of portable speech recognition and text-to-speech software.

Currently mobile devices do not have the processing power required to accomplish speech recognition. Speech recognition would mean that any text could be entered into a device merely by dictating it. Pocket PCs can, however, be used with voice command recognition when either simple commands (with a limited recognition vocabulary) or a string of commands (a command with recognized variables e.g. read > next item) are entered.

Text-to-speech software uses a synthetic voice to read out text from document, diary entries or simple notes.

Students with a specific learning difficulty may find audio feedback useful because they may have slow reading speeds and/or poor reading comprehension skills. Most users may also find the use of text-to-speech a good way to review their own writing and to highlight grammatical errors.

Students who have a visual impairment or whose study environment makes visual concentration difficult, might prefer text-to-speech as a more effective reading method.

Freedom Scientific has developed a screen reader that allows students with visual impairments to access the GUI for Pocket PC, which is available with the PAC Mate (http://www.freedomscientific.com/).

Symbian operating system phones

The Symbian operating system has an increasing presence owing to its use on smartphones. The Royal National Institute for the Blind (RNIB) in the UK and Vodaphone have recently been working together to research into the mobile phone accessibility needs of the blind and visually impaired (http://www.vodafone.co.uk/Mike_Duxbury_interview.pdf). The most recent development in mobile device accessibility has been in the development of a screen reader (text-to-speech for the blind and visually impaired) and screen magnifier for Symbian OS mobile phones (e.g. Nokia 9110i) (http://www.codefactory.es/products.htm).

In addition, there is a new GUI that has been designed for the visually impaired, which provides an easily adaptable high-visibility interface and text-to-speech (http://mobileaccessibility.codfact.com/).

Accessibility issues for disabled students

Mobile devices are useful tools for many students with and without disabilities. The following uses of an inclusively designed mobile device would be helpful to all students:

- note taking – using a text editor or word processor for taking notes (in most cases this would also require a peripheral keyboard);
- viewing/storing reference materials – using a customized PDA database, text editor files, or e-book and e-doc files to store and present information (such as sections of a textbook, old essays, lecture notes, etc.);
- a diary planner – using an electronic diary and planner for an academic timetable.

However, most mobile devices are not fully inclusive and have features that present difficulties for students with disabilities. The following sections provide summaries of the features of PDAs and other mobile devices that affect students with disabilities. These summaries are only generalizations and every student is different.

Blind and visually impaired

Students with a visual impairment may find using a handheld device problematic because of the size or clarity of the display. They may also find the layout of hardware buttons on a device difficult to distinguish and use.

Features that may hinder accessibility:

- small screen size;
- low screen resolution;
- small standard font size;
- short sentence wrapping distance;
- small touch-screen sensitivity areas;
- poor screen contrast control;
- poor (front, back or side) lighting for the screen;
- buttons with a low tactile quality or poor layout;
- buttons with small labelling or symbolism.

Features that make accessibility better:

- 'live' text-to-speech (screen reading and document reading);
- speech recognition (both text transcription and for initiating commands);

- an external screen magnifier;
- keyboard commands with navigational prompts.

Specific learning difficulties (e.g. dyslexia)

Students with specific learning difficulties may find that some of the accessibility features mentioned in the blind/visually-impaired section will also apply to them due to a visual-processing deficit.

Features that may hinder accessibility:

- counter-intuitive layout of hardware buttons that action functional commands (e.g. badly aligned hardware);
- buttons for cursor navigation control;
- counter-intuitive location or actions of fixed on-screen buttons;
- poor use of symbolism/icons and visual representations of actions or commands;
- lack of multimedia options;
- poor quality calendar or diary functions that could be invaluable for those with short-term memory difficulties.

Features that make accessibility better:

- 'live' text-to-speech (screen reading and document reading);
- speech recognition (both text transcription and for initiating commands);
- simple graphical navigational aids;
- clear menu structures.

Deaf/hearing impairment

Many of the difficulties that deaf or hearing-impaired students encounter with handheld computers are often the same issues that arise when using mobile phones.
Features that may hinder accessibility:

- alerts that are purely auditory (e.g. a sharp tone when user errors occur);
- complex use of mobile device-specific language.

Features that make accessibility better:

- vibrating alert;
- flashing LED;
- flashing display and/or light.

However, mobile phones and some PDAs routinely offer Short Message Service (SMS) texting and this is a near-universal accessibility tool across many different communities.

Manual dexterity

Students with manual dexterity problems may find manipulating or using a mobile device with their hands cumbersome or difficult. They may lack the dexterity needed to coordinate simultaneously holding and operating a mobile device. Most of the devices on the market have a touch-sensitive screen and can be operated using a stylus (or finger). The devices can also be operated using the physical buttons.

Features that may hinder accessibility:

- holding and supporting a device for 'in hand use';
- stiff or cumbersome buttons or other physical controls;
- small size buttons and/or non-ergonomic shapes of buttons;
- when a stylus or touch screen controls are the only control option;
- a small, thin, hard-to-grip stylus;
- poor operating system support for hardware accessories (such as additional keyboards).

Features that make accessibility better:

- device cases designed with materials that increase friction and grip;
- an overall ergonomic shape that allows the device to be held comfortably in the hand;
- larger, more ergonomic styli that are more easily gripped;
- the availability of peripheral keyboards or other hardware data input devices;
- speech recognition (both text transcription and for initiating simple commands).

Mobility impairment

Students with mobility impairment may have difficulty in moving from place to place, due to a physical or medical constraint. They may find the portability of a mobile device useful.

Features that may hinder accessibility:

- the 'handheld' nature of mobile devices;
- poor portability due to a heavy device weight;
- a short battery life requiring regular charging.

Features that make accessibility better:

- the availability and/or feasibility of mounting brackets for use with a desk, wheelchair or in a fixed location;
- a means of portable battery recharging;
- speech recognition (both text transcription and for initiating simple commands).

Speech and language difficulties

Students with speech or language difficulties may find it hard to cope with complex technical language and may prefer to use symbol or graphical-based communication systems.

Features that may hinder accessibility:

- poor use of symbolism/icons and visual representations of actions or commands;
- poor speech output from written text or picture grids, i.e. audible text-to-speech;
- poor quality built-in speakers;
- lack of multimedia options.

Features that make accessibility better:

- 'live' text-to-speech (screen reading and document reading);
- a high performance central processor to provide the power required to produce good quality speech.

Mobile devices as assistive technology

Students with major mobility and communication difficulties have been using Alternative Augmentative Communication (AAC) and remote control devices for a few years now.

Students with speech impairments can use AAC devices to generate synthetic speech and/or visual displays. Remote control devices can be used to control computers, domestic appliances and environmental controls using infrared and short-range radio frequencies. These specialist devices are often much larger than the usual PDA but now examples of the Pocket PC with speech output and a simple interchangeable GUI system are being used.

Mobile devices such as PDAs and 'smart keyboards' provide a relatively low cost option for portable computing. As a result, the use of mobile devices for supporting disabled students is increasing within UK colleges and universities.

Students with specific learning difficulties (such as dyslexia) have been using 'smart keyboards' as portable word processors or note takers for several years. Smart keyboards, such as the AlphaSmart Dana (www.alphasmart.co.uk/dana/), have bridged the gap toward PDAs and now offer students a much greater range of facilities. With the use of additional software, students can now use one device for:

- reference databases (e.g. dictionaries);
- electronic material readers (e-doc readers);
- electronic reminders;
- to-do or task lists;

- outline tools or mind/concept mapping;
- text editing (or word processors, for note-taking).

Accessibility and mobile learning

Features of mobile learning that promote accessibility include:

- anywhere, anytime access to learning material and general information;
- the integration of portable communication tools (message boards, text messaging and e-mail) to create a mobile collaborative learning environment;
- anywhere, anytime access to learning scaffolds and support tools (dictionaries, diaries and electronic reference materials, etc.).

Developing a mobile learning component of a course should address accessibility thoroughly in advance. Accessibility should be integrated into the design process early, not 'bolted-on' later as a remedy. Developing an accessible alternative to a course after the initial development phase will be time-consuming and expensive. In this context, the choice of mobile technology used will have a significant impact on the learning experience of the students. The design and content of the learning materials will be the most important factors for developing a mobile learning course.

The role of inclusive learning design

The primary aim of accessibility in mobile learning should be to ensure the accessibility of the learning experience. Students should be provided with the opportunity to meet the learning objectives and this might involve alternative course material or assessment methods. Mobile learning and its technologies are in their infancy and there are not always easy or technology-based solutions to accessibility problems.

In the UK, institutions providing mobile learning courses must plan to make reasonable adjustments under SENDA 2001 to accommodate the needs of all students. This may simply mean the provision of loan laptops or making the course material available in a desktop PC format.

No two students learn the same way. Even within the normal range of performance, skills and ability, students vary greatly in their ability to see, hear, move, read, write, organize, communicate, focus, engage and remember. Universal Design strives to encompass all these abilities through good design principles. Applying the principles of Universal Design for Learning (http://www.cast.org/udl/) to the learning materials and activities will increase access for all students, including those with disabilities.

In order to promote accessibility, when developing a mobile learning course:

- a named individual within the development team should be responsible for investigating the accessibility issues;

- where possible someone who is familiar with the range or requirements for accessibility should be asked to evaluate the course;
- the technical requirements of the course should be made widely available to enable students and support staff to effectively evaluate any possible accessibility difficulties;
- ways of adapting the course for disabled students should be fully explored when the course is evaluated through the normal institutional quality assurance procedures.

Creating accessible mobile learning materials

Producing learning materials that are accessible for disabled students takes much less time and effort than most people realize. Whether providing a batch of PDAs or specifying supported models in the course requirements, it is essential to consider the needs of students who might be using alternative models or technologies to access the material due to their accessibility needs.

This means that ensuring the maximum interoperability of the materials is a key factor to the inclusion of students with disabilities. As a rough guide, the following should be considered:

- static information and basic course text should be available on request in text files (.txt) or HTML;
- course materials developed using proprietary formats should be provided in a format accessible using the host computer (such as Macromedia Flash or TomeRaider http://www.tomeraider.com/);
- where bespoke applications have been developed, an accessible host computer version should ideally be available, or the content and interactivity of the system should be available in an accessible format for use on the host computer;
- provide user preferences to adapt the user interface for display on a mobile device or using a computer monitor;
- provide user preferences to modify the main background and font colours.

Conclusion

The mobile technology sector is developing rapidly and as similar technologies merge (e.g. smart keyboards or mobile phones) into multipurpose devices, the functionality offered by these devices could enrich the lives of many disadvantaged groups (including disabled students). However, the speed of development may also hinder the advancements in accessibility if lessons are not learned from problems with current technologies.

The use of mobile devices as assistive technologies is likely to increase as inclusively designed devices become more widespread and as such provide more opportunities to develop innovative technology solutions for accessibility problems.

Mobile learning brings a new dimension of portability to e-learning, which itself has already started to engage with a wider range of students. More than anything, those providing mobile technology or mobile learning courses need to be cognisant of the needs of disabled students and integrate accessibility into the initial development phases of any new technology or curriculum.

References

Phipps, L., Sutherland, A. and Seale, J. (2002) *Access All Areas: Disability, Technology and Learning.* Report published by JISC TechDis and ALT. On-line. Available HTTP http://www.techdis.ac.uk/index.php?p=1_1_20042209080936_20040610021026 (accessed 28 November 2004).

Chapter 6

Case studies

Introduction and overview

John Traxler

This part of the book consists of twelve case studies. This introduction pulls together some common themes and issues from them. They are all structured in a similar way and based around a common framework designed to facilitate comparison. They are all first-hand accounts drawn from contemporary projects with a direct relevance to training and education around the world. The accounts of the case studies have been written specifically for this book and they draw on research and development done by the respective authors within the last few years. Different authors each bring their own specific emphasis to bear.

Each one consists of sections that address:

- the context and setting;
- the problem statement;
- the aims, objectives, resources;
- technology, systems and infrastructure;
- the issues of engaging with students, and of teaching and learning;
- evaluation, monitoring and outcomes, with feedback from major stakeholders;
- institutional aspects, the wider impact and possible future developments.

In reading these case studies, we are looking at a snapshot across the developed world of pilots and trials that have taken place over the years from 2000 to 2004. These case studies, along with other work in schools, corporations, universities and colleges, suggest that mobile learning is emerging – perhaps unsteadily – from an early phase of technological innovation and subject-specific delivery. It is now approaching a critical phase in its development when its advocates must address the twin issues of 'blending' with other forms of delivery, both traditional and electronic, and of devising sustainable, reliable, generalized and large-scale formats across whole departments and institutions. We return to these latter issues in Chapter 19.

The case studies start with the most ubiquitous and stable mobile technologies, namely Short Message Service (SMS) texting, then move on to more technologically sophisticated examples based on current PDA technology and finish with some even more technologically complex case studies.

SMS texting has assumed a vast social importance over the last five years and has transformed cultural life and social behaviour with the take-up of mobile phones in many parts of the world (Plant 2001; Katz and Aakhus 2002; Tamminien *et al.* 2003). There has been a growing understanding of mobile phones' potential for supporting learning (Attewell and Savill-Smith 2003). There is now experience of using mobile phones to deliver educational content. One recent study looks at SMS in learning tourist Greek (Pincas 2004), another at learning literature (Hoppe 2004). There is also experience in using mobile phones to address retention (Stone 2004), to provide study support at a departmental level (Traxler and Riordan 2003) and possibly across a large academic institution (Traxler and Dalziel 2004). This has been based on earlier work (Stone *et al.* 2002; Garner *et al.* 2002; Briggs and Stone 2002) that suggested students would prefer SMS and e-mail to websites or notice boards as ways of receiving up-to-date information, and will welcome SMS texts that were perceived as timely, appropriate and personalized. This work shows that SMS can be used to provide support, motivation and continuity; to provide alerts and reminders; to deliver bite-size content, introductions, and revision tips; to give study guide structure. A gradual transition of an SMS service from operational issues, through tutorial and pastoral support, to fully moderated asynchronous conferences is anticipated (Salmon 2000). This is the context for our first case study.

The remainder of the case studies are based firmly around PDA technology and smartphone technology. Whilst there is some general guidance on good practice in mobile learning (Smith 2003; Perry 2003), there is still not a large consolidated literature on mainstream subject-specific mobile learning using these technologies in the post-compulsory education sectors. Table 6.1 shows the spread of technologies in our case studies.

Several authors have previously addressed teacher training (Seppala and Alamaki 2003; Sariola and Rionka 2003). This is clearly one specialist niche, along with medical and para-medical education, where one would expect to see early adoption of mobile devices. In all of them, there is an emphasis on practical on-the-job training (in the ward or in the classroom), a large volume of facts and procedures to be absorbed and a substantial investment by the state in the associated sectors of education and healthcare. There is already also a small literature that describes projects and programmes that use mobile devices to enhance the wider student experience, for example providing advice and guidance (Vuorinen and Sampson 2003), developing job-seeking skills (McKay *et al.* 2003) and supporting personal information management (Traxler and Riordan 2004a). Our case studies draw on medical and para-medical education but also on engineering, economics, Italian, informatics, music, human-centred systems and include three more broadly based studies where the focus is more organizational.

We ought to examine the extent to which our case studies and other work described in the literature reflect the current global extent of mobile learning. Our case studies and the other work are drawn mainly from the English-speaking developed world and are clustered in the USA, the Far East/Pacific Rim,

Table 6.1 The case study technologies

Levy and Kennedy	Phones
Ramsden	PDAs
Trinder *et al.*	PDAs
Smørdal and Gregory	PDAs
Kneebone and Brenton	PDAs
Luckin *et al.*	PDAs
Kukulska-Hulme	Laptops, PDAs
Polishook	PDAs
Sharples *et al.*	PDAs
Weber and Yow	Laptops, Tablets, phones, PDAs
Hackemer and Peterson	PDAs
von Koschembahr and Sagrott	Laptops, PDAs

Scandinavia and the UK. The use of mobile technologies in developing countries is constrained by a rather different environment but holds out considerable promise (Traxler and Kukulska-Hulme 2004).

Many if not all of the case studies describe work supported on a short-term basis, perhaps looking at the feasibility of some larger proposal. This raises several problems in relation to both implementation and evaluation. Short-term projects may not become embedded in the core or compulsory parts of courses because staff perceive them as both short-term and untried. Students may be reluctant to invest time and effort putting personal data (birthdays, dental appointments, relatives' addresses etc.) into handheld devices if they know the devices have to be returned at the end of the project. Consequently, the students may also feel encumbered by carrying two devices, a personal mobile phone and a project handheld device, rather than just one. In some projects (Traxler and Riordan 2004b) students have also felt that the handheld devices issued as part of a mobile learning project were inferior to their own up-to-date high specification mobile phones and that these sophisticated mobile phones were better for what they perceived to be their information management needs.

At the start of a mobile learning project, lecturers and researchers will have had to predict training needs for staff and students, and to anticipate usability and accessibility problems with very little previous experience to guide them. Inevitable technical problems and delayed or reduced start-ups may mean that summative evaluation at the end of the pilot is squeezed or rushed. Devising appropriate evaluation procedures may itself be problematic and sometimes produces outcomes of questionable value, and ones that may not scale up and understandably not address questions of embedding and sustainability.

Many of the case studies hint at a further hidden barrier to increased mobile learning, namely access to hardware. Many of the current case studies obtained one-off grants from public bodies or small-scale loans from equipment manufacturers. These will probably have represented a risk or outlay of less than £10,000. Breaking through to sustained or institutional commitments is clearly a challenge, hinging on finding ways to conduct trials and pilots several orders of magnitude larger than currently, with corresponding larger sets of equipment over longer timescales.

In this context, it is worth examining the subsequent institutional consequences of each of our case studies. Clearly, pedagogic and technical evaluation, outcomes and implications were generally more obvious and more significant than institutional, financial or organizational ones. These may not even become viable research questions until a further round of small-scale and fixed-life pilots and trials has made the pedagogic and technical characteristics of mobile learning much more explicit.

The balance of hardware and software platforms is interesting in the light of Chapter 2, which looked at technology and systems. Bear in mind that this balance may not be the result of purely technical and pedagogic factors. If nothing else, major equipment manufacturers take differing positions on engagement with education, with research and with corporate sponsorship. The Palm Academy, mentioned in the University of South Dakota case study, is one example of a particularly distinctive corporate strategy. That said, there is some representation from both of the two major software platforms, PalmOS, running on Sony and Palm machines, and Windows PPC, a smaller proportion, running on HP and XDA machines. The software complement beyond the basic pre-installed Personal Information Management (PIM) functions is surprisingly modest and may be just one or two relatively standard applications. This last observation should be seen however in the context of each project's champions. Some are technologically sophisticated and prepared to push or develop the technology, others are technologically less sophisticated and driven more by a need to develop or deliver teaching and learning in a particular pragmatic situation. Some people involved in our case studies clearly fall into both categories.

Furthermore, it is worth examining the case studies in the light of the pedagogic ideas set out in Chapter 3. Some of the case studies are based on an explicit pedagogic position but the technical and organizational difficulties of mounting and evaluating innovative projects may obscure this. Some of the other case studies are reacting to the more pragmatic needs of students.

Many case studies, both here and in the wider literature, report technical problems and these often account for an apparent failure to deliver the full, anticipated pedagogic potential. These technical problems are hardly surprising for projects that by their nature are technically innovative but are seldom related to the handheld devices themselves, which seem robust and reliable. (We should also bear in mind that PDAs and smartphones are never developed with an educational market in mind and hence any educational use is likely to involve adaptation, appropriation and compromise.) The technical problems are usually those of usability – either finding usable applications, or converting documents into usable formats – or are problems of interoperability and integration – with pre-existing systems such as Virtual Learning Environments (VLEs) or wireless networks. In addition, we can see that many case studies understandably show mobile devices being used largely as mobile and connected PCs to deliver a portable version of e-learning. We have yet to exploit the full potential of the extra functionality associated with many mobile devices, for example cameras, MP3 players, Global Positioning Systems (GPS) etc. and so to define mobile learning as distinct and different from e-learning.

The case studies may come from a skewed sample of institutions in terms of funding and resourcing, or in terms of innovativeness and infrastructure. This may mean that the kinds of approaches used in the current round of trials and pilots, including those described in our case studies, do not map out a template for subsequent developments nor travel successfully to other institutions. Only time will tell.

The value of these case studies is their diversity and their honesty – a 'warts-and-all' approach in the words of one contributor. They are not case studies in any formalized methodological sense (Yin 1993) but are nevertheless a source of valuable systematic evidence. Research and development in mobile learning is still testing the technologies, identifying a role amongst learning technologies and within institutions, and defining priorities and research questions. These case studies and the efforts of their authors make a considerable contribution to moving this process forward.

References

Attewell, J. and Savill-Smith, C. (2003) *Young People, Mobile Phones and Learning*, London: Learning and Skills Development Agency.

Briggs, J. and Stone, A. (2002) *ITZ GD 2 TXT – How To Use SMS Effectively in M-Learning*, in Proceedings of MLEARN 2002, Birmingham: LSDA.

Garner, I., Francis, J. and Wales, K. (2002) *An Evaluation of an Implementation of a Short Message System (SMS) to Support Undergraduate Student Learning*, in Proceedings of MLEARN 2002, Birmingham: LSDA.

Hoppe, H. U. (2004) *SMS-based Discussions – Technology Enhanced Collaboration for A Literature Course*. Proceedings of International Workshop on Wireless and Mobile Technologies in Education (WMTE), National Central University, Taiwan.

Katz, J.E. and Aakhus, M. (eds) (2002) *Perpetual Contact – Mobile Communications, Private Talk, Public Performance*, Cambridge: Cambridge University Press.

McKay, E., Thomas, T. and Martin, J. (2003) Research Note – an Interactive Job-Seeking System for Vocational Rehabilitation, *Journal of Computer Assisted Learning*, 19(3): 396–8.

Perry, D. (2003) *Handheld Computers (PDAs) in Schools*, Coventry: BECTa.

Pincas, A. (2004) *Using Mobile Phone Support for Use of Greek During the Olympic Games 2004*, in Proceedings of MLEARN 2004, Odescalchi Castle, Lake Bracciano, Italy.

Plant, S. (2001) *On the mobile – the effects of mobile telephones on individual and social life*, Motorola. On-line. Available HTTP http://www.motorola.com/mot/doc/0.234_MotDoc.pdf (accessed 5 April 2005).

Salmon, G. (2000) *e-Moderating – The Key to Teaching and Learning Online*, London: Kogan Page.

Sariola, J. and Rionka, A. (2003) Mobile Learning in Teacher Education – The LIVE Project. In H. Kynaslahti and P. Seppala (eds) *Mobile Learning*, 79–90. Helsinki: IT Press.

Seppala, P. and Alamaki, H. (2003) Mobile Learning in Teacher Training, *Journal of Computer Assisted Learning*, 19(3): 330–5.

Smith, T. (2003) *Personal Digital Assistants (PDAs) in Further and Higher Education*, York: TechLearn.

Stone, A. (2004) *Blended Learning, Mobility and Retention: Supporting First Year University Students with Appropriate Technology*, in Proceedings of MLEARN2004, Odescalchi Castle, Lake Bracciano, Italy.

Stone, A., Alsop, G., Briggs, J. and Tompsett, C. (2002) *M-learning as a Means of Supporting Learners: Tomorrow's Technologies Are Already Here, How Can We Most Effectively Use Them in The E-learning Age?* in Proceedings of Third International Conference: Networked Learning 2002: A Research Based Conference on E-learning in Higher Education and Lifelong Learning, University of Sheffield.

Tamminien, S., Oulasvirta, A., Toiskallio, K. and Kankainen, A. (2003) *Understanding Mobile Contexts*, Udine: Springer.

Traxler, J. and Dalziel, C. (2004) *Texting and Retention*, Exeter: Association for Learning Technology.

Traxler, J. and Kukulska-Hulme, A. (2004) *Mobile Learning in Developing Countries* (G. Chin, ed.), Vancouver, BC: Commonwealth of Learning.

Traxler, J. and Riordan, B. (2003) *Supporting Computing Students at Risk Using Blended Technologies*, Galway, Ireland: ICS-LTSN.

Traxler, J. and Riordan, B. (2004a) *Supporting Students with Mobile Devices*. Wolverhampton: University of Wolverhampton. On-line. Available HTTP http://www.wlv.ac.uk/ee2004 (accessed 22 November 2004).

Traxler, J. and Riordan, B. (2004b) *Using PDAs to Support Computing Students*, Belfast: ICS-LTSN. On-line. Available HTTP http://www.ics.ltsn.ac.uk/pub/ltsn5/papers/john%20traxler%2014.doc (accessed 16 April 2005).

Vuorinen, R. and Sampson, J. (2003) Using Mobile Information Technology to Enhance Counselling and Guidance. In H. Kynaslahti and P. Seppala (eds), *Mobile Learning*, 63–70. Helsinki: IT Press.

Yin, R.K. (1993) *Applications of Case Study Research*, Vol. 34, London: Sage Publications.

Chapter 7

Learning Italian via mobile SMS

Mike Levy and Claire Kennedy

Context and background

Widespread acceptance and use of new communication technologies in the world
at large does not necessarily point to effectiveness or value in the educational
context. Effective transfer depends to a large degree on the nature of the particular
technology, its strengths and limitations both as a technology and as a pedagogical
tool, and the social and cultural conditions that surround its use. There is always a
possibility that mobile phone users will see any educationally motivated use of
this technology as an unwanted incursion into their own personal, social space
and as a result, would strongly reject this kind of usage (see Dias 2002a:18). On
the other hand, within certain parameters and for certain kinds of students such a
use might be welcomed. Dias' findings are encouraging. In his survey study, when
students were asked would they study/practise English using their cell phones, if
they knew a way to do it, 57.9 per cent of girls replied positively and 47.4 per cent
of the boys replied favourably too (Dias 2002b: 4). Still, overall, careful evaluation
needs to occur before new technologies that have been accepted in the wider world
can be welcomed into formal, educational contexts.

Some work has been done already on the use of mobile phones in language
learning, as the study by Dias indicates. This approach is still very new, however.
Most of the work completed so far has emanated from Japan or the US (see Dias
2002a, 2002b; Lewis 2002; Houser *et al.* 2002). In Japan, mobile technology use
for language learning is almost exclusively in relation to the teaching of English
as a foreign language; in the US, a wider range of languages is represented, although
French and German tend to dominate (Godwin-Jones 1999).

Rationale and problem statement

Learning a language involves learning in the domains of phonology, grammar,
vocabulary and discourse. There is growing evidence to suggest that particular
technologies, through their design and functionality, lend themselves more to one
or other of these domains or levels of language learning (see Levy 1997, 2003).
The evidence so far suggests that mobile Short Message Service (SMS) technology

might prove especially effective for vocabulary learning. Vocabulary items can be presented through relatively short, discrete definitions and examples that suit the screen dimensions and general handling capabilities of a mobile phone. For groundbreaking work in this area, see the work of Houser, Thornton and Kluge (Houser *et al.* 2001; Houser *et al.* 2002; Thornton and Houser 2002; Kluge 2002).

In fact, already there are commercial services that deal with vocabulary learning utilising mobile technologies such as Mobile-Lingo that provides interactive language training on the mobile phone. The vendors describe their exercises as follows: 'Each daily session features a new word and includes five related SMS sessions: the vocabulary word with its definition, followed at intervals by entertaining practice sentences and questions in context'. Features include immediate feedback, a step-by-step methodology, and a choice of weekly topics, including career English, popular culture and travel.

The deeper reasons for the likelihood of a match between mobile technology and vocabulary learning lie in well proven findings from memory research in general (Baddeley 1990) and second language vocabulary learning research in particular (Bloom and Shuell 1981). Research shows unambiguously that spaced repetition in vocabulary learning results in more robust learning than massed repetition (Nation 2001: 76). In other words, repetitions undertaken across a period, usually at ever-increasing intervals, are a more effective way to learn and retain new words than sustained repetition during a single, continuous period. SMS messages sent at intervals via a mobile phone have the potential to meet this requirement rather well.

The nature of the way in which the repetition is activated is critical too. It is advantageous to provide learners with an appropriate trigger or prompt so that they have to make an *effort* to guess or recall what they have learnt previously. Thus in vocabulary learning, after the learner has first encountered a new word – where it is best to present the word and its meaning simultaneously – subsequent encounters are best managed by providing learners with some kind of prompt so they have to try and remember the corresponding word or phrase. In other words, effort is required. It is argued that such a tactic is beneficial because retrieval of this kind is more akin to the performance required in normal use (Nation 2001:79).

The work described in this chapter builds upon the initiatives of Houser *et al.* (2001) and Dias (2002a,2002b) on vocabulary learning, and applies these ideas to the learning of Italian within an Australian university context. A particular focus in these studies concerns the timing and the number of repeated messages, and the nature of the recall prompts to enable effective vocabulary learning. It is important to note, however, that although vocabulary learning will be one of the central focal points in this project, it will not be the only one. Other purposes were tested too, especially those that are consistent with the informal, social and entertainment functions of mobile phones in the world outside the educational institution. Ideas that will be tested alongside the main theme of vocabulary learning will be course reminders, related Internet sites, quizzes, information messages, film titles, proverbs, translations (e.g. idioms), and questions to do with song titles, themes, first lines and authorship. The first trial related to a course on Italian literature and society and a second, which will follow later, concerns Italian and the news.

The project described here was conducted over a seven-week period with third-year students of Italian in the course entitled 'Italian Literature and Society'. We decided to pitch the project at this particular course and language proficiency level (i.e. higher intermediate) for a number of reasons. We believed we could really make a difference at this level and in this course because we believed we had an approach that could assist with the large amount of new vocabulary the students would encounter for the first time at this point. Also student feedback over the years for this course showed that students sometimes felt daunted by the more elaborate language introduced through the novels and short stories. This work was very challenging in terms of new vocabulary, especially when compared with the reading material they had worked with prior to the course such as newspapers and magazines, so the time seemed right to test an additional vocabulary teaching strategy.

Through the course, students were sent new words, definitions and example context sentences at appropriately spaced intervals by their mobile phone (using the 'Once Only' and 'Recurring Delivery' options available with this service) in between the scheduled lessons and tutorials of their mainstream Italian course. Eighteen students took part in the study and participants were surveyed through a questionnaire and focus group interview to gauge attitudes and expectations toward mobile phone technologies in an educational setting.

The vocabulary items were selected from the novel the students study in the course. It is called *Una Storia Semplice* (A Simple Story) by Leonardo Sciascia. Though the language is demanding, the novel is short; furthermore, it is a detective story and past experience has shown that different groups of students have enjoyed it very much.

Technology and infrastructure

The technology service used in this project was the Telstra Mobile Online SMS Business service. The system allows SMS text messages to be prepared in advance and then, when required, they may be sent to a large group of people via e-mail and a PC. The sender can create instant, scheduled and delayed messages across all networks, regardless of the carrier. So, for example, a message may be prepared in advance and then scheduled to be sent to a group of students' mobile phones on a certain day at a certain time in the future. Messages may also be sent 'Once Only' or as a 'Recurring Delivery' (a feature explored in the studies), in which case the sender can nominate the intervals at which the message will be sent again. The message limit and screen size of the phones used in the project was 160 characters and 22mm by 33mm respectively. Overall, we were very pleased with the Telstra Mobile Online service. The interface was intuitive and easy-to-use and, with rare exceptions, due to occasional congestion we believe, all messages were sent out on time according to plan.

Engaging with students

Preparing the mobile phone messages did take some time, about four hours a week in fact. At first glance, it may seem odd that short messages of no more than 160 characters should require so much time and effort to construct. However, looking a little closer there are good reasons why this amount of time was necessary and justified. First, the content of the messages was context-embedded. The material was closely bound up with the syllabus and the learning objectives of the teacher, together with the language of the novel the students were studying. Message preparation therefore required a very close reading of the novel in order to select new vocabulary, plus further careful consultation with the teacher on vocabulary choice and interpretation. The character limit also imposed a constraint requiring the ingenuity of the author in creating messages that were both motivating and instructive while remaining within the limit. In general here it is important to remember that it is not the length of the message that matters so much as the extra study and the new vocabulary learning that each message could potentially initiate, especially when the message content is thoughtfully and appropriately constructed by being fully integrated into the broader scheme of work.

A representative sample of the messages that were sent to students is given below. They include vocabulary-related messages (the main emphasis), as well as messages concerning grammar, literature and general information. The messages were all in Italian of course and they related to the sections of the book that were being studied in that particular week of the semester (page numbers were given).

- How do you say, 'Forget it', or 'Drop it'?
- Is the noun 'tesi' masculine or feminine? And 'ipotesi'?
- Match the adjectives to the nouns: 'duro, feroce, greve, grezzo, incredulo … [etc.]'
- Did you notice these adjectives … [etc.]?
- Here are some expressions from the world of the church: …
- Which of these works is not by Pirandello: …?
- Don't miss 'Inspector Montalbano' tonight at 10 on SBS TV.
- Have you bought your second novel from the bookshop yet? There are only two copies left and we need to know if we should order some more.
- Do you know the song 'Garibaldi'? Maybe Rosalia [the teacher] will sing it for you in class!

In terms of content, student preferences were for messages on grammar, vocabulary, news, literature and administration. Therefore, in spite of the study's principal focus on vocabulary, students still saw grammar as the topic on which they primarily wanted to receive messages.

A special point of interest in this study related to the timing of the messages. Timing here covered such matters as the preferred time of day to receive messages, the intervals between them, as well as the rate and intervals between repeated or recall prompts messages. In all matters of timing, we sought a clearer sense of student preference relating to indications of effectiveness.

Evaluation and outcomes

Feedback from students was obtained in four ways at key stages during the project using a range of procedures from the more informal at the start to the more formal towards the end. The four methods included feedback via telephone, a snap poll in class, a questionnaire and a focus group. First, in the second week of the project a number of students were phoned for their general reactions and asked to report any specific problems. No significant problems or concerns were noted here. Second, a snap poll was held in class about three weeks into the project and students were asked if they were having any difficulties and whether they felt the frequency of messages was about right. Feedback at this point led to a reduction of messages per day from three to two. Third, a questionnaire was designed and distributed during the last week of the project. Then, finally a focus group was organised and held about two weeks after that at the end of the semester. The summary results from the questionnaire and the focus group are now reported.

The vast majority of students enjoyed receiving the messages (17/18 = 94.4 per cent). The single student that answered negatively had a general dislike of mobile phones for any purpose.

Overall, these student responses in the focus group interview were representative:

> I like the fact that it keeps you in contact, keeps you in touch, between one Monday [class] and the next Monday [class].

> I think I enjoyed the messages with regard to, um, things on TV and things like that. I found those really enjoyable to receive because they were, sort of, day-to-day language, they told me something I wouldn't have figured out otherwise …

The majority of students preferred to receive messages at 9 am or 10 am, although generally there was an even spread each hour in the survey responses from nine in the morning to six in the evening. As far as the number of messages per day was concerned, two a day (10/18 = 55.6 per cent) or three a day (6/18 = 33.3 per cent) were the clear majority preferences. On the question of repeated messages, the feedback was not as positive: only one-third of the participants found repeated messages useful whereas two-thirds did not.

As far as vocabulary learning was concerned, we were particularly interested in the effectiveness of the messages containing recall prompts. It is advantageous to provide learners with an appropriate trigger or prompt two or three days after the initial message when a new vocabulary item was first introduced, so that they have to make an effort to recall it. Although in retrospect this approach to vocabulary learning was not made sufficiently explicit to students at the outset of the project, many students implicitly understood what was intended. Two students reported:

> I liked the repetition; I liked the presentation of a question and the coming round again at the back door, what was the word? To reinforce whatever was the issue.

> The part I liked … it comes at you from a different angle. Then you go 'oh yeh', and it sinks in better. But I liked the fact that between, we have Monday and Tuesday classes here and then nothing till the next Monday so it keeps you in contact, keeps you in touch, keeps you thinking in Italian. The expressions I liked I really learnt, I wrote them down and I learned them properly.

Other more general suggestions made by students for improving message content were:

- Don't make the messages too challenging.
- Add translation in English for hard words.
- I thought the mix was very good – and I really enjoyed the 'double bite' on various themes towards the end, i.e. a message was reframed to make sure it was understood.
- Messages advising any cultural activities in the community would be good.
- Maybe grammatical 'irregularities' if they occur?
- Homework reminders.

One very important finding that emerged from the survey findings and the focus group was the 'knock-on' effect of the SMS messages that were sent. That a message may trigger the receiver to actively engage in language learning between classes is enormously beneficial, especially for vocabulary learning. We were greatly surprised by the number of times students wrote down messages; for example, one student said:

> I actually found most of the time I got it [the SMS message] on the bus … and then when I get home again and I'm sitting down I look at it again and I write it down.

As a result of the messages received, students wrote down words in their person-alised dictionaries, looked up words in dictionaries and grammar books, and carefully considered translations. Though the SMS message itself may be short, we realised that the impact educationally may reach far beyond the initial message, especially with the more motivated students. This was a powerful finding in this study.

Of course, this interconnectedness between in-class and out-of-class activity only occurs successfully when the mobile phone messages are very carefully integrated into the content and goals of the wider scheme of work, in this case a course in Italian Literature and Society and the topic of the novel that was being studied. In addition, the technology selected must fit the pedagogical purpose, as mobile SMS technology fits vocabulary learning in this case study.

Institutional aspects and what next

The project will most certainly continue both in Italian and we hope with the other languages taught in the School of Languages and Linguistics at Griffith University. In Italian, the plan is to run the study again, in a different course, 'Italian in the News', to refine our approach to vocabulary teaching via SMS, and to see how different course content may influence message content. More broadly, there is interest not only in the School of Languages and Linguistics, but across the Faculty of Arts at the University. A number of seminars are planned presenting the results of this and follow-up projects to other members of staff at the university. The wider institutional reaction has been very positive, amongst colleagues and institutional management.

References

Baddeley, A. (1990) *Human Memory*, London: Lawrence Erlbaum Associates.

Bloom, K.C. and Shuell, T.J. (1981) Effects of massed and distributed practice on the learning and retention of second-language vocabulary, *Journal of Educational Research*, 74: 245–8.

Dias, J. (2002a) CELL phones in the classroom: boon or bane? *Calling Japan*, 10(2): 16–22.

Dias, J. (2002b) CELL phones in the classroom: boon or bane? [Part 2], *Calling Japan*, 10(3) 8–14.

Godwin-Jones, B. (1999) Emerging technologies: mobile computing and language learning, *Language Learning and Technology*, 2(2): 7–11.

Houser, C., Thornton, P. and Kluge, D. (2002) Mobile learning: cell phones and PDAs for education. JALTCALL, 18–19 May 2002. Hiroshima Jogakuin University, Hiroshima, Japan.

Houser, C., Thornton, P., Yokoi, S. and Yasuda, T. (2001) Learning on the move: vocabulary study via mobile phone e-mail, ICCE 2001 Proceedings, 1560–5.

Kluge, D. (2002) Tomorrow's CALL: The future in our hands, in P. Lewis (ed.) *The Changing Face of CALL: A Japanese Perspective*, Lisse: Swets & Zeitlinger.

Levy, M. (1997) *CALL: Context and Conceptualisation*, Oxford: Clarendon Press.

Levy, M. (2003) Effectiveness of CALL technologies: finding the right balance, in R. Donaldson and M. Haggstrom (eds) *Changing Language Education Through CALL*, Lisse: Swets and Zeitlinger.

Lewis, P. (ed.) (2002) *The Changing Face of CALL: A Japanese Perspective*, Lisse: Swets & Zeitlinger.

Mobile-Lingo: Interactive language training on the mobile phone. On-line. Available HTTP http://www.smarttrust.com (accessed 22 November 2004).

Nation, I. S. P. (2001) *Learning Vocabulary in Another Language*, Cambridge: Cambridge University Press.

Telstra Mobile SMS. On-line. Available HTTP http://www.telstra.com (accessed 22 November 2004).

Telstra Mobile SMS Demo. On-line. Available HTTP http://onlinesms.telstra.com/demo/index.html (accessed 22 November 2004).

Thornton, P. and Houser, C. (2002) M-Learning: learning in transit, in P. Lewis (ed.) *The Changing Face of CALL: A Japanese Perspective*, Lisse: Swets & Zeitlinger.

Chapter 8

Evaluating a low cost, wirelessly connected PDA for delivering VLE functionality

Andy Ramsden

Context and background

The primary aim of this study was to evaluate if the tools and features of a virtual learning environment (VLE) could be delivered to a wirelessly connected Palm Pilot. In other words, could students access, in a usable format, course documents (lecture PowerPoint slides, essay titles, reading lists), participate in discussion boards, communicate through email and collaborate on group work using an Internet-connected Palm Pilot with a mobile telephone in the same manner that they would interact with a VLE using a computer. A requirement was that students were not expected to 'hotsync' their PDA to a PC to download material. The secondary aims focused on the non-technical issues. In particular, would the model be sustainable and scaleable in terms of greater student numbers and courses? What benefit did the use of PDAs offer this particular student group? These aims reflect Kristiansen's (2001) views that the successful implementation of mobile learning is an outcome of technology, management and pedagogical design.

The pilot study ran from August 2002 to March 2003, and the sample group comprised 13 students, none of whom had previously owned or had regular access to a PDA.

The selected course was a first-year undergraduate course taught face-to-face in the Department of Economics at the University of Bristol. The course was structured as a weekly lecture followed by a small group seminar. The course was intended for non-economists who wished to study and receive a credit in Economics.

On further analysis the sample group appeared to be a good representation of the whole group. The sample group appeared to have a similar level of IT competence compared with other students on the course. In particular, they had similar ratings in terms of confidence at using computers, the frequency of checking their email and accessing the Internet (based on a Computer Knowledge Survey).

For training purposes the sample group was divided into groups of two or three who underwent an initial 1.5 hours training on the Palm hardware and software.

The taught course was supported by an available course on the University of Bristol's virtual learning environment (Blackboard). A review of the previous year's course and a discussion with the lecturer suggested the VLE use was primarily a 'content and support model', where relatively unchanged course material from lectures and the course handbook is uploaded to the supporting VLE course (Mason 1998). This is evident as the file types employed on the course tended to be either PowerPoint slide shows (50 per cent) or Microsoft Word documents (33 per cent), while the most frequently used feature in Blackboard was the course document area.

This type of use indicates that the Palm Pilots will need to be able to access large amounts of content. However, to further test the hardware and software the students would be required to complete a set of tasks. These included monthly surveys, participation in discussion boards, visiting web sites and downloading learning materials. The success of these tasks and an evaluation of the student experience were assessed through a series of monthly questionnaires and an end of project interview.

The tasks were intended to use the common features of a VLE to facilitate a complete learning and teaching experience as outlined by O'Leary (2002):

1   communication tools to promote discussion between tutors and students, e.g. email, discussion boards and virtual chat facilities;
2   delivery of learning resources and materials;
3   self-assessment and summative assessment;
4   shared work groups for students to upload files and communicate with each other;
5   support for students;
6   management and tracking of students.

Technology and infrastructure

The study employed low-specification Palm Pilot technology (Palm Pilot M105). The rationale for this was associated with the widening participation agenda in UK Higher Education and concerns over a widening digital divide.

The M105 Palm Pilot included a black and white screen, 2MB of memory and no expansion slots. The software used within the study reflected the need to use the Palm bundled software. However, each Palm included an email client (MultiMail SE) and web browser (Palmscape – trial version) and a PDF reader (on request). Students were also given advice on appropriate free and shareware software. The telephone was an Ericsson T39M, with a GPRS tariff for data transfer.

The use of this technology did impose certain constraints in terms of accessing the web. The Palm Pilot web browser was not sophisticated enough to access the University of Bristol's VLE (Blackboard). This was due to the browser having poor support for frames, script languages and stylesheets. Consequently, a require-ment was to develop an equivalent and accessible version of the content for the Palm Pilot. The material was distributed through the use of static and dynamic web pages (HTML and ASP).

The method by which the material was developed and distributed reflected the method by which the material was authored. In general the material was authored in Microsoft Word or PowerPoint, and converted to an appropriate web format for delivery as the student would access the web site. Communication focused on the use of SMS text messaging and email. In addition the file transfer via FTP was evaluated.

When designing a PDA-friendly web site or web page, the design principles should be similar to those employed for a large-screen web page. However, for a small screen device the design needs to channel its creativity into planning for economy (Kacin 1999).

The need for economy is due to three interrelated factors:

1   The PDA has a small screen (150 × 150): the design problems associated with small screens include the use of images, while paragraphs appear relatively long and require significant scrolling.
2   Online web browser limitations: the web browser did not support Java script, or cascading stylesheets. Therefore, the bulk of the material tended to be marked up using a limited range of HTML tags.
3   Transfer speeds: the GPRS transfer rates are relatively slow compared with PC modems. The longer download time raises concerns about the stickiness of the site. For instance, Nielsen (2000) suggests that if download time is more than ten seconds then people lose interest and leave the site.

Overall, the characteristics of the hardware and access method meant that there is a need to minimize the file size, while balancing the need to emphasize a text-intensive design with minimal site hierarchy.

An important design rule is the need to examine each item on its merits and decide what information is essential and what can be excluded, while maintaining a high degree of usability. This process requires the designer to continuously question all choices. For instance, on a staff information page, what task is the student's priority? What is the minimum information the student will need to complete the task? If it is assumed that the primary task is to contact the person to arrange a meeting then it would be effective to simply provide the person's name and email address.

Evaluation and outcomes

The study identified seven key findings.

Finding 1: students could read all the course documents, announcements and supporting material – after the material was converted to a suitable format

If students are expected to spend a significant amount of time reading onscreen then the ease of reading needs to be maximized. The study identified that onscreen readability could be enhanced through using devices with higher resolution screens. There is also the need to design the material specifically for small screens through incorporating white space and content chunking, and to provide training or advice to students in terms of how they can change the preferences of their software to meet their needs.

Finding 2: the academic needs to be consulted about the file format they are likely to use when authoring material to minimize the difficulties of the file transfer process

The study found that it was very difficult to transfer files from Microsoft Office formats to Palm OS formats without hotsyncing third-party software, such as Documents to Go and eBook readers. Admittedly, these problems are diminishing with improvements in technology (see 'What next?' below). However, it does raise the issue that academics (material developers) need to be included in the discussion of authoring material.

Finding 3: students found it straightforward to participate in discussion boards using relatively long sentences and undertake online activities such as surveys and quizzes

Many lessons were learnt concerning text entry. It was evident that the e-learning design should focus in reducing the need for free-text entry on a PDA. For instance, the length of discussion board contributions: these are likely to be shorter than contributions written on a PC. It was evident that students need to be made aware of hardware or software solutions that might improve the speed and accuracy of text entry. This observation is supported by a usability test where the sample group entered the following sentence: 'I'm having a great time. Hope all is well with you; chat soon. My new number is 55 what's yours?'

Table 8.1 illustrates that text entry on a PDA is slow and prone to errors compared to the use of a keyboard.

Table 8.1 Text entry speeds and accuracy tests

	Average time	Average number of errors
Graffiti users ($n = 9$)	110 seconds	1.8
Onscreen keyboard users ($n = 4$)	91 seconds	0.8
PDA keyboard (the project manager)	31 seconds	No errors
PC keyboard (the project manager)	26 seconds	No errors

Finding 4: students could access web links from the PDA site and surf the Internet on their PDAs

The interviews implied that Internet browsing was limited due to a majority of web sites not rendering in a usable format on small screens. This raises the need to engage with the academic to make sure wherever possible that the web site they recommend renders on the small screens. Students also implied that the technology acted as a barrier. The requirement of using infra-red (line of sight) connectivity with the telephone meant that Internet access was not viable on the move.

Finding 5: students could send and receive email for their university email accounts using their Palm Pilot

Finding 6: collaborative group work was possible through sharing Palm memo files via FTP, using SMS text messaging, discussion boards and email

A key component of many e-learning activities is the need for students to learn collaboratively through sharing ideas and documents. The technology employed limited the degree of collaboration in terms of the file types that could be written on the Palm and transferred. This is becoming less of a problem as technological developments have meant that file formats and delivery methods are now available to which students are more accustomed, in particular Microsoft Office products and email attachments.

Finding 7: the use of mobile technology offered a new dimension in the lecture theatre

Students were able to submit questions and answers during the lecture on a discussion board. This was well received by students, however, they did find it difficult to participate in the discussion board and follow the lecture.

Overall, the findings imply that there was not a significant technical barrier to the use of a wirelessly connected PDA to deliver the same functionality of a VLE through a password-protected web site. However, within the context of this study there were questions regarding its effectiveness.

The results of the study indicate that the primary aim has been achieved. Students could access course documents (lecture PowerPoint slides, essay titles, reading lists), participate in discussion boards, communicate through email and share work using an Internet-connected Palm Pilot with a mobile telephone in the same manner that they would use a VLE such as Blackboard via a PC. The study illustrated that the system was relatively easy to create and worked with low specification Palm Pilots. However, the findings for the secondary aims were less clear.

The study did raise concerns in terms of support needs for both the academic and the student. In particular, the time needed to support an individual student and the apparent limited scope for economies of scale within the support process. Therefore, a scaling up would require a more sophisticated support structure with the emphasis on student to student help networks. These points taken, the administration and support issues are surmountable with an appropriate level of resource.

The student interviews indicated the majority of the students in the group (11 out of 13) thought that the Internet-connected Palm Pilot had little to contribute to their current learning experience. The reasons cited included:

1   The PC offered advantages over the PDA in terms of being easier to read onscreen, easier to input information, quicker to access materials, and the materials could be printed. Therefore, there was little motivation to use the PDA when there was relatively easy access to PCs.
2   The students' current learning strategy tended to focus on taking notes or annotating the PowerPoint slides during the lecture. This strategy was not suited to a PDA.

Interestingly, two individuals did use their Palm Pilots during the lecture to read and input information. They also used them before and during seminar sessions. Their strategy tended to use the Palm Pilot as an extension of the PC, through constantly transferred information between their Palm Pilot and computer.

The overall outcomes support the view outlined by Kristiansen (2001) that the success of using mobile technology in learning has more to do with the pedagogical task than the technology. The mismatch between the required e-learning task and the PDA technology is evident from the characteristics of the student and course:

1   It is a first-year undergraduate course and many of the students are likely to have poorly developed independent learning skills and have a learning strategy that is heavily reliant on pen and paper and taking notes from the lecture.
2   The course is face-to-face and there exist good informal communication networks between the lecturer and the students.
3   There is a good provision of PCs on campus.
4   All the e-learning tasks tended to focus on reading static content.

The use of the technology by the student mirrors the demands of the e-learning tasks designed by the lecturer. For instance, a low order skills activity of acquiring knowledge through reading a PowerPoint slideshow would be best undertaken on devices that render PowerPoint slide shows in an easily digestible format, i.e., large screens or print. Therefore, students who are required to complete this type of e-learning task are unlikely to find much application for a PDA.

However, e-learning tasks that require reflection, communication (via discussion boards or chat rooms) and are 'content lite' would favour the use of this PDA technology. In particular, if the active learning process is based on a period of reflection and then engaging in dialogue with peers.

Further research is needed in areas where the technology is most likely to meet the purpose and need of the e-learning tasks. For instance, courses with dispersed learners, synchronous and asynchronous communication intensive courses, and the application of reflective logs and personal development profiles.

Institutional aspects

The nature of this case study meant that the institutional aspects where not specifically evaluated, although many aspects can be inferred from the findings, especially on training support needs. These have been covered in the section on evaluation and outcomes.

What next?

Many of the findings of this study have become less of an issue due to advancements in mobile technology. The study raised the issues of how the material should be authored to maximize accessibility while minimizing the need for repurposing. However, there have been significant advancements in Palm OS web browsers, combined with advancements in Palm OS software that can view Microsoft file formats. For instance, the bundling of Documents to Go as part of the 'free' software package on many Palm OS devices has meant that web-enabled Palm OS devices are able to open Microsoft file types direct from a web site. In addition, other software developments have had major impact on this type of study: these include the growth of software that can be used on different operating systems. For instance, the delivery of material to different devices, such as Palm OS, Pocket PC and PCs is relatively straightforward using software such as Mobipocket eBook reader. The material is converted to a MobiPocket format and the student downloads the Mobipocket reader that is appropriate to their device.

At the same time there have also been developments within virtual learning environment software which is likely in the near future to deliver improved access to material for PDA users via online-offline synchronization.

These advances are making the technical obstacles of using a PDA to access VLE content less problematic. In the near future the technology will be readily available whereby students can seamlessly move content and participate in e-learning activities between different computers and their mobile devices at their convenience with the minimum of effort. However, two major challenges still exist. First the interaction and screen design of the material needs to account for the device on which it will be accessed. This is especially important as the student switches between large and small screen devices, and the increased use of multimedia within education. Second, as inferred in the outcomes and evaluation section the pedagogical design needs to harness the unique potential benefits that mobile technology offers to further promote learning.

References

Kacin, M. (1999) 'Optimizing web pages for handheld devices', *PalmPower Magazine*. Available HTTP <http://www.palmpower.com/issuesprint/issue199902/avantgotips.html> (accessed 21 April 2004).

Kristiansen, T. (2001) 'Telenor mLearning WAP project: mLearning Initiatives in 2001', in D. Keegan (ed.), *The Future of Learning: from e-learning to m-learning.* On-line book, available HTTP <http://learning.ericsson.net/mlearning2/project_one/book.html> (accessed 21 April 2004).

Mason, R. (1998) 'Models of online courses', *ALN Magazine* 2(2) (October 1998). Available HTTP <http://www.usdla.org/html/journal/JUL01_Issue/article02.html> (accessed 21 April 2004).

Nielsen, J. (2000) *Designing Web Usability: The Practice of Simplicity,* Indianapolis, IN: New Riders.

O'Leary, R. (2002) Virtual learning environments: learning and teaching support network. Available HTTP <http://www.ltsn.ac.uk/application.asp?app=resources.asp&process=full_record&section=generic&id=36> (accessed 12 April 2005).

Chapter 9

Expect the unexpected

Practicalities and problems of a PDA project

Jon Trinder, Jane Magill and Scott Roy

Context and background

This chapter reports on the progress of a project at the University of Glasgow to investigate the benefits of Personal Digital Assistants (PDAs) as teaching, learning and revision tools and the practicalities of deploying PDAs and measuring their use. This case study describes what happened at the pilot stage and the problems we encountered. Had everything worked as it should have done we would have collected more data, unfortunately we had overestimated the students' willingness to co-operate.

For several years staff in the Departments of Electronics and Electrical Engineering and the Robert Clark Centre for Technological Education at the University of Glasgow have been collaborating on projects to enhance access to, and provide effective delivery of, university course material. The work has previously focused on the application of computer-based learning and assessment methods to a range of undergraduate courses. The results have demonstrated that the use of regular formative assessments and appropriate student feedback can have a marked effect on overall course results.

In this pilot project we wanted to enhance access to assessment and learning materials by utilising portable devices to increase accessibility and flexibility of learning for students.

The one-year pilot project was funded by a Learning and Teaching Support Network (LTSN) mini-project grant. The mini-project was titled 'Portable Learning and Assessment – Towards Ubiquitous Education'. The budget of £3,000 was used to purchase 25 entry level PDAs plus spare parts, software and batteries.

The students selected for the pilot were from a level three course in Semiconductor Design and Technology, which is part of the degree of Electronics and Electrical Engineering. In addition the PDAs were used during the university summer schools for school leavers.

The main objectives of the project were:

- evaluate to what extent a PDA can help student learning;
- monitor when PDAs are used by students and for what purpose;
- investigate interface and usability limitations within the educational context;

- identify mechanisms to evaluate the use of PDAs in education;
- identify practical problems of PDA use in education.

Rationale

Portable devices are becoming increasingly important within education and it is recognised that 'mobile devices can become efficient and effective teaching and learning tools' (Roibas and Sanchez 2002). PDAs now provide computing performance comparable to previous generation laptop PCs, whilst benefiting from battery lifetimes measured in weeks, and prices some 20 times less than modern desktop systems. The ability to readily up- and down-load information to and from central university systems also makes PDAs an attractive tool for delivery of teaching and learning materials on a regular basis.

Assessment is an important component of education as it enables students to evaluate what knowledge they have gained and to identify areas in which their knowledge is weaker. Computer Aided Assessment (CAA) can provide the opportunity for rapid feedback enabling students to direct their studies to areas where they have identified a gap in their knowledge. Using a PDA for CAA provides the benefit of a portable 'on demand' formative assessment system with which a student can test their knowledge in a regular and flexible manner.

With many students also working part-time their available spare time for study has been reduced so any learning resource that can be utilised during the rare gaps in a contemporary student's busy schedule is a valuable asset to them. The immediate readiness of PDAs (switch on and use, no boot-up time) makes them ideal to grab a few moments useful working time at times and in locations where even a laptop would not be useful. The organisational, diary and note-taking tools that are built into most PDAs may also help the student to develop better time management skills.

Other studies have noted the importance of portable systems to provide opportunities for learning:

> Our team carried out a detailed study of how radiology is taught and practised. One clear finding was that trainees have very little spare time. They can't take the time to sit in libraries or computer labs, and so any computer-based learning must fit into the gaps in their busy schedule – in the hospital, at home, when travelling – which means a personal and portable system.
>
> (Sharples 2000: 5)

Other studies have relied on questionnaires and observations to determine how and when PDAs are used (SRI 2002). We wanted to collect more objective data and so developed an automatic logging system that records time stamped entries to identify when the PDA was used and which applications were used.

Using objective data enables us to make a quantitative analysis of student learning patterns, i.e. how often the students break from the CAA tool, how long the breaks last and what they do with the PDA during those breaks.

Technology and infrastructure

The PDAs used in our project use the PalmOS operating system. Among the practical factors that influenced our decision were:

- one of the team was a PalmOS application developer. This meant we could arrange for custom applications to be written and gave us Palm technical support expertise;
- PalmOS-based PDAs currently have the biggest market share. We hoped that this would mean the students would exchange data with other PDA users outside the project and that the experience of using the device could be useful to them for their future employment.

The PDA used was the Sony Clié SL10 with a monochrome screen and 8MB of memory. We used both custom written and proprietary software. The PDAs were supplied with an application to facilitate the editing of Microsoft Word and Excel documents on the PDA. The students were given the CD that is supplied with the PDA so that they could install software on their personal computer, to allow the transfer of documents between their personal computer and the PDA.

It was important for us that the students did hotsync to our server so that we could collect our logging data. When the batteries run out the PDA loses all its stored data and third party applications, such as our logging data. A machine was made available at specific times for students to hotsync with our server. On occasions we synced their machines for them during lab sessions.

The initial log files showed that most of the students had connected their PDA to a PC so they were aware of hotsyncing, but they had no incentive to hotsync to our systems. We offered to provide batteries hoping this would encourage the students to contact us and provide us with an opportunity to hotsync their machines; unfortunately the students preferred to buy their own batteries or to just let the batteries run out.

The type of questions we wanted to use determined the choice of quiz application. There are many PDA 'Quiz' applications but the majority of these only display plain text or images. As the subject of the questions was engineering, it was essential that mathematical symbols could be displayed.

Application logging

To log what applications were used on the PDA we wrote our own application called AppLog (Ninelocks 2002). There are other applications that can record similar data but none of them provided the detail of information we required. AppLog records the time, date and application identifier whenever an application is used.

When the PDA is synchronised with the desktop application the log file on the PDA is processed to produce a text file on the desktop system containing:

- application identifier;
- date and time the application was started;
- how long the application was used for.

Objective analysis techniques such as the logging can be time-consuming to analyse and cross reference (Traxler and Riordan 2003). We automated some of the processing of the log files produced by AppLog to give summary reports and pre-process the data for analysis using a custom graphing package. The graphing application can display the data as:

- the number of times an application has been used;
- the cumulative time for which an application has been used;
- the session history for an application.

From the logs, we could see patterns of application usage and make guesses about how the PDA was being used. For example, if the log showed that the applications used were the quiz, the calculator, the quiz, then this suggests that the calculator was used to help solve a quiz question.

Engaging with students

The first phase of the project was treated as a pilot study to uncover any problems in the support and the deployment of PDAs. It was impractical and undesirable in the initial phases of the project to issue PDAs to an entire class. Working with a smaller group made support issues easier to handle.

Two groups of students have been involved in the project. The first was a group of 14 undergraduate students in advanced level electronic engineering classes. The students chosen had already worked together for a term and knew each other. They were Joint Honours computer science students described as being well motivated and with a good electronic systems background; it was thought that these qualities would mean only the most critical technical problems would require assistance from support staff. They were issued with PDAs for three months. The students who were not selected to use the PDA were issued with the same study materials in printed form: this was also intended to give us a control group of students to compare performance against.

The second group was initially five 'summer school' students. The summer school is for school leavers who have applied for a university place but need some preliminary study, and/or have attended schools which rarely send students to university and are therefore participants in 'widening participation' programmes. Summer school ran for ten weeks and consisted of two three-hour sessions per week. The students used the PDAs during lecture and practical laboratory sessions and were allowed to take the device home.

Students in both groups were loaned a PDA that contained a quiz application to deliver formative self-assessment questions and our logging application.

Additional applications were pre-installed on each PDA; the applications included chemical tables, a scientific calculator and document readers. The students were encouraged to install their choice of additional applications.

The students were given basic training in the use of the PDA and its applications. If PDAs are to be deployed in larger numbers, training could be a significant overhead so we were interested to find out how much training is required. Initially we supplied the PDA so that it started in the built in 'set-up application' which provides a guide of how to use the PDA.

Technical support for the students and the configuration of the PDAs was provided by one of the team who is also a member of the computer support group within the department.

The ability to 'beam' items between PDAs encouraged collaboration and communication both between the students and between the students and their tutor. Exchanging of eBooks became popular with the summer school students when it was discovered that the tutor had a large collection. The tutor was very positive about this aspect stating that: 'We don't normally get to know the pupils beyond our own subject area, so this put a whole new slant on the summer school'.

The course tutor reported that the quiz application generated useful subject related queries from students. For example, one student thought that one of the quiz answers was incorrect until it was explained that they had not considered other aspects of the question. The discussion with the tutor about these aspects helped all of the students' understanding of the subject.

Evaluation and outcomes

We did not gather enough data with the small pilot sample to satisfy all of our objectives. However, in conducting the project we did identify many important factors that need to be addressed to make future studies more successful.

With the undergraduate students, the first log data, collected after a few weeks, showed that the students were using the PDAs and were installing applications on them. Most had connected their PDA to a desktop computer. All had installed at least one game. What is not certain is whether all the applications were installed from a desktop machine or beamed from another PDA. The logging software has now been modified to record when 'beaming' occurs.

Although the students used the PDAs for a further two months, only a limited amount of data was collected. The students repeatedly failed to synchronise their PDA to our server as requested. In addition, the data actually collected was not comprehensive making it difficult to analyse systematically. All the students were given a questionnaire to fill in to give us feedback about the project. Even though the students were reminded on numerous occasions, no feedback forms were returned.

To avoid the poor return of questionnaires a different strategy was used with the next group. The summer school students were issued with a questionnaire at the end of the project, but this time they were distributed after their final exam and they were asked to complete it before leaving. This method produced a 100 per cent return of questionnaires and will be adopted for future studies.

As the students attended lectures at regular times each week it was easier to ensure that the devices were synchronised more frequently. The students' machines were hotsynced during the laboratory sessions in order to collect data more successfully than in phase one of the project.

Principal findings from the data collected and our observations

Ergonomic aspects

Some students reported problems with seeing the PDA display. The PDAs used had a monochrome screen, and while this is not in itself a drawback the screen contrast of this particular model was very poor. The screen is only easy to read in very good lighting conditions or by using the backlight (which uses more battery power).

During observations the on-screen keyboard was being used more often, whereas in the questionnaires three out of the four remaining summer school students who completed the course said they used the handwriting recognition software most often.

Some students reported that trying to write on the screen or indeed select items was not easy when 'on a bus'. However reading in such situations was not identified as a problem. Use while travelling is one of the advantages we perceived of using PDAs for educational purposes, but we wondered if reading the screen while travelling might be a problem. In fact, this issue has not been highlighted so far.

Quiz use

The students commented that they liked the mixture of questions, from the easy ones that 'could be done on the bus' to the more difficult ones that required additional time and calculation to answer. One complaint about the quiz questions was that there were not enough of them.

Technical aspects

In each phase of the project, we lost usage logs due to battery related problems such as: the batteries had not been replaced in time, the batteries had fallen out of the PDA, the PDA had been accidentally switched on e.g. while in a well-packed bag.

It is essential that the students synchronise their PDAs regularly to minimise the impact of any data loss. The synchronisation process must be easy and convenient to use and this is something we will improve in our future projects. In the next phase, we will use rechargeable PDAs so battery failure is less likely to be a problem but there is still the possibility of the students not keeping the devices charged.

Institutional aspects

To satisfy the requirements of the Data Protection Act each student was required to read and sign an approved statement agreeing to take part in the project. This statement explained what data would be collected, who it would be seen by, and what it would be used for. The students also signed a statement acknowledging receipt of the PDA and associated accessories.

Developing the project?

We have received additional funding from our institution to expand the project. The next phase will be to issue up to 50 first year entrants with a PDA to be used throughout their time at university. As the student will be given the PDAs on a permanent basis they will have a stronger sense of ownership of the PDA. If they own the PDA the students are more likely to buy and install applications to tailor the device to their learning needs.

References

Ninelocks (2002) AppLog: An Application Logging Application for PalmOS PDAs: NineLocks. On-line. Available HTTP http://www.ninelocks.com/applog (accessed 22 November 2004).

Roibas, A. C. and Sanchez, I. A. (2002) Pathway to m-learning. Proceedings of MLEARN 2002, European Workshop on Mobile and Contextual Learning, University of Birmingham, 20–21 June 2002.

Sharples, M. (2000) Disruptive Devices: Personal Technologies and Education. On-line. Available HTTP http://www.eee.bham.ac.uk/handler/ePapers/disruptive.pdf (accessed 22 November 2004).

SRI (2002) Palm Education Pioneers Program; March 2002 Evaluation Report. On-line. Available HTTP http://www.palmgrants.sri.com/PEP_Final_Report.pdf (accessed 22 November 2004).

Traxler, J. and Riordan, B. (2003) Evaluating the Effectiveness of Retention Strategies Using SMS, WAP and WWW Student Support. On-line. Available HTTP http://www.ics.ltsn.ac.uk/pub/conf2003/John%20Traxler.pdf (accessed 22 November 2004).

Chapter 10

KNOWMOBILE

Mobile opportunities for medical students

Ole Smørdal and Judith Gregory

Context and background

KNOWMOBILE (Lundby 2002) – 'mobile opportunities for medical students' – was a research and development project from 2000 to 2002. The aim of the project was to develop and evaluate net-based and mobile solutions for knowledge access in distributed training of medical students, leading up to their lifelong learning. The focus was on the students' needs for just-in-time knowledge in training situations as future health workers, and on the learning processes in such distributed, net-supported training.

The project looked into how dispersed learners, in a variety of local contexts, could use the net to access and apply relevant knowledge and information for their training practice with patients. It also focused on how students in face-to-face situations, as well as in distributed communities of learners, used the net to access and apply relevant knowledge sources and build collaborative support structures for their training practice while away from campus.

Intended for lifelong learning in a variety of health professions, the KNOWMOBILE project involved medical students during their assignments in the primary healthcare sector. The field study was carried out during the tenth semester of the new curriculum of the School of Medicine, University of Oslo, while the medical students were on assignments in clinical training in the surgeries of general practitioners (GPs) and in hospitals in southern Norway.

Project partners were the Faculty of Medicine, University of Oslo, Department of Informatics, University of Oslo, Telenor R&D, Ericsson Norway, Hewlett-Packard Norge and the Centre for Educational Technology at Umeå University. MedCal (under The Council for the Renewal of Higher Education in Sweden) is a Nordic reference body for the study. The project was co-ordinated by InterMedia, University of Oslo.

The Nordic Council of Ministers funded half of the project costs with a grant of 2,000,000 NOK (*c*.€250,000) under the Nordunet2 programme. The partners paid the other half. Hewlett-Packard contributed to the project with the handheld devices that were used in the field study.

Rationale and problem statement

We believe that the use of mobile and wireless technology in healthcare will increase due to its potential for supporting many functions, e.g. to document and communicate about patient information electronically, to make and share memos, to use medical references when needed etc. Thus, it seemed natural to use Personal Digital Assistants (PDAs) and other technology support also for educational purposes. Since the outcome of the future healthcare will much depend on the use of technology, professionals must not only be supplied with appropriate technology, but must also be educated in its use and possibilities.

In parallel with the issues around technology itself, KNOWMOBILE has tackled the new educational approaches with a shift from delivery to more active learning when the individual searches for information needed for the task and situation – from instruction to construction. This new learning approach put high demands on supporting tools with regard to learning styles and settings for an increased number of mobile students (Petersson 2002).

The focus of the KNOWMOBILE project lead to the following questions: how could just-in-time knowledge access to net-based educational resources be performed and utilized in practical problem solving by learners with mobile terminal equipment in a distributed work-like training situation? What is the learning outcome, and how were the technological and sociological conditions during the project? The research question, then, is related to just-in-time learning, and to just-in-time access to knowledge as a condition for such learning.

Technology and infrastructure

PDAs and various network infrastructures were introduced into three distinct types of local settings, in order to experiment and learn from situations where various technical solutions may be used in differing practical settings.

Setting A: the problem-based learning (PBL) group

The PBL groups, with eight students and one tutor in each, normally met face-to-face. During the tenth semester, the same groups solved two PBL assignments using a web-based learning management system. The medical students were spatially dispersed in their assignments to GPs' surgeries, their hospital and where they lived. One of the PBL groups was selected to participate in the KNOW-MOBILE project, and was offered the use of PDAs during the semester. The PDA did not have any direct connection to the internet, but content from the internet could be downloaded during synchronization with desktop PCs.

Setting B: living together

More often than not, medical students are required to move temporarily and live in a local apartment during their assignments in clinical practice. Five medical students sharing an apartment for the period of their tenth semester assignments were offered PDAs. The PDA in setting A and B had a small form factor, suitable for carrying around in the pocket of a doctor's white coat. The PDA had no keyboard, and was operated with a stylus pen on a touch screen. It was equipped with standard applications, such as a note taker, off-line e-mail, off-line web browser and a voice recorder. A wireless network with internet connection was operated at four locations: at two GPs' surgeries, at the apartment and in the teaching facilities in the local hospital. The PDAs could access this network by means of a small wireless network card that fitted into the PDA.

Setting C: commuting

Some of the medical students continued to live at home and commuted to their assigned hospital and GP surgeries. A group of five students assigned to the same local hospital were offered a larger PDA model with a keyboard and a larger screen. Global System for Mobile Communication (GSM) cellular phone cards were fitted into the PDAs. Thus, the students had access to the internet at home, during commuting, and in the GPs' surgeries. Hospital regulations prohibited use of the PDAs for internet access or mobile communication within the local hospital.

In terms of technology, the KNOWMOBILE project was not just-in-time with expected products on the market. The project design had to be adjusted accordingly. For setting C, we relied on new PDAs with General Packet Radio Service (GPRS) network connectivity to be out on the market. This was not the case when the field study started. Accordingly, we had to change to GSM and use a mobile phone card with 3xGSM (Hi-Speed) connectivity. For setting B, we wanted to test on-line communication services based on a local wireless network (WLAN); we relied on a card which we got to the KNOWMOBILE students one week after its arrival on the market, which was four weeks after the announced introduction course with the students. This, of course, subdued their enthusiasm for the project to a certain degree.

Engaging with students

Each medical student worked in a general practitioner's surgery for six weeks, then switched to a local hospital for the remaining six weeks of the tenth semester in medical school. Each of the medical students had already obtained a medical doctor's licence before the tenth semester assignment. The curriculum design for the semester is to follow patient cases across levels in the health system, and to gain experience for decisions about specialization in later medical training. In both the general practitioner's surgery and the hospitals, the medical students have a tutor. In the beginning, the tutors have responsibilities for the students' work but eventually the medical students work independently as physicians in the general practitioner and hospital assignments.

Norwegian medical students are encouraged to use information sources on the internet in their work. This is part of a larger plan in the School of Medicine to make use of the internet as an arena for learning and for access to Evidence Based Medicine websites. This effort, originally begun by local enthusiasts, included installing desktop computers in all the general practitioner's surgeries and in the local hospitals, organizing a team of medical students that work as IT-support (as 'super users'), developing a net-based schedule for the medical school and creating collections of pointers to medical information on the net.

There were about as many technical support personnel as medical students (18) in the project. Those providing technical support were students from the School of Medicine who were 'super-users' with special interests in ICT, and Masters students from the Department of Informatics, whose Masters thesis research and writing were based on the KNOWMOBILE field studies. The field studies where conducted by the Informatics Masters students who actively participated in the project. In the first part of the project (weeks 1–4) the Masters students did interviews, observations and walk-throughs with the medical students at their workplaces, their apartment and while commuting (see settings A, B and C), but this changed in the latter half of the field study when the Masters students designed and introduced interventions, e.g. they set up experiments with instant messaging and use of the electronic handbook (in settings B and C). Certain of the field studies by the Informatics Masters students were framed by the principles and methods of 'contextual inquiry' (Beyer and Holtzblatt 1998), a user-oriented approach to technology design.

Video documentation has been used to create resources for analysis and reflection upon social practices and technology design.

Evaluation and outcomes

The video documentation was conceived as video ethnography, part of the overall contextual inquiry and participant observation approach, building on the field studies by the Informatics Masters students and, crucially, on the working relations, rapport and trust established with the participating medical students. The foci for the video documentation were also framed by the substantive concerns of the KNOWMOBILE project's multidisciplinary research partners and by an activity theoretical approach to delineation of units of analysis (Kuutti 1991, 1999). Colleagues carried out the video documentation in consultation with the Informatics Masters students and KNOWMOBILE project director during one week close to the end of the field study (November 2001). The video documentation has proved useful to communicate concepts and findings of the KNOWMOBILE research regarding experimentation with the PDAs and problems of PDA use in practice, in ways that facilitate discussion of future research directions and implementation.

The main findings from the field study point to several factors that act as barriers to widespread use of PDAs. All students were eager to test the PDAs and wanted to investigate how the PDAs could be useful in their learning. However, the medical students did not use the PDA for information gathering.

Usage patterns involving other informational artefacts, various reference books and other information sources are well established. The use of PDAs never challenged the usability of these (Hsu 2002). Hsu found that few websites are adapted to the PDA screen size, and hence they are not very usable in terms of overview and interaction. For the GSM connected PDAs (see setting C) the slow transmission of web pages was also an important factor.

The information that was specially prepared for and downloaded to the PDA by means of a medical handbook in the format of an e-book was not used (Gallis and Kasbo 2002). They found a misfit between the e-book and the purposes for which it was used, the PDA did not to a sufficient degree support just-in-time interactions, and the PDAs' version of the medical handbook did not carry many of the properties of paper-based artefacts.

Field experiments showed that students experienced problems in working across different applications and information resources on the PDA, for example, there were problems in cutting and pasting material from one application to another, which limited the usefulness of the PDA as a communication device (Ellingsen 2002). While the field studies indicate that the PDA was useful for sending and receiving Short Message Service (SMS) messages, this feature only proved to be useful to organize social events after hours.

The experiment in the project offering a messaging service that was designed for and around the group of learners in order to support collaborative learning was not successful (Finkenhagen and Haga 2002). They found several reasons for this, both technical (messages were delayed, contacts lists were not updated), and social (the 'instant messaging' service could not compete with the existing communication infrastructure of pagers and telephones in hospitals, as these work very effectively).

It was found that many of the problems that confronted possible uses of the PDAs – resulting in non-use – are related to complexities of infrastructure. On the one hand, there are numerous technical requisites for viable PDA use that must be in place, maintained and learned (including acquiring new habits of caring for and interacting with a new technology). On the other hand, existing infrastructure – availability of stationary PCs, SMS via cellular phones, rapid and systematic paging systems in hospitals – also mitigated against PDA use. Yet it is necessary to reconceptualize information and communication infrastructures carefully to gain deeper appreciation of their socio-historical character as a critical step in expanding understandings of the complexities of such infrastructures.

Institutional aspects

Our main finding is that a better understanding is needed of the commonalities and divergences between and amongst the networks of designers of wireless and mobile technologies, medical practitioners in general practice and in specialized hospital-based care, and medical educators concerned with problem-based learning and the promotion of evidence-based medicine.

Design should not only be concerned with creating a standardized and possibly closed information and communication environment which is mediated by PDAs, but should also be based on existing information sources and communication means already implemented and used. This could be achieved by creating gateways between networks, which would thus integrate parts of existing institutional, social and technical resources, and make them available on the PDAs. This implies finding ways to relate and align multiple activity systems, which will be the subject of further theoretical research.

The experiences of the participating medical students and researchers and multidisciplinary research collaborators suggest practical insights for technology design and implementation. They also provoke a reconceptualization of information and communication infrastructures to emphasize their social historical constitution and how vitally they are embedded in social and technical networks. From such a socio-historically rich perspective, it is proposed that the PDAs should no longer be regarded only or primarily as Personal Digital Assistants, but rather as potential gateways in complicated webs of interdependent technical and social networks.

What next?

This kind of technology is still at a very early stage. The project is now closed and was itself not just-in-time in respect to the possibilities of mobile and wireless technology. However, the situation changes rapidly in terms of technology development as well as in use situations. It is very much a question of timing.

The authors have been engaged in further research in the health sector. In the MEDMOBIL project (see Smørdal et al. 2004a, 2004b) a user participatory approach using video scenarios addresses future support for co-ordination and communication in a professional mobile health team using wireless infrastructure and handheld devices.

References

Beyer, H. and Holtzblatt, K. (1998) *Contextual Design: Defining Customer Centered Systems*, San Francisco, CA: Morgan Kaufman.

Ellingsen, K.B. (2002) Bruk av håndholdt datamaskin i medisinstudenters utplassering (Medical students' use of PDAs during their assignments in the primary healthcare sector). Cand. Scient. Thesis (in Norwegian), University of Oslo.

Finkenhagen, K. and Haga, Ø. (2002) How can Instant Messaging Support Communication in a Wireless Environment? – Medical Students' use of Personal Digital Assistants for Messaging in the Knowmobile Project, Department of Informatics, University of Oslo.

Gallis, H.E. and Kasbo, J.P. (2002) Walking away from the PDA: a contextual study of medical students' use of mobile terminals and services in relation to their clinical practice. Cand. Scient. Thesis. Department of Informatics, University of Oslo.

Hsu, D. (2002) Hva hindrer og fremmer bruk av PDA'er i medisinstudenters praksisperiode? (Barriers and triggers for medical students' use of PDAs during their assignments in the primary healthcare sector). Cand. Scient. Thesis (in Norwegian), University of Oslo.

Kuutti, K. (1991) The Concept of Activity as a Basic Unit of Analysis for CSCW Research, in Proceedings of ECSCW '91 (eds, L. Bannon, M. Robinson and K. Schmidt), 249–64, Amsterdam: Kluwer Academic Publishers.

Kuutti, K. (1999) Activity Theory, Transformation of Work, and Information Systems Design, in *Perspectives on Activity Theory* (eds, Y. Engeström, R. Miettinen and R. Punamaki), 360–76, Cambridge: Cambridge University Press.

Lundby, K. (2002) Knowmobile. On-line. Available HTTP http://www.intermedia.uio.no/prosjekter/knowmobile/ (accessed 22 November 2004).

Petersson, G. (2002) KNOWMOBILE guides the implementation of technology in medical education, in *KNOWMOBLE Knowledge Access in Distributed Training. Mobile opportunities for medical students. Report 5* (ed., K. Lundby), 231–43, InterMedia, University of Oslo.

Smørdal, O., Moen, A., Kristiansen, T., Refseth, Y., Mortensen, B. and Osnes, T. (2004a) Participatory Design and Infrastructures for Coordination and Communication in Interdisciplinary Mobile Health Teams. Presented at MedInfo 2004 in San Francisco, USA.

Smørdal, O., Moen, A., Kristiansen, T., Refseth, Y., Mortensen, B. and Osnes, T. (2004b) Information Sharing in Interdisciplinary Mobile Health Teams. Presented at IT in Health Care: Sociotechnical Approaches – To Err is System, Portland, Oregon, USA.

Chapter 11

Training Perioperative Specialist Practitioners

Roger Kneebone and Harry Brenton

Background

This case study discusses the use of handheld computers (Personal Digital Assistants or PDAs) within a group of mature healthcare workers who undertook training in a new professional role between April 2003 and March 2004. After a brief introduction to the role, we present our experience during a 12-month training programme, critically evaluate our pilot and summarize key points for the future.

The European Working Time Directive has placed great pressure on arrangements for medical cover within UK hospitals. In 2002, the National Health Service (NHS) Changing Workforce Programme at the Department of Health established 19 pilot projects to address the mandatory reduction in junior doctors' workload to 56 hours a week, scheduled to take effect in August 2004. One such project, the Perioperative Specialist Practitioner (PSP), pilots a new professional role that aims to expand the surgical team by providing patients with integrated care before and after an operation. The goal of integrated care is to provide patients with a stable relationship with a single PSP throughout their stay in hospital, rather than a fragmented series of contacts with different healthcare workers. PSPs will assume many of the diagnostic and procedural responsibilities currently carried out by junior doctors.

The 12 PSPs in this pilot were mature professionals with many years' experience of working in the NHS. Before leaving their previous posts to train as PSPs, nine of the participants were nurses, two were operating department practitioners and one was a physiotherapist. The PSPs were geographically dispersed across Britain, working in eight hospitals within five National Health Service trusts (NHS trusts provide a general range of services to local communities through health centres, clinics and centres of expertise in specialized care).

The creation of a new professional group presents challenges to trainees, clinician colleagues and course designers alike. There is no established template for training, nor was there an existing professional identity for the PSPs to assume.

Team structure

The PSP pilot project was run by a team at Imperial College London consisting of a clinical leader, a manager, an administrator, an educational consultant and a workforce designer from the Department of Health. A learning technologist was appointed six months after the project began. PDA software was developed in collaboration with The Department of Information Systems at the London School of Economics (LSE). The LSE team consisted of a departmental head, a PhD student and two MSc students. They provided technical assistance and advice, together with initial programming, but remained at one remove from the everyday running of the programme.

Pedagogic approach

The PSP training programme was full time and lasted for one year. Intensive one-week training modules at Imperial College London alternated with longer periods of supervised clinical practice within the surgical team at each participant's hospital. This arrangement allowed skills learnt during training sessions to be consolidated and extended in the workplace. As well as factual knowledge, PSPs gained procedural skills in a range of professional settings: clinics, hospital wards, operating theatres and laboratories. Skills included:

• Pre-operative investigation to assess the suitability of a patient for an operation.
• Understanding of normal and abnormal states relating to surgical procedures.
• Identifying and treating common and important complications.
• Carrying out clinical procedures including taking patient histories, ordering tests, taking blood and putting up intravenous infusions.

Taught modules used a range of teaching styles: didactic lectures, scenario-based learning, skills training and computer simulations of surgical procedures. Technical, professional and communications skills were taught on an integrated basis; for example, a PSP would learn techniques for taking blood while simultaneously answering questions from an actor taking the role of a patient. This method is designed to recreate how healthcare skills are deployed in practice on the hospital ward (Kneebone *et al.* 2002).

Because the training programme was an innovative combination of centralized instruction and situated learning in the workplace, we adopted a flexible pedagogic approach with continual revision and restructuring of training modules. Ongoing evaluation allowed us to assess the changing educational needs of the PSPs and feed these into the training design. Evaluation questionnaires and group interviews at the end of every module (conducted by an independent, professionally accredited psychologist) explored negative as well as positive feedback.

Initial aims

Creating a portfolio of evidence

It was essential that each PSP built up a portfolio of evidence, both as a 'map' of their training and for future accreditation of the role. In order to withstand external scrutiny and maximize learning, the portfolio needed to provide detailed and accurate evidence of clinical activities, prior learning competencies, course materials and certificates. Records of clinical activity needed to be made contemporaneously while fresh in the memory, protected by regular backup in case of loss or theft.

Remotely monitoring clinical activities

In order to identify possible gaps in training we wanted a method of remotely monitoring the professional duties performed by the PSPs, to check they had adequate opportunities to practise the clinical and motor skills they had been taught. The PSP's duties meant they were rarely in one place for long and it was essential that they could log data on the move.

Written reflections

We wanted each PSP to keep a learning diary, allowing them to reflect in writing on knowledge gained while providing clinical care in their own hospitals. Learning diaries help to consolidate learning and play an important part in the transition from one professional role to another. Although the use of learning portfolios is well established within medical education (Snadden and Thomas 1998), there are few published examples of PDAs being used for reflective diaries within medicine (Savill-Smith and Kent 2003; Alderson and Oswald 1999).

Access to learning resources

We wanted each participant to have access to learning resources such as clinical guidelines and medical reference works on the internet. Ideally, participants would be able to access this material on a standard desktop computer or by using a PDA.

Rationale for using PDAs

We realized that not all PSPs would have easy access to desktop or laptop computers, therefore we decided to explore the use of handheld computers as a convenient alternative. PDAs are increasingly being used in UK healthcare and are common in America where is has been estimated that 50 per cent of US doctors will be using a mobile device by 2005 (Harris Interactive 2001). A recent survey has reported that medical students are the largest undergraduate users of PDAs within UK Higher Education (Savill-Smith and Kent 2003).

PDAs combine the portability of paper forms with the technological advantages of a personal computer. Although paper based logs have the benefit of simplicity they are hard to share with others, may be filled in incorrectly, become bulky and are easily lost. Desktop computers are tied to one location and may not be readily available within a clinical setting. Laptop computers are more portable but are expensive and too cumbersome to be used on the ward. Other advantages of PDAs include:

- PDAs can be carried at all times and provide guaranteed access to a computer.
- Data can be emailed to the Training Centre to build a cumulative pattern of PSP activity.
- PDAs are password protected to prevent unauthorized access in case of loss or theft.
- A backup is created every time the PDA is synchronized with a PC.
- Software can be written to meet custom requirements.
- PDAs are independent of local IT infrastructure that varies within each hospital and NHS Trust.
- Clinical activities can be recorded contemporaneously.

There are other documented uses of mobile computers within healthcare that we did not implement at the start of the project (Fischer *et al.* 2003; McAlearney *et al.* 2004). These include point of care assistance (e.g. drug information, clinical guidelines, decision aids and medical reference works); software to track the results of common clinical tests such as blood analysis; electronic drug prescription.

Implementation

Hardware and software

We provided each PSP with a Compaq iPAQ 3970, running Pocket PC 2002 OS. This model comes supplied with an inbuilt appointment calendar, address book and cut down 'pocket' versions of Microsoft Word and Excel. The MSc students from the LSE developed and installed two additional components: a prototype clinical activity logging database and a learning diary template (developed with ABCDatabase).

We initially considered using wireless PDAs operating over a wireless Internet connection or the mobile phone network. However, the technology at that time (early 2003) was not mature enough and the costs were prohibitive. Possible devices such as the XDA from British Telecom were considered unreliable. There is a major problem in British hospital wards with legal restrictions on the use of mobile phones and wireless networks on the grounds that they interfere with medical equipment. However, many believe that these fears are groundless and based on unsubstantiated evidence (Myerson and Mitchell 2003).

Activity logging database

The activity logging database records details of patient encounters on the wards. Clinical activities are selected from a predefined 'pick list' by tapping a stylus directly on the screen. Additional data includes initials of any supervisor and whether the activity is elective or emergency. The patient's age and gender are recorded but in accordance with data protection legislation their names are not recorded (Principles of Data Protection website).

Learning diary template

The learning diary consists of a set of templates with headings such as 'Thoughts and feelings' and 'What worked and what didn't?'. These questions are intentionally open-ended, allowing the PSPs to frame the answers as they wish. Reflections are typed using a detachable keyboard that folds into a compact case.

Training sessions with students

When the PDAs were first distributed, all PSPs attended a group training and induction session to accustom them to the PDA and learn to use its basic functions. Each PSP received a manual explaining how to use the clinical activity database. They were also given instructions on how to email clinical activity data back to the training centre. The PSPs were unfamiliar with PDAs, except for one of the trainees who owned a Palm Pilot and required minimal instruction.

Outcomes

Evaluation strategy

Our evaluation strategy was twofold:

*   Ongoing technical evaluation of software prototypes to address any problems as they arose. This took the form of repeated interviews with the PSPs, both in groups and individually, to explore their experiences of using the database as it evolved.
*   A broader evaluation of how PDAs could be used within a professional healthcare context.

Testing the prototype

After their induction, the PSPs tested activity logging software and written reflections at their home sites for four weeks. Initial responses appeared to be positive, but barriers subsequently emerged.

Positive experiences

*   PSPs appreciated being given their own device and liked the inbuilt applications, in particular the appointment calendar and address book.

- One PSP reported that writing reflections in the learning diary helped them to contextualize their training by building beneficial connections between previously separate areas of theory and practice.

Negative experiences

- After an initial period of enthusiasm, the PSPs felt a loss of engagement with the PDAs.
- Some PSPs were unsure about why we were asking them to use PDAs and saw no immediate professional benefit from logging their clinical activities.
- The activity logging software ran too slowly to use effectively in a clinical setting.
- Only one activity could be recorded for each patient record. For example, if a patient had a blood test followed by an X-ray, the patient's details had to be entered twice.
- Several PSPs did not have easy access to a desktop computer, which was required to synchronize data with the PDA.
- One PDA failed to synchronize when the number of patients stored on the database exceeded 60.
- Entering significant amounts of text (learning diaries) on the PDA was cumbersome, even with the foldable keyboard.
- No participants emailed clinical data back to the training centre.

Mid-term evaluation

An interim evaluation took place six months after the project started. At this point, there was a crisis of confidence, and it became clear that major dissatisfactions were threatening the viability of the entire PDA project. There was a widespread feeling amongst the PSPs that PDAs were irrelevant and burdensome. Key technical reasons were:

- The PSPs needed an intuitive and quick tool, but the software we provided was too slow and awkward to use in a clinical setting.
- We were not able to monitor clinical activities continuously because the basic data entry function of the software was not working satisfactorily and this prevented the transmission of information back to the training centre.

In addition, it appeared that the PDAs represented a focus for other anxieties that the PSPs were experiencing:

- The PSPs were undergoing profound upheaval in their professional lives through taking on a new role and the PDAs represented another change they were expected to accommodate. During stressful periods, the PDAs sometimes became a focus for other professional anxieties; as a tangible object they make an easy target.

- At a particularly difficult stage in the PSPs' training, feelings of frustration towards the PDAs were shared and amplified amongst the group. As a measure of this frustration, two PSPs were ready to hand back and stop using them altogether.

Remedial action

On reflection, we had underestimated the need to communicate our vision of the potential long-term training benefits of PDAs. In addition, we had not provided a full time dedicated member of staff from the start of the project to give technical support and act as an intermediary between the participants, the teachers and the project managers. At this crucial six-month stage, we took the following actions:

- Appointed a learning technologist to provide dedicated and personalized technical support.
- Established formal and informal forums and encouraged PSPs to voice their concerns openly.
- Abandoned written reflections on the PDAs and reverted to a paper-based system (with the option of continuing with the PDAs if they wished).
- Abandoned ABCdatabase in favour of a faster development tool (HanDbase).
- Re-wrote the activity logging software from scratch using HanDbase. The new design incorporated continuous input from the PSPs.
- Installed relevant reference material on each PDA (Oxford Handbook of Clinical Medicine, and a medical calculator Archimedes).

Final evaluation

By the end of the pilot, the PSPs were very positive about the new database and reported it was fast enough to use on the wards. However, technical problems persisted and some PSPs reported an error in the iPAQ synching software that corrupted data being synched at the time including the HanDbase data.

At the end of the pilot, a one-day evaluation workshop explored participants' responses to the PSP programme as a whole, including the PDA component. Individual and group interviews revealed a surprisingly high level of support for the PDA concept, although all PSPs acknowledged that technical issues had prevented the technology from being as useful as we had initially hoped.

Summary from PSP pilot

Although we did not use PDAs as extensively as we initially planned, we learnt some extremely valuable lessons. We underestimated the delicate interplay between technical development and the requirements and attitudes of users. Testing a concept within a real world scenario provides invaluable information, yet may risk alienating users if devices do not perform efficiently in the workplace.

It takes time for mature professional learners to absorb new technology into their culture. Unless participants feel a sense of ownership towards their PDA the technology may be regarded as an 'imposed gift'. It is vital to involve participants in software development from an early stage and clearly explain the training benefits of using PDAs. The provision of an expensive hi-tech device is not enough of a benefit in itself, as the novelty of having a new gadget soon wears off.

Ensuring that the software functions correctly is essential, but it means nothing without a dedicated member of support staff who can talk about PDAs in plain English. The more hi-tech a solution, the greater the need for human interaction to aid its introduction.

Key lessons

- To be accepted, PDAs must save time and not create additional work.
- The needs of the user should drive the technology, not vice versa.
- Designing PDA software requires careful management and iterative development. Programming, planning and training often take longer than expected.
- Technical support should be provided in plain English.
- Personal involvement between support staff and users is highly valued.
- Learning technologists fulfil a useful role by bridging the barrier between technology and education.
- PDAs can become a focus for unrelated professional frustrations.
- Users, software developer and project managers may have completely different perspectives on PDAs.
- Electronic medical reference works are highly valued as they have an immediate professional use.
- When technical problems cannot be resolved immediately it is important to make clear that users' concerns are recognized.
- Mobile technology works best when it becomes 'transparent' and does not interfere with the goal that the user is trying to achieve.

Further developments

The PSP pilot finished in March 2004. The project was widely regarded as success-ful, and a new cohort of 15 PSPs started training in October 2004. PDAs will again be used, but we have made a number of modifications in the light of the experiences outlined above.

Due to the synching and software problems experienced in the pilot, we decided to abandon using iPAQ in favour of Palm Pilots (Tungsten T3s). The synching procedure on a Palm is simpler than that on an iPAQ and a Palm software developer has advised us that they are less likely to crash when synching. They also have a greater available library of medical software. At the time of writing (October 2004), we are thoroughly testing the 15 Palms by simulating usage for one month. By intensive synching with a number of PCs, we aim to eliminate problems before distributing devices to the PSPs. We have installed a comprehensive set of medical reference works on every PDA (Dr Companion website). This comes on an external memory card and includes a wide range of clinical reference works and drug formularies.

A dedicated learning technologist will actively manage the process of introducing PDAs and ensuring that PSPs are confident and competent in using them. This will include a greater openness about the potential difficulties PSPs may experience when using their PDAs. By being honest about the limitations as well as the advantages of PDAs, we hope to manage the expectations of the PSPs and not give them an unrealistic view of what the technology can offer.

Conclusions

In conclusion, our study has shown that PDAs can offer significant benefits within a new healthcare role. If inexpertly managed, however, such technology can cause more problems than it solves. If mobile computing is to succeed, it must meet a perceived need by potential users. Well-designed software and efficient data synchronization are necessary but not sufficient conditions for success. The process must be mediated by a real person, who is able to recognize, understand and allay the anxieties associated with the introduction of unfamiliar technology in a new professional role.

Acknowledgements

We wish to acknowledge the support and advice of the following:

*   Dr Carsten Sorenson, Gamel Wiredu, Jennifer Blechar, Csaba Horvath (Department of Information Systems, London School of Economics).
*   Heather Fry (Head of Centre for Education, Imperial College London).
*   Jacqueline Younger (Lead Workforce Designer for Practitioners and Prescribing, NHS Changing Workforce Programme).
*   We would also like to thank all the PSPs.

References

AbcDB database website (2004) On-line. Available HTTP http://www.pocketsoft.ca/ (accessed 22 November 2004).

Alderson, T.S.J. and Oswald, N.T. (1999) Clinical experience of medical students in primary care: use of an electronic log in monitoring experience and in guiding education in the Cambridge community based clinical course. *Medical Education*, 33: 429–33.

Archimedes drug calculator website (2004) On-line. Available HTTP http://www. pocketpccity.com/software/ppc/Archimedes-The-Intelligent-Medical-2001-3-14–ce-ppc.html (accessed 22 November 2004).

Dr Companion website (2004) On-line. Available HTTP http://www.drcompanion.com/products/uk/overview/index.html (accessed 22 November 2004).

Fischer, S., Stewart, T.E., Mehta, S., Wax, R. and Lapinsky, S.E. (2003) Handheld computing in medicine. *Journal of the American Medical Informatics Association*, 10: 139–49.

HanDbase website (2004) On-line. Available HTTP http://www.ddhsoftware.com/handbase.html (accessed 22 November 2004).

Harris Interactive (2001) Physicians' Use of Handheld Personal Computing Devices Increases From 15% in 1999 to 26% in 2001. On-line. Available HTTP http://www.harrisinteractive.com/news/allnewsbydate.asp?NewsID=345 (accessed 22 November 2004).

Kneebone, R., Kidd, J., Nestel, D., Asvall, S., Paraskeva, P. and Darzi, A. (2002) An innovative model for teaching and learning clinical procedures, *Medical Education*, 36: 628–34.

McAlearney, A.S., Schweikhart, S.B. and Medow, M.A. (2004) Doctors' experience with handheld computers in clinical practice: qualitative study, *British Medical Journal*, 328: 1162.

Myerson, S.G. and Mitchell, A.R. (2003) Mobile phones in hospitals, *British Medical Journal*, 326: 460–1.

Oxford Handbook of Clinical Medicine website (2004) On-line. Available HTTP http://www.franklin.com/estore/details.aspx?ID=OCM500734DLDP (accessed 22 November 2004).

Principles of Data Protection website (2004) On-line. Available HTTP http://www.informationcommissioner.gov.uk/eventual.aspx?id=34 (accessed 22 November 2004).

Savill-Smith, C. and Kent, P. (2003) *The Use of Palmtop Computers for Learning – A Review of the Literature*. Learning and Skills Development Agency. On-line. Available HTTP http://www.lsda.org.uk/pubs/dbaseout/download.asp?code=1477 (accessed 14 April 2005).

Snadden, D. and Thomas, M. (1998) The use of portfolio learning in medical education, *Medical Education*, 20: 192–9.

Chapter 12

Whether it's m-learning or e-learning, it must be ME learning

*Rosemary Luckin, Diane Brewster,
Darren Pearce, Benedict du Boulay and
Richard Siddons-Corby*

Context and background

The learning context at the heart of this case study is a course called Interactive
Learning Environments, which is offered to third year undergraduate students and
to postgraduates from a variety of Masters programmes at the University of Sussex.
The course aims to offer informatics students a mix of theoretical grounding, case
study examples and hands-on experience with developing technologies. During
the course, students were required to develop and evaluate their own interactive
learning experiences in collaboration with their fellow students. For example, one
group of students was required to design a learning activity for their peers supported
by technology. Both groups of students were required to design and conduct an
evaluation of this learning activity.

As an institution, the University of Sussex has decided to promote the
development of in-house technologies such as its Managed Learning Environment
(MLE): Sussex Direct, and to encourage small projects that expand upon novel
solutions to particular problems or issues within a learning context. As part of this
policy, the Teaching and Learning Development Unit at Sussex offered financial
support for a mobile learning theme to be developed for the Spring term of 2003.
This funding enabled a course team to be set up and hardware and software to be
purchased for what became known as the SMILE project (Sussex Mobile Interactive
Learning Environments). The total budget for the SMILE project was £21,300 for
the period from October 2002 to May 2003. The project offered the university a
viability study for future larger scale implementations of mobile learning devices;
an evaluation of relevance to the MLE and Virtual Learning Environment (VLE)
programmes under development at the university; and a model of how learners
collaborate and learn using mobile on-line devices.

The budget allowed the purchase of 18 combined mobile phone and Personal
Digital Assistant (PDA) devices. At the time of purchase (November 2002), the
range of devices available on the market with the required functionality was limited
and the XDA was selected as the one most appropriate for our needs. The XDA
offered integrated phone and PDA, along with Pocket PC and General Packet
Radio Service (GPRS) so that the phone connection was 'always-on' for web
browsing or email applications. The functionality it therefore offered included

internet access and email both via a browser and to the university mail server (available for POP3 or IMAP4). The device has a touch-sensitive colour screen, applications such as Word, Excel, Outlook and Explorer and can record audio.

The course team consisted of two technical experts, two lecturers and a teaching assistant. The students were allocated devices for the term and were expected to use them 'as their own'. Postgraduate students had a device each, whilst the under-graduates had to share them in small groups of three or four students. This constraint resulted in undergraduates only having access to their personal email via a web browser on the device and not via direct access to their accounts on the university mail server. The course team also provided a website for information along with access to lecture slides. Two one-hour lectures each week were used to cover the syllabus content, whilst the seminar time, two hours for postgraduates, one hour for undergraduates, was given over to an exploration of the issues surrounding the use of mobile technology for learning. Seminars for both groups of students consisted of practical activities using the mobile device, as well as workshops on topics such as personalisation, collaboration, design and evaluation.

Rationale and problem statement

Initial results on the use of mobile technology, such as those reported in MLEARN 2002 and in the 2002 IEEE workshop (Milrad *et al.* 2002) have been encouraging. Researchers have suggested, for example, that mobile learning enhances autonomous and collaborative learning (Cereijo Roibás and Arnedillo Sánchez 2002), and that it can be applied to a wide age range of students (Inkpen 2000; Perlin and Fox 1993; Sharples *et al.* 2002; Soloway *et al.* 2001). But how do we help our students to understand what this really means with respect to the design of a mobile learning experience?

The XDA technology was introduced to the course in order to give students the opportunity to experience what it would be like to use mobile technology to support and enhance their own learning. When students then came to design a session for their peers using this technology, their approach was grounded in this experience as well as in their understandings of pedagogy, system design and the work of others. From the perspective of the teachers on the course, it gave us the opportunity to assess the potential of such devices for use in higher education and to increase our understanding of the ways in which learners use these devices in their own right and in combination with the other course resources. We were particularly interested in the potential of the technology for collaborative work and for increasing students' appreciation of their own learning processes.

Technology and infrastructure

The functionality of the XDA technology we used has already been described. Here we consider the implications of adopting this technology and the infrastructure into which it was integrated. The XDA itself was far from the 'out of the box' experience it had promised. The devices were purchased from a local supplier, along with a phone account with a service provider in order for students to use both the mobile phone functionality and the on-line web browsing. Each device had to be tested and all parts logged. This was to be expected. What was more of a surprise was the difficulty we faced in taking all the devices on-line. This required several interactions with both device supplier and service provider. All devices were subsequently connected, but the fact that this was less than straightforward was an early sign of what was to be an unexpectedly tiresome feature of the project: what we were trying to do was not within the normal patterns of service provision. For each account (associated with each device), we had to set up a method of payment to ensure that the rental and usage costs were paid to the service provider. We also had to ensure that students were unable to run up huge bills that would be the university's liability, for example by downloading large files from websites. Students signed an acknowledgement of their responsibility for payments in excess of the stipulated maximum. In order to try to help students track the amount of material they were downloading we purchased third party software to monitor data traffic. This was unreliable and with no figures available from the service provider, a climate of nervousness was created among the students; they were concerned about incurring debt if they used data above the agreed tariff. No students did in fact run up an excessive bill. There is insufficient space within this chapter to give any detailed account of the time and effort that went into managing our relationship with the service provider and ensuring that the devices were kept on-line without exceeding our budget. Suffice it to say that this was a significant cost to the project.

In addition to the XDA itself, the students had access to a course website that contained all the lecture notes and slides plus references and web links. In addition to this standard content the website also gave students information about all their peers' contact details, email addresses and XDA phone numbers. The access to the course website was logged in a manner that enabled us to distinguish between XDA and desktop access. Information about access was presented back to students through the website so that they were constantly aware of how many times each resource had been accessed. Students also agreed that their email traffic, when between course participants, could be logged from week four (out of ten) onwards (but not the content of messages). When an email was sent between two or more people involved in the course, we knew whether it was sent via the XDA or not. In addition to the website, students were invited to join an on-line discussion group and at one point in the course, this discussion group was explicitly linked to a lecture time slot. Students did not need to turn up to the physical location of the lecture, but were encouraged to view the slides and join in the discussion from whatever location they wished. The group and the website could be accessed via the XDA, any of the desktop machines on campus or in the students' homes. Students were enthusiastic about being offered the devices and all signed up willingly to take responsibility for them and to ensure, as far as they could, that they were returned in good working order at the end of the course. The management of the process of allocating devices was an overhead for both staff and students, as was the management of the finances. This included the offer to back up the files in the devices on a weekly basis, so that data would not be lost and any software updates could be easily downloaded. This was further complicated by having the ongoing running costs associated with mobile phone network service provision.

Engaging with students

In the first session of the course students were given a training session with the devices and technical support was freely available throughout. Our evaluation of the course, a fuller account of which can be found in Luckin *et al.* (2003), involved multiple data sources. Here we restrict our discussion to the student questionnaires and discussions, the email and website logging data and an on-line poll.

What did the students think?

Student attitudes to the introduction of the devices and other related technology into the course were assessed in two ways: an end-of-course questionnaire and qualitative data from notes taken during an end-of-course evaluation session with the postgraduate students.

Most students tried at least half of the functions offered by the device, although email came out a clear winner as its most useful feature with 48 per cent of the votes and web access second with 19 per cent. This suggests that it was the connectivity of the device that students really appreciated. However, only 57 per cent of students could see a clear educational use for the device, with the remainder being unconvinced. The views expressed by students ranged from enthusiastic to antagonistic, with most students recognising the potential of the technology but making statements such as 'the device isn't quite there yet'.

Email and web logging data

Hits on the course website were grouped into those made by members of the course team who had an XDA each, those made by postgraduate students who also had an XDA each and those made by undergraduate students who shared an XDA between three or four students. Hits were differentiated as coming either from the XDA or from a desktop machine on campus or in the students' homes. Figure 12.2 illustrates that postgraduate students made more website hits using the XDA than did undergraduate students. Postgraduates made an average of 35 hits per device as opposed to 24 hits for each undergraduate device. However, undergraduates made more use of desktop technology than their postgraduate counterparts, with an average of 231 hits per undergraduate as compared to 200 for each postgraduate across the term (see Figure 12.3).

The logging of email traffic between course participants showed that, not surprisingly, the course admin team sent the most emails to course members, both using the device and not using it. The postgraduates were more frequent users of the device overall for email, but the undergraduates were at the severe disadvantage of sharing devices so not being able to use it as easily to access their personal email.

The on-line poll

We designed the poll to enable us to ask students their views about the key features that need to be part of the design of both face-to-face and technology-mediated educational experiences. The poll was offered to students through the course website as part of an on-line lecture. The poll was also conducted with students taking the same course in the following Spring (2004), which enabled us to draw upon evidence over a longer period of time and from a greater number of students.

In both 2003 and 2004 students felt that the most important feature to the success of face-to-face learning was *Approachable, knowledgeable and enthusiastic tutors*. The chance to get hands-on experience of material being discussed in the course such as offered by the XDA, finished third in 2003 and second in 2004. There was a similar consistency between 2003 and 2004 with respect to the feature that students considered vital to the success of on-line learning; this was *Tutor support on-line*, which finished top in both years with *Conference environments* and *Student collaboration* also proving popular choices. Web resources were considered to be less important for on-line education in 2004 than in 2003, a change which is carried through into students' views about the types of technology that are most important for students in both face-to-face and on-line learning contexts. Unsurprisingly *Internet access* was voted the most important technology for on-line learning in both 2003 and 2004, receiving 95 per cent and 85 per cent of the votes respectively. However, the top three technologies for face-to-face learning in 2003 were:

1   Internet access: 33 per cent of votes cast
2   Notebook and pen: 24 per cent of votes cast
3   On-line multimedia course materials: 14 per cent of votes cast.

Whereas in 2004 they were:

1   Notebook and pen: 58 per cent of votes cast
2   Books: 19 per cent of votes cast
3   On-line multimedia course materials *and* Internet access: 12 per cent of votes cast.

Evaluation and outcomes

The evaluation of this learning experience, as discussed above, suggests that as a device the XDA can allow students to experience learning in whatever context they happen to be. The website usage statistics indicate that learners will access

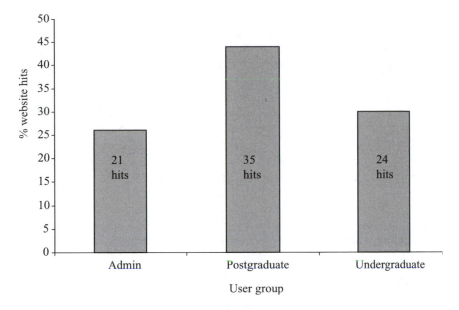

Figure 12.1 Average website access per XDA device

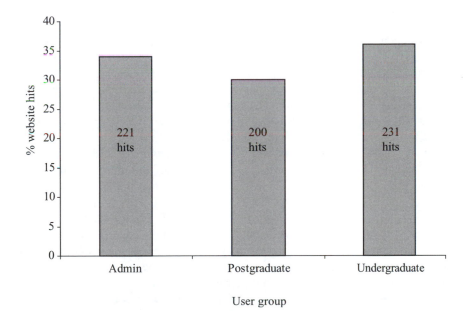

Figure 12.2 Average website access per user (not using the XDA)

resources at any time of the day if given the opportunity. The student evaluations suggest that it is the connectivity of the device that learners appreciated, as opposed to the word processing or other applications. However, the device alone is far from enough. Even those students who were lucky enough to have sole use of an XDA for the term, with all reasonable bills paid for them, still used standard desktop technology to a much greater extent both for course assignment preparation, resource access and email communication. Always-on personal digital assistants are not a replacement for other more familiar artefacts and should not be seen as such. The key feature needed is the provision of a means of communication with others who can offer encouragement and support. As we mentioned in the previous section, we also collected data from an on-line poll. These poll results suggest a rise in the popularity of non-digital technology, such as notebooks, pens and textbooks. Is this evidence that students now take for granted the existence of good quality Internet access, or could it also be evidence of a disappointment in the digital technology on offer or the manner in which it is deployed?

Conclusions and institutional aspects

The overall feeling from both the course team and the students was that the project had been a worthwhile exercise, allowing as it did an investigation of the use of combined mobile phone and PDA devices within an educational context (Luckin *et al.* 2003). It illustrated that the provision of coherent learning opportunities and episodes mediated by technology and accessible through multiple devices is certainly possible. However, the success of the technology as an educational tool depends upon the extent to which it is integrated into a pedagogically grounded framework. The technology is merely a medium through which the learner can communicate with others. Those others may be the writers of course modules that the learner is reading on a screen, they may be fellow students with whom a discussion is being conducted through an on-line forum, or they might be a teacher who is offering some advice. Whatever the situation, the technology itself should not be the focus. There is a tendency to add a fresh letter to the start of the word 'learn' or 'learning' and to then assume that a new paradigm has been created. The words 'e-learning' and 'm-learning' are examples of this phenomenon. The fundamental feature is still, of course, the learning and that should always be the focus of any educational experience. If we wish to offer learners a particular technology such as a mobile PDA in order to increase their access to the learning experience, the focus of attention should remain upon the concepts to be taught and learnt, not on the technology. We may have to make some changes to the packaging, to the size of the modules for example, but the concepts we want the learner to understand should remain our primary concern.

An analogy with a good take-away springs to mind here. If I fancy a Chicken Tikka for supper, I have various options available to me: I can cook it myself, I can go to a restaurant that I know serves that dish or I can order a take-away to be delivered to my door. My choice will probably be dictated by various constraints including cost and convenience. However, whichever mode of delivery I choose, the meal I eat will still be Chicken Tikka. In fact, it may even be the identical meal, since many outlets that offer a take-away service also offer a sit-down restaurant alternative. The food is precisely the same in both instances. The chef does not differentiate the ingredients or the method because the food is going to be taken away and eaten off the premises. The same should be true for education.

So why is there a problem? In the main, the problems occur because the technology or the way in which it has been integrated into a particular learning context results in it becoming the focus of attention. The XDA we introduced to the Interactive Learning Environments course fell prey to this deficiency to an extent. It was not reliable and not all its features were deemed useful or indeed easy to use. The overhead of staff time in terms of technical support, account administration and finding workarounds for features that did not work as required was enormous.

What next?

As we stated at the outset, Sussex University encourages small projects that expand upon novel solutions to particular problems or issues within a learning context. The SMILE project we have discussed in this case study increased our understanding of what it means to offer a learning experience that encompasses multiple technologies across varying contexts such as on campus and at home. For the Interactive Learning Environments course in Spring 2004 we opted away from sophisticated kit that requires a lot of maintenance and chose to offer all students a Universal Serial Bus (USB) pen-drive, complete with all course materials. Students were required to find their own new resources to add to those we provided and to create a portfolio that they could share with other members of the course by bringing it along to seminar sessions on the pen-drive. The work could then be displayed via a laptop and projector and discussed. We also once again used the XDA devices. However, despite the students' desire for connectivity, the overhead of administering the on-line access and managing a relationship with the service provider was too great for us to contemplate its repetition. In 2004, the XDA was offered as a portable mobile computing resource, but with no on-line or mobile phone functionality. Students could, for example, use it to view and listen to the course material provided, a contrast to the 'black box' of the pen drive, which is merely a storage device. Once again, the web resources were available, but this time with the addition of audio lectures for students to download along with a piece of experimental software which enables textual annotation of this audio stream. The emphasis was upon providing learners with simple tools to help them link together the different elements of the course content.

References

Cereijo Roibás, A. and Arnedillo Sánchez, I. (2002) Pathways to M-learning, Proceedings of the First European Workshop on Mobile and Contextual Learning, pp. 53–6, Birmingham, UK, June 2002.

Inkpen, K.M. (2000) Designing Handheld Technologies for Kids, *Personal Technologies*, 3(1–2): 81–9.

Luckin, R., Brewster, D., Pearce, D., du Boulay, B. and Siddons-Corby, R. (2003) SMILE: The Creation Of Space For Interaction Through Blended Digital Technology, Proceedings of the Second European Conference on Learning with Mobile Devices – MLEARN 2003, pp. 87–93, 19–20 May 2003, London.

Milrad, M., Hopper, H.U. and Kinshuk (eds) (2002) Proceedings IEEE International Workshop on Wireless and Mobile Technologies in Education, 29–30 August, 2002, Växjö, Sweden. IEEE Computer Society.

Perlin, K. and Fox, D. (1993) Pad: An Alternative Approach to the Computer Interface, Proceedings of SIGGRAPH '93: 20th Annual Conference on Computer Graphics and Interactive Techniques, 2–6 August 1993, Anaheim, California, USA, 93: 57–64.

Sharples, M., Corlett, D. and Westmancott, O. (2002) The Design and Implementation of a Mobile Learning Resource, *Personal and Ubiquitous Computing*, 6: 220–34.

Soloway, E., Norris, C., Blumenfield, P., Fishman, B., Krajcik, J. and Marx, R. (2001) Handheld Devices are Ready at Hand, *Communications of the ACM*, 44(6): 15–20.

Chapter 13

Reading course materials in e-book form and on mobile devices

Agnes Kukulska-Hulme

Context and background

Open University (OU) students, who are distance learners, typically have to fit their learning activities around other tasks, such as work and family commitments. On most courses they receive printed course materials, presented as course books, study guides, assignment guides and readings. They may also be sent other resources, such as video, audio or software, and may be able to make use of electronic resources and on-line conferencing. Providing access to learning resources in an easily portable form can enable students to make more effective use of time while away from the home or office environment. At the same time, use of a computer as a medium for reading and interacting with course materials offers advantages such as efficient searching, convenient storage of large amounts of information, and navigation via hyperlinks that connect sections of text. Given that handheld computers such as Personal Digital Assistants (PDAs), along with e-book reading software, are becoming more widely available, we have been considering what implications the possibilities and constraints introduced by these tools have on the activity of reading for learning purposes.

An evaluation study was first undertaken at the Institute of Educational Technology during 2001, centred on the Open University Masters level course, Applications of Information Technology in Open and Distance Education (Kukulska-Hulme 2002; Waycott and Kukulska-Hulme 2003; Waycott 2004). The study was funded by an OU Teaching Fellowship Award in recognition of the course team's 'innovation and excellence' in global on-line course delivery. Students were supplied with Palm m105 PDAs and WordSmith, a commercially available document editor and viewer, enabling them to read some course materials on the PDA. Findings showed that while the portability of the device was welcomed by students, and the electronic format was advantageous, limitations such as the small screen size, navigation difficulties, and slow and error-prone methods for entering text, made it difficult to read and interact with documents. The PDA also changed the way students interacted with the study text: they were less likely to take notes and highlight text on the PDA, compared with the strategies they employed when reading print-based materials. However, students devised strategies to overcome limitations of the PDA, such as using abbreviated notes which they transferred to their desktop computer, and they used the PDA in conjunction with print materials and paper. The study recommended that documents should have more salient contextual clues about the reader's location within the document and more flexible navigational tools such as hyperlinks.

At approximately the same time, the Open University launched a project on e-book production and deployment (the E-Book Pilot Project 2001–3) funded by a university initiative in e-learning. The project set out to investigate technical aspects of producing Open University course books and other course materials in e-book form without increasing overall production costs. A pilot study was conducted to trial and to investigate the use of such e-book materials on a number of courses with a view to their future general use as an alternative study medium, and this was accompanied by a formal evaluation by staff from the Institute of Educational Technology. Following on from this, the university is in the process of distributing course material e-books to students on around 200 courses. It is expected that most students will access these on their desktop computer, but growing numbers of students are also users of laptop computers and PDAs. This case study describes the evaluation of the E-Book Pilot Project, focusing on teaching and learning aspects and the use of laptops and PDAs, rather than e-book production issues.

Rationale and problem statement

The evaluation was undertaken in order to identify the perceived value of e-books from the point of view of OU students, as well as course teams, i.e. the authors and developers of course materials. In relation to student use, we needed to find out:

- whether students welcomed the possibility of having materials in e-book format;
- what problems were encountered and how they were overcome;
- how e-books might change the learning experience;
- what it would take for students to make the most of this technology;
- how disabled students cope with the technology and whether they can benefit from this means of delivery.

OU students largely fall into the 25–45 age range, although there are many outside that range. The university takes special responsibility for making higher education accessible to people with disabilities; well over 7,000 students belong to this category. The e-book files formed a part solution to implementing the requirements for compliance with the Special Educational Needs and Disability Act 2001 of the UK Parliament. This came into force in September 2002 (incorporated as Part 4 of the Disability Discrimination Act, 1995) and concerned students with various categories and degrees of disability, such as motor impairments giving difficulty in handling books, or visual impairments needing large print display or a degree of screen read out of text. Most of the e-books provide access to course texts via keyboard command and screen reader software. The files can be used as an 'intermediate' file format for printing to Braille printers.

From a teaching perspective, the evaluation sought to establish:

- the opportunities and drawbacks for course teams;
- whether the opportunities were understood and valued;
- what kinds of material might be delivered in e-book format to students;
- what impact this technology would have on course team and tutor skills and roles;
- any cost implications for course production.

Interviews were conducted at the start of the evaluation to establish expectations and experiences that participants already had with the technology, how they anticipated that e-book materials would be produced, and to answer and further refine the questions that the evaluation would try to address. Focus group meetings were organized at the end of the evaluation project. They enabled course team participants across the university to share their experience, and to discuss some evaluation findings and their implications.

Participants were drawn from the five courses that took part in the pilot project, from the faculties of Arts, Science, Social Science, and Maths and Computing: Exploring Psychology, Philosophy and the Human Situation, The Molecular World, Governing Europe, and User Interface Design and Evaluation.

Technology and infrastructure

E-books were created from existing printed course materials by the university's Learning and Teaching Solutions (LTS) unit. It was decided to use Adobe Acrobat file format which could be used on desktop and laptop computers and PDAs. Students could download the e-book files and instructions for using them from their course website in addition to receiving the printed materials. To read the e-books, they were expected to use the Adobe Acrobat eBook Reader software, version 2.2 (Adobe has since combined the eBook Reader and the general Reader in a single application). This software was made available via their course websites, and on a generic CD-ROM containing a number of applications and tools, which is sent out annually to students on a wide range of courses. The eBook Reader software included facilities for managing a personal library of e-books, facilities for different kinds of annotation and for book-marking, and to hear the text read aloud. Hyperlinks were not available in the e-book texts in the pilot project, but it is intended to make them available in the future.

The E-Book Pilot Project determined that e-books should be complementary mirror images of existing print material to give added services to students. The e-book file is created from the PDF file that is used to print the course material. The e-book PDF files were processed to ensure small file sizes for ease of downloading from a website, and screen readability. They were produced to other technical specifications to improve appearance on screen. The aim was to make the file size no larger that 2–3MB, with 4MB being a maximum. This equated to download times on a normal internet modem connection of approximately six minutes, nine minutes and 12 minutes respectively. Where file sizes exceeded this size, the files were split into a number of constituent parts at logical points, e.g. at the beginning of a chapter. Pagination, page numbers and references were exactly the same as for the print versions.

Course teams specified which items they wished to deploy as e-books, and the deployment of e-books on a course website was undertaken by LTS. It was also possible to give some students e-book files on a course-specific CD-ROM. Students could run the e-book files directly from the CD-ROM if they so wished; any notes or highlights they made were automatically stored on their own local hard disk and the software automatically associated these with the correct files on the CD-ROM. Students could copy the files to their local hard disk if they so wished or to a laptop. They could also be transferred to PDAs such as Palm or Pocket PC, although no specific support for this was offered during the pilot project.

Engaging with students

Students were not given training in the use of e-books; however, along with the e-book files they could download a set of instructions for installing and using the Adobe Acrobat eBook Reader software. The instructions covered aspects such as opening a file and creating a library, and the main features of the software. The document also explained that Acrobat Reader (though not Acrobat eBook Reader) was also available for the Palm PDA, and for the Pocket PC platform, and that they could transfer PDF files to these handheld computers and read the e-book files there if they wished. The document went on to say that the university would not be able to offer any support for use of platforms other than the standard Windows environment. Furthermore, it was pointed out that the university offers students and staff a telephone helpdesk service, dealing with course-related technical computing queries.

Students on the courses involved in the project were offered the opportunity to respond to two questionnaires – one administered early on in the course, and one at the end – regarding their expectations, experiences and opinions of e-books. The questionnaires were administered via the First Class asynchronous on-line conferencing system used by the students, accessed through the course websites. Students were given the option to submit their answers directly through the website, by e-mail, by printing the questionnaire and posting it, or they could request a printed version to submit by post. Not untypically for Open University students, who are mostly mature learners, 70 per cent of respondents to the first questionnaire (and 65 per cent to the second questionnaire) were in the 31–50 age bracket. The questionnaires gathered information about students' previous experience of e-books and computers, their expectations of how they might use Open University e-book files, actual frequency of use, specific functions of the eBook Reader software, where the e-books were used, and whether they were read on screen or used to print selected sections of the course materials. They addressed disability issues such as whether e-book use might be restricted by disability and whether e-books could make studying easier.

There were also direct observations of four volunteer students. These enabled us to establish specific usability issues involved in accessing and using e-book materials, to look at how effectively students performed tasks and used software functions, and to observe student reactions. The participants undertook a series of tasks using two e-book files produced for an Arts course in philosophy. The sessions were audio and video recorded in the Data Capture Suite at the Open University's Institute of Educational Technology, capturing images of the computer screen, participants' behaviour and mouse movement.

Evaluation and outcomes

Findings relating to students

Our evaluation participants turned out to be largely confident and experienced IT users. Overall, they were very positive about e-book provision. A high proportion of those who responded to the first questionnaire had access to computers at work and at home, nearly half were regular laptop users and over a fifth were regular PDA users. They saw the main advantages of e-books as being portability, especially on laptops, and they felt that e-books made it easier for them to study at work. E-books could provide a useful extra copy of materials, and were considered good for searching, cut and paste, printing extracts, and highlighting. There was some suggestion of possible benefits from the ability to enlarge print, and for dyslexic students.

Although the majority of respondents used their e-book course materials on their desktop PC, we found that over a quarter used them on a laptop, and a small number of students used them on a PDA. Most felt that e-books should not replace print. The main usability and ergonomic issues were slow downloading of large files, some problems navigating the documents, and some discomfort in terms of eye-strain. Students appreciated being able to access course materials at work, read on the train, and print summaries for revision and study. Other positive aspects identified were using e-books as stand-ins for lost or late print materials, and easier referencing and highlighting. 'Copy/paste' and 'find' (search) were well-used facilities. Some functions of the e-Book Reader appeared to have been under-used, which we can speculate may have been due in some measure to students not accessing or reading the instructions. The students who took part in the observations certainly tended to use 'trial and error', rather than referring to the user instructions. They encountered problems with downloading files, with getting satisfactory page and font size and text clarity, and with navigation and cursor control. They were confused by similar operations (select/highlight; go to page/go to bookmark), and missed some 'hidden' features which could only be revealed by right-clicking their mouse.

Findings relating to course teams

Course teams were of the opinion that the use of e-books needed to be integrated more closely into learning and teaching strategies. They indicated that pedagogical advice on e-book use would have been helpful and that the impact on study strategies should be considered. They wanted a general statement about what e-books enabled students to do; they also wondered what an e-book could not do, for example it was thought that individual diagrams could not be printed from an e-book, whereas student feedback indicated that some students would want to, or try to, print diagrams. They wanted a reference to more detailed pedagogical advice that they could perhaps adapt for their course and pass on to students. It would include advice on learning strategies, e.g. effective use of book-marking (to deter students from book-marking 'everything in sight'), and the dangers of 'accidental' plagiarism. There were concerns that pagination might be different in e-books and print, resulting in confusing or incorrect page references. They were unclear as to what differences there might be between using an e-book on a PC and on a PDA.

Course teams also wanted to see advice for tutors. This would focus on plagiarism issues and the fact that e-books can inadvertently 'prioritize' some course materials, as a result of their portability and easy access for students on the move. Finally, course teams wanted to know whether the computing service would be providing plagiarism detection software.

Institutional aspects and 'what next?'

The production of e-book versions of printed material is now done as an automated process as a by-product from the print production process, thus ensuring that the service can be rolled out at very little cost. We concluded from our evaluation study that e-books were welcomed, but largely regarded as a complementary technology. E-book users relied on intuitive, sometimes inefficient, ways of working, and some potentially useful facilities remained undiscovered. However, there were indications of new study possibilities, such as printing extracts to read on the train, making summaries and compilations for revision, and reorganizing texts. Implications of the use of 'cut and paste' invite further investigation, both because of current concerns that studying with electronic texts may encourage plagiarism and more positively, because there are potential benefits of being able to quote and reference with precision and to discuss extracts with other students or tutors in on-line conferences. We have continued improving user instructions and the incorporation of hyperlinks is on the agenda for the future.

The E-Books Pilot Project was a preliminary investigation which enabled us to identify key issues. We are looking to develop pedagogical advice for course teams and students and will continue learning from research and published guidelines (e.g. Schcolnik 2001; Simon 2001; Wilson *et al.* 2002; Wilson and Landoni 2002; Bellaver and Gillette 2003; Ingraham and Bradburn 2003). Further research should explore student rationales for selecting technology, i.e. their reasons for choosing to access materials in print, on their desktop, laptop or PDA, along with patterns and contexts of mobile use, and any differences between use patterns across disciplines and pedagogical approaches in various courses. It will be important to explore the extent to which students are accessing other e-books available through the Library and on the internet, and any accessibility problems that may be encountered when downloading older versions of e-books and PDF files. E-books are available from many websites such as the University of Virginia's E-book Library (University of Virginia 2004) and through subscription arrangements with publishers such as the Taylor and Francis Online eBook Library (Taylor and Francis 2004).

Future research should also seek to determine which properties of the printed document are successfully modelled on the PDA and which ones are not. It may be the case that a strong focus on the document perspective is in fact counter-productive on a PDA, and that the device is more valued for making notes, quick references, audio notes and perhaps location specific reading. We are also interested in the move toward the sharing of annotations and content between users (Desmoulins and Mille 2002).

References

Bellaver, R.F. and Gillette, J. (2003) The Usability of eBook Technology: Practical Issues of an Application of Electronic Textbooks in a Learning Environment, *The UPA Voice*, 5(1), January 2003. On-line. Available HTTP http://www.upassoc.org/upa_publications/upa_voice/volumes/5/issue_1/ebooks.htm (accessed 22 November 2004).

Desmoulins, C. and Mille, D. (2002) Pattern-Based Annotations on E-Books: From Personal to Shared Didactic Content, IEEE International Workshop on Wireless and Mobile Technologies in Education (WMTE '02), Växjö, Sweden, 25–30 August 2002.

Disability Discrimination Act (1995) What The Law Says. On-line. Available HTTP http://www.disability.gov.uk/law.html (accessed 22 November 2004).

Ingraham, B. and Bradburn, E. (2003) *Sit Back and Relax: Issues in Readability and Accessibility for Electronic Books*, A TechDis/ILTHE Case Study Report, November 2003. On-line. Available HTTP http://readability.tees.ac.uk/Techdis%20report.htm (accessed 22 November 2004).

Kukulska-Hulme, A. (2002) Cognitive, Ergonomic and Affective Aspects of PDA Use for Learning, Proceedings of European Workshop on Mobile and Contextual Learning, University of Birmingham, 20–1 June 2002. On-line. Available HTTP http://kn.open.ac.uk/public/document.cfm?docid=2970 (accessed 22 November 2004).

Schcolnik, M. (2001) A Study of Reading with Dedicated E-Readers, PhD dissertation. On-line. Available HTTP http://12.108.175.91/ebookweb/survey.miriam.schcolnik.pdf (accessed 22 November 2004).

Simon, E.J. (2001) Electronic Textbooks: A Pilot Study of Student E-Reading Habits, *Future of Print Media Journal*, Winter 2001, Institute for Cyberinformation, Kent State University. On-line. Available HTTP http://www.futureprint.kent.edu/articles/simon01.htm (accessed 22 November 2004).

Taylor and Francis (2004) Online eBook Library. On-line. Available HTTP http://www.jisc.ac.uk/index.cfm?name=coll_tandf_ebooksandsrc=alpha (accessed 22 November 2004).

University of Virginia (2004) E-book Library for the MS Reader and Palm Devices. On-line. Available HTTP http://etext.lib.virginia.edu/ebooks/ebooklist.html (accessed 22 November 2004).

Waycott, J. (2004) The Appropriation of PDAs as Learning and Workplace Tools, unpublished PhD thesis, The Open University, Milton Keynes, UK.

Waycott, J. and Kukulska-Hulme, A. (2003) Students' Experiences with PDAs for Reading Course Materials, *Personal and Ubiquitous Computing*, 7(1): 30–43.

Wilson, R. and Landoni, M. (2002) Electronic Textbook Design Guidelines. On-line. Available HTTP http://ebooks.strath.ac.uk/eboni/guidelines/index.html (accessed 22 November 2004).

Wilson, R., Landoni, M. and Gibb, F. (2002) Guidelines for Designing Electronic Textbooks, Sixth European Conference on Research and Advanced Technology for Digital Libraries (ECDL 2002), Rome, Italy, 16–18 September 2002.

Chapter 14

Handheld composing
Reconceptualizing artistic practice with PDAs

Mark Polishook

Context and background

In the 2001/2 academic year, I used handheld computers to teach music composition to undergraduate and graduate students in a grant-funded project at Central Washington University. The purpose of the project, which was called Handheld Composing: Reconceptualizing Artistic Practice with Personal Digital Assistants (PDAs), was to see how mobile computing devices could be used to teach music composition. The assumption of the project was that if handheld use could guide students to think critically about composing then it could also help students to reconceptualize artistic process, that is, to see it differently than they would have without the use of PDAs. The point of asking students to reconceptualize their composing process was not to create a new or better way of writing music but, rather, to help students to take a broad look at how interfaces influence artistic process and technique. Therefore, the key question was could handhelds lead composition students to discover techniques that exceeded the bounds of usual practice?

The project participants included nine undergraduate and three graduate students. Most of the undergraduates were composition majors in the Music Department. They came to their musical studies with strong performing skills and limited composing experience. The graduate students, all of whom were pursuing Masters degrees in composition, had more extensive backgrounds writing and performing music. Common to the studies of all the participants, as would be the case in college and university music programmes across the States and internationally, was focus on composing for traditional acoustic instruments as used in orchestras and jazz ensembles. Of course, most of the undergraduate and graduate students were computer-literate; they had experience working with desktop or laptop machines running music-related software applications. But only a few of the students had worked previously with handhelds. And none of them had used handhelds subversively, that is, as a means to raise questions about conceptual rather than practical dimensions of artistry.

Rationale and problem statement

One way to ask how handheld use might influence the composing process is to look at how a transition from one technology to another influences production. For example, in *The Language of New Media* (Manovich 2001), Lev Manovich examines the transition from print media to new media. Manovich points out that computer interfaces control how we work with media objects (text, sound, and video files) and what we can do with them, just as natural language determines what and how we think.

If, as Manovich suggests, an interface is analogous to a language and thus a determinant upon what we can communicate, we should ask how traditional composing tools, such as manual writing tools and score paper, shape what we can say through music. Does the interface of manual writing tools and score paper support particular modes of expression and technique? How might the interface of a handheld computer, with its tiny display screen, its stylus for entering data, its menu-driven interface, and its assortment of collage-style cut-and-paste operations shape music composition? Throughout the Handheld Composing project, questions of this sort, about how handhelds influenced artistry, were key.

Technology and infrastructure

In the spring of 2001, the Northwest Academic Computing Consortium (http:// www.nwacc.org) provided funding, in the form of a Proof of Concept grant, for the proposal (http://www.nwacc.org/grants/2001/Polishook.html) I had submitted in the late winter of that same year. The grant allowed the acquisition of twelve very portable handheld workstations. Each station consisted of a Palm VIIx handheld, a Portable Palm keyboard, an SG-20 MIDI module (from SwivelSystems at http://www.swivelsystems.com), and software including NotePad, BeatPad, and Theremini (from MiniMusic, http://www.minimusic.com).

The NotePad software allowed students to write four separate single-note lines onto a grand staff. Thus, it was ideal for sketching string quartets or four-part chorales in the style of Bach. NotePad played the four lines through a tiny matchbox-sized SwivelSystems MIDI module that attached to the serial port at the bottom of the handheld. The module, which was very, very small, added only a few inches of length and a few ounces of weight to a Palm handheld.

The SwivelSystems module allowed its users to access a General Midi sound set such as are available on PC sound cards for games. Among the available sounds were instrumental timbres (pianos, clarinets, violins, and assorted percussion sounds), ensemble simulations (string sections, choirs, and orchestras), artificial sounds (imitations of commercial synthesizers) and various effects (gunshots, helicopters, audience applause, and breaking ocean waves).

None of the SwivelSystems timbres were of a particularly high quality and under no circumstance could they replace the sounds they imitated. However, this was acceptable because the project participants recognized the SwivelSystems module provided an abstract, rather than a realistic, reference to naturally occurring and synthetic sounds. The point was to work experimentally and subversively with resources that were, literally, at hand.

The BeatPad software, which also played through the Midi module, used as its interface the model of a simple pattern-based drum machine. The drum-machine model is very similar to the grid-like interface that many mobile phones now offer so users can compose ring tones. The idea of graphical pattern-based composing, while not novel in itself, was nonetheless interesting; it provided an alternative to common-practice notation (notes and rests on a staff). Through such capability, BeatPad provided a means to initiate discussion about how interfaces shape common practice.

The Theremini software allowed students to control sound by drawing (gesturing) along an x-axis and a y-axis. The students exploited this capability by using the handhelds to create long, drawn out glissandi to explore textures rather than melodies. The name 'Theremini' is a pun upon the well-known electronic instrument, the Theremin, which can be heard in film scores such as those for *Spellbound* and *The Day the Earth Stood Still* and in pop music, most notably in *Good Vibrations* by the Beach Boys. The pun also became part of the conceptual fabric of the project. This was because the students saw the Theremin, with its history that spans concert music to film to pop, and their 'mini-Theremins' as subversive and at the fringes of common practice.

Through NotePad, BeatPad, and Theremini in combination with the SwivelSystems module, students thus had a general-purpose system that supported common-practice music notation, graphical pattern-based drum machine styles, and gestural possibilities. The sum of such things far surpassed in general-purpose computing capability what could be done in 2001 (or now in 2004) on devices such as mobile phones or Gameboys. However, the handheld systems did not provide enough features or computing power to replace desktop or laptop composing systems. Rather, it was the generality of the handhelds coupled with their size and portability that made them so useful. The handhelds thus were centre-pieces on which to base discussion about the theory and practice of composing.

Engaging with students

Throughout the project year, I asked students to write music directly with and for their handhelds and I also requested that they consider how the handhelds might allow for artistic expression that couldn't be duplicated with other tools. For example, a technique I encouraged and which the students reinterpreted was exploiting the extremes of the MIDI sound modules, the highs and lows, rather than using the more conservative middle register.

The students amplified this by organizing the sounds they used into arhythmic, fragmented collages rather than harmonious, synchronized ensembles. These collages, based upon the density of sounds, rather than the alignment of notes, became a standard of sorts. As the Handheld Composing project progressed, student works featured graphical scores (students drew their scores into the interfaces of the software), 'just-in-time' composing (students saw writing music as a group activity to be done on the spot), theatrical gestures (students swept their PDAs up into the air when drawing into the Theremini software), and networking (students shared data during performances through infrared ports).

One could speculate that any of these things could be done just as well with laptop or desktop computers and Wacom graphics tablets. But such speculation doesn't account for how the students were using PDAs to devise strategies to overcome limitations – instead of giving in to restrictions. In retrospect, one could also say that working with the limitations, the constraints, of the PDAs was similar to what Igor Stravinsky described in *The Poetics of Music*:

> My freedom thus consists in my moving about within the narrow frame that I have assigned myself for each one of my undertakings. I shall go even further: my freedom will be so much the greater and more meaningful the more narrowly I limit my field of action and the more I surround myself with obstacles. Whatever diminishes constraint, diminishes strength. The more constraints one imposes, the more one frees one's self of the chains that shackle the spirit.
>
> (Stravinsky 1956: 68)

Another feature of the PDAs that set them apart from desktop and laptop computers was the sheer portability of the handheld form. It was the case that students took the handhelds where and when they pleased. For example, one of the graduate students literally took to wearing her PDA around her neck so that she could use it at a moment's notice. For other students, portability provided alternatives to extra-musical concerns. For example, gender preferences in computer use can be seen easily enough in most college and university computer labs (Verbick 2002). Handhelds, because they are portable, allowed students to outmanoeuvre such circumstances.

To emphasize the aesthetic transformations that were taking place, some project participants began handheld performances with the phrase 'Palms up!'. Other students raised the subversive possibility of a handheld opera (which unfortunately never moved past the initial idea). Two graduate students co-wrote *Pilot This!* (unpublished, by Joyce Barnes and David Blink 2002) for multiple handhelds; PalmOne has since used an excerpt from the piece in a television commercial it ran during the Super Bowl in the winter of 2004. A colleague wryly punned Stravinsky's famous *Symphony of Psalms* by suggesting *Symphony of Palms* – which four project participants brought to fruition in a collaborative work for twenty-eight handhelds attached to fifty-six speakers (*Out of the Box*, unpublished, by Joyce Barnes, David Blink, Kathy Frasier and John Sanders 2002).

Evaluation and outcomes

Some colleagues and students who heard about the handheld composing project in the spring of 2001, shortly after the grant was awarded and several months before the acquisition of the equipment for the project, were intrigued. Other colleagues were astonished and some were sceptical. The array of reactions reflected the fact that handheld composing appeared to be everything from a creative idea to a bizarre episode of Ripley's *Believe It or Not*. The issue was whether or not handhelds were (simple) toys, (real) tools, or (frivolous) gadgets, gimmicks, or gizmos.

Student participants provided further perspective. In a *Seattle Post-Intelligencer* newspaper article (Schubert 2001), one said 'We're composing in a way we never thought of ... Once you step back and look at it, not for what it can't do, but what it can do, it starts to open up the possibilities'. Another student said: 'I'm going places that I never would have been able to go myself ... It forces you to go outside of what you can do'. And another student stated, also in the same article: 'We've all got things woven into our musical fibre that weren't there before.'

Yet, it was not the case that all of the project participants were enamoured of handheld capability. This was because the handhelds couldn't simply replace full-featured desktops or laptops running Finale™ or Sibelius™ software for notation or Digital Performer™ for MIDI sequencing and hard disk recording (standard production software then and now). Students who withdrew from the project thus did so because they found that composing with handhelds was clumsy, tedious, and akin to torture. For these individuals, reading notes on small, poorly-lit, low-resolution screens, poking at tiny dialogue boxes with a stylus, and attaching extra wires to connect serial and MIDI ports did not seem productive or intellectually challenging. This suggested that handheld composing tools worked best when participants used them specifically to think critically about how to work creatively within a given set of constraints.

What next?

The Handheld Composing project didn't continue in the 2002/3 year and there are no plans to run the project again. There are two reasons for this. First, the NWACC grant provided project funding for a year only. Second, over the course of the project year it became clear that endeavours such as Handheld Composing require support past what one individual can supply through a one-time grant. Of course, neither of these issues are unique to mobile computing or the Handheld Composing project.

Yet, interest in Handheld Composing has continued. I presented a poster session on Handheld Composing at an EDUCAUSE conference in Portland, Oregon. Joyce Barnes, one of the graduate student participants in the project, gave a presentation on her work with handhelds at a conference for women composers at Stanford University in the late spring of 2002. In the fall of 2002, I described the Handheld Composing project in a presentation at the National College Music Society Conference in Kansas City, Missouri. In the summer of 2003 a PalmOne media producer posted a web feature about Handheld Composing (http://www. palmone.com/us/education/studies/study54.html).

Early in the winter of 2004, PalmOne made a television commercial based on the idea of Handheld Composing; the commercial featured music by CWU graduate student composers (Joyce Barnes and David Blink), and it ran on Super Bowl

Sunday in select markets and, again, in August of 2004 (in the States) in select markets. In the autumn 2004 issue of the *Australian Journal of Emerging Technologies and Society*, Mark Finn and Natalie Vandenham refer to the Handheld Composing project (Finn and Vandenham 2004).

It may be that pervasive, portable technology held in the hand has a role that iconic monoliths, such as and including desktop computers – and pianos – will never fulfil. Perhaps this is because the personal computing devices we hold in the palms of our hands, in best post-human fashion, extend not just what we can do but also who we are. We feel differently about devices we can hold, like handhelds or mobile phones, in contrast to devices that require us to sit in front of them, such as desktop computers or even pianos. If, as Lev Manovich argues, interfaces, like language, influence what it is that we can communicate, it may be that handhelds reveal perspectives that are unique to the circumstances in which we use them. In the case of the Handheld Composing project, such conjectures speak directly to how PDAs helped student project participants to think critically and reflectively about artistic practice.

References

Finn, M. and Vandenham, N. (2004) The Handheld Classroom: Educational Implications of Mobile Computing. *Australian Journal of Emerging Technologies and Society*, 2(1). On-line. Available HTTP http://www.swin.edu.au/sbs/ajets/ (accessed 28 November 2004).

Manovich, L. (2001) *The Language of New Media*, Cambridge, MA: MIT Press.

Polishook, M. Handheld Composing home page. On-line. Available HTTP http://www.cwu.edu/~handheld (accessed 22 November 2004).

Schubert, R. (2001) Students Have Music Composition in the Palms of Their Hands. Seattle, Washington: *Seattle Post-Intelligencer*, 20 November 2001.

Stravinsky, I. (1956) *The Poetics of Music in the Form of Six Lessons*, New York: Vintage Books.

Verbick, Tabatha (2002) Women, Technology, and Gender Bias, Journal of Computing Sciences in Colleges, Volume 17 Issue 3. On-line (with ACM subscription). Available HTTP http://portal.acm.org/citation.cfm?id=772674&coll=Portal&dl=GUIDE&CFID=42299885&CFTOKEN=5028919.

Chapter 15

The Student Learning Organiser

Mike Sharples, Dan Corlett, Susan Bull, Tony Chan and Paul Rudman

Context and background

Mobile organisers, including an electronic diary, notebook and to do list, have been successful in providing employees with a range of tools to manage their activities outside the office. The aim of the Student Learning Organiser project was to explore whether university students need a similar set of tools to help them manage their studies and to assist their learning.

Surveys indicate that over 95 per cent of university students in the UK own a mobile phone (Dundee University 2003) and over 30 per cent own a laptop computer (University of Leeds 2003). Many students also have mobile devices for entertainment, such as MP3 players and handheld games machines. Thus, a secondary aim of the study was to explore how students would manage a further device, a wireless personal digital assistant (PDA), alongside their other mobile technology.

From an activity theory perspective (Engeström *et al.* 1999), students are embedded in complex activity systems within the university and beyond. Students attempt to organise their studies through the mediation of tools that have been created for them, such as course notes, study plans and timetables, and those they create themselves, such as revision notes. A difficulty many students experience is that the tools are constantly being created and transformed, so they must search for study material in many places (departmental office, lectures, library) and they are in a perpetual state of uncertainty as to whether they have the latest versions.

Students participate in many overlapping communities with different rules and divisions of labour. These include the formal activity system of university study and examination with its regulations and academic awards; the communities of practice into which they are being apprenticed, including academia and the professions; and also their social and family communities. Each of these has different modes of communication and collaboration. So, for example, many university students tend to use e-mail for communication with academics and for maintaining more ephemeral contacts, but mobile phone texting for organising their social life (Longmate and Baber 2002).

Rationale and problem statement

This analysis raises many questions for the design of mobile technology to help students organise their activities, including:

- Which software tools are of value to students in organising their studies?
- Do students need specialised tools to manage their learning, or would they benefit more from using standard office management tools?
- If students are provided with a broad set of organiser and communication tools, what patterns of activity and technology usage emerge?
- What institutional support is needed to help the students make good use of the technology?

The aim of the study was to provide some initial answers to these questions. The intention was not to measure learning gains, but to investigate how the technology altered the patterns of study and communication activity among students, and to assess the users' attitudes towards the new technology in a context where the students were already heavy users of information technology.

The study was carried out during the academic session 2002/3 in the Department of Electronic, Electrical and Computer Engineering at the University of Birmingham. Seventeen students on the Human Centred Systems MSc course were recruited to the trial, together with a number of their lecturers. One student dropped out after a few weeks, but another joined about halfway through. All the students were familiar with computer technology and they had access to the university web Outlook software, including e-mail and calendar, accessible from a web browser. Most students had limited personal information management tools available on their mobile phones.

Technology and infrastructure

The seventeen participants of the study were each loaned a Compaq iPAQ 3760 handheld computer, running Pocket PC 2002, with 64MB memory. The students were allowed to use the machine within the university and outside it, and they were provided with a 'docking station' to synchronise their data with their home PC. Each iPAQ was supplied with an expansion sleeve and an 802.11b wireless network card, able to transmit data at up to 11MB/sec. When attached, the sleeve and card roughly double both the size and weight of the device.

The Pocket PC 2002 includes cut-down versions of Windows Word, Excel, Outlook, Internet Explorer and Media Player. In addition the students were provided with a custom-designed Learning Organiser. Developed at the University of Birmingham, the Learning Organiser provides an integrated suite of tools for students to access course materials and organise their studies, consisting of a Time Manager, Course Manager, Communications Manager and Concept Mapper. The students could also download any other applications or documents they wanted for their study or entertainment.

The Time Manager tool (Figure 15.1) allows the students to create, delete and view timetable events and deadlines. Software on a desktop PC enables lecturers to create a folder of course materials and a timetable of events and deadlines that the students can import to their iPAQs. The front screen of the iPAQ is also customised to show a strip with the events for the day (in red) arranged in timetable slots as well as a note of the time and location of the next scheduled teaching event (Figure 15.2). The Time Manager is integrated with Microsoft Outlook, so that any events or to do items created in Outlook appear as timetable events and deadlines.

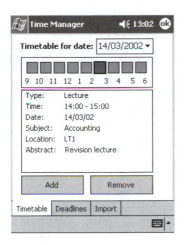

Figure 15.1 Learning Organiser screen showing the Time Manager

Figure 15.2 Learning Organiser front screen with timetable strip and next teaching session

The Course Manager (Figure 15.3) allows a student to download and view packages of course material via the wireless network. The packages can be created by academic staff using the complementary tool, called Course Builder, that runs on a Windows PC. The Course Manager tool allows students to browse locally stored course material as well as providing a seamless link to remotely stored data. It can show Microsoft Word and PowerPoint files as well documents in PDF, Microsoft Reader and HTML format.

The Communications Manager just provides a screen with buttons to launch standard e-mail, instant messaging and contacts tools.

Two concept-mapping tools were designed at the University of Birmingham for the Learning Organiser. Both enable students to create and browse information by following topic links, but they differ significantly in design and operation. Map-It! (Figure 15.4) uses a logical tree structure whereby the current topic node is shown in the centre of the screen with linked surrounding nodes. The user navigates by clicking on one of the outer nodes which brings it to the centre, displaying the topics related to it. Clicking on the centre node displays any document associated with that node. The user adds a new node by selecting a document from the file list, which attaches it to the central node.

Concise Concept Mapper (Figure 15.5) provides a free-form concept map based on user-positioned nodes and links. Interaction is by pen gestures: a node is moved around the map by dragging it with the pen, scrolling the map as necessary (by dragging into the eight 'arrows'). Nodes may also be grouped for dragging. To add a new node at an unoccupied place on the map the user taps at that place, opening an input area for the node's text. Nodes may subsequently be linked by dragging one node on top of the other. The dragged node then snaps back to its original position with the link attached.

Engaging with students

The students were given an induction session on using the iPAQ and its tools including the Learning Organiser, but were left to decide for themselves how and where they wanted to use the technology, and for what purposes. They were encouraged to use the devices for their own personal activities and to install any software they wished.

Not surprisingly, amongst the most popular downloads were various games and an additional media player. Several different Personal Information Manager (PIM) applications were tried as alternatives to the ones included with Pocket PC or the integrated Learning Organiser. Other installations included a money manager and a photo album.

Two students used Microsoft Portrait (a Pocket PC equivalent of NetMeeting). One of these students reported to have used this to contact his family living on another continent. He received audio and video of them, and was able to speak to them, using the iPAQ as a mobile internet phone.

Several of the students installed Chinese character support for their communication with one another and their friends and family at home. Only two on-line

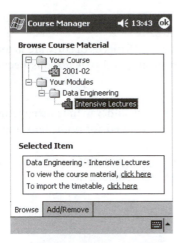

Figure 15.3 Learning Organiser screen showing the Course Manager

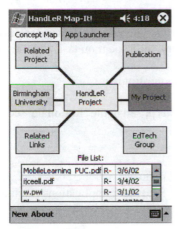

Figure 15.4 Screen display of Map-It!

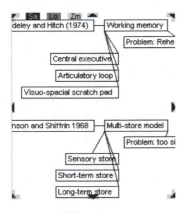

Figure 15.5 Screen display of Concise Concept Mapper

services were accessed by any students. Three students used AvantGo on a regular basis to synchronise web content including news.

Only eight students installed additional software, 18 pieces of software in total. This was explored further in the final focus group, and two reasons became apparent:

- most students saw the value of the iPAQs as being either in time management or in e-mail/messaging. These were already catered for with the standard software;
- since the devices had to be returned within the year, participants were reluctant to invest much of their own money or time in personalisation.

Evaluation and outcomes

Data were collected in three different ways:

- questionnaires at 1, 4, 16 weeks and 10 months;
- logbooks during the early stages of the trial, where students were requested to record each use of the iPAQ, the activity, time spent on task and the tools used;
- focus groups to coincide with each of the questionnaires.

These aimed to uncover answers to the questions posed in the 'Rationale' section, by exploring:

- students' attitudes to the technology;
- students' attitudes towards the Learning Organiser;
- patterns of usage of the technology and the software applications (including any they had downloaded themselves);
- ease of use issues;
- issues relating to institutional support for mobile learning devices.

Usability

One of the most reported issues was the usability of the hardware. At the final focus group the students were unanimous in expressing discontent about the form-factor, memory size and battery life.

The sleeve and wireless PC card made the iPAQ too heavy and too large for comfortable use and the ability to store in a pocket. But within the department, the wireless sleeve was indispensable since it provided valuable communications functions.

The iPAQ memory was considered to be too small to hold the course resources, additional PDF and media files and any added software, whilst leaving any space for games and music files. As the participants were required to return the iPAQs at the end of the year, they were not willing to invest in additional memory modules.

The battery of a recharged unit would generally perform adequately for one day, but if left uncharged for a number of days, the unit lost all data and programs added by the user since these were stored in volatile memory. On a few occasions (generally during the vacations) students unwittingly left their devices disconnected from mains power for longer than a week, and as a result had to reinstall all their software and data that had not been synchronised with a PC.

All of these problems are being addressed in a new generation of PDA devices, with integrated wireless communication, larger internal memory, and removable memory cards that can be transferred to other devices. Battery life remains a significant problem, with the improvement in battery technology being offset by the power drain of larger screens and wireless connectivity.

Usefulness

No single tool stood out as being likely to revolutionise the students' learning or personal organisation. Table 15.1 shows the perceived usefulness of the various tools at the 4 week, 16 week and 10 month stages of the trial. Communications tools and the timetabling features were consistently amongst the most useful. Course content and the concept mapper show a trend of decreasing usefulness over time. It should be noted, however, that the students were provided with less course content and materials later in the course, and at the 10-month survey most students were involved more heavily with project work.

The participants were also asked to name the applications or tools that made the greatest impact on their learning, personal organisation and entertainment. The answers to this free-response question were collected under generic headings. Table 15.2 shows that, for learning, course materials are regarded as having the most impact, despite the lower perceived overall usefulness. Concept mapping was not considered of greatest importance by anyone in any category.

Other responses to the questionnaires and at the focus group sessions indicated that:

- the Student Learning Organiser software frequently ran too slowly to be usable;
- much of the content made available by lecturing staff over the web was not optimised for Pocket Explorer, making it difficult to read;
- the concept mapping tools were difficult to use without further instruction. The free-format concept map appeared to be better for note taking and for experienced users, while the tree structure was better for highly structured information and novice users;
- participants were reluctant to use the concept mapping software since its content could not be transferred to other applications.

Patterns of usage

As can be seen in Figure 15.6, use of the iPAQs overall declined over time. However, the number of participants using the devices many times per day stayed much the

Table 15.1 Perceived usefulness of tools ('useful' or 'very useful') after 4 weeks (n = 17), 16 weeks (n = 14) and 10 months (n = 17)

	4 Weeks	16 Weeks	10 Months
Timetable	59% (10)	64% (9)	82% (14)
Web browser	65% (11)	64% (9)	71% (12)
Instant messaging	59% (10)	50% (7)	71% (12)
E-mail	76% (13)	79% (11)	65% (11)
Course materials	59% (10)	43% (6)	41% (7)
Supplementary materials	53% (9)	43% (6)	24% (4)
Concept mapper	35% (5)	14% (2)	0% (0)

Table 15.2 Perceived impact of tools on learning, personal organisation and entertainment; number of students after 10 months, who named the tool as having greatest impact (not all participants answered all three questions)

Learning	Personal organisation	Entertainment
Course materials (6)	Timetable and deadlines (6)	Media player (7)
Browser (3)	Calendar (5)	Games (3)
Timetable and deadlines (2)	Writing/note taking (2)	Messenger (2)
Writing/note taking (1)	E-mail (2)	Browser (1)
Calendar (1)	Task manager (1)	Writing/note taking (1)
		Reader (1)

same. Starting with a more even spread, usage became more polarised between those who used them very frequently and those using them very infrequently.

Participants were asked to say how frequently they used the iPAQs in four different locations, and whether this was for MSc-related work or other activities. Table 15.3 shows the rank order of these locations during the study.

Early in the study, students used the iPAQs at home and in the Department for MSc and other activities. By the end, 'travelling' was a more frequent location than the department for other activities. It is worth noting again that more project work is carried out towards the end of the course, so it is likely that students will spend less time in the university. Alternatively, this result may also suggest that the students were finding more uses for the devices and beginning to see their value as mobile tools.

Students were invited to describe their own patterns of use. Some interesting observations include the following:

- although e-mail is synchronised to the device for off-line use, students only tended to use e-mail when connected by the wireless LAN;
- email and instant messaging were frequently mentioned together as if they were complementary tasks;
- participants used the calendar and timetabling in all locations;
- in the 4-week survey, there were many references to using the device for listening to music and playing games. By the 16-week survey, these activities had been largely replaced by e-mail and instant messaging;

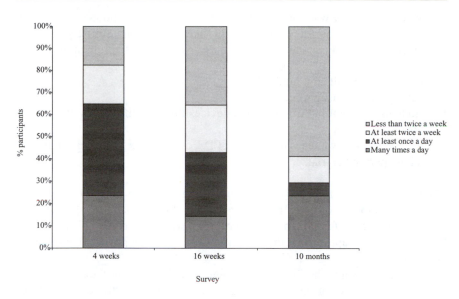

Figure 15.6 Frequency of use of the iPAQ during the trial

Table 15.3 Rank order of frequency of use at four locations, for work and, in parentheses, other activities

	4 Weeks	16 Weeks	10 Months
Home	1 = (1)	2 (1)	2 (1)
Department	1 = (2)	1 (2)	1 (3)
University (elsewhere)	3 (4)	4 (4)	3 (4)
Travelling	4 (3)	3 (3)	4 (2)

- a number of students reported regularly reading course materials, off-line web content and e-books when at home. This was surprising, since all the participants had their own desktop or laptop computers in their homes;
- for a few students, this was the first time they had kept their personal organisation information in an electronic format. Among those, some only made use of this information through the PDA, even though it was synchronised and available on their laptops or desktops.

A separate question on how their use of the iPAQs had changed over the course of the year did not yield any noticeable trends. Some students attempted to use it for everything in the early stages before accepting that some tasks were better done on a normal PC. Others who were sceptical at first, later became frequent users of the devices. Either way, after ten months, students had evaluated the capabilities of the PDAs, adapted them to their needs and settled into a personal pattern of use.

An attitude survey was conducted as part of the final questionnaire. Students were asked to rate statements on a five-point Likert scale from 'Strongly Agree' to 'Strongly Disagree'. Four statements were associated with significant results:

- using the iPAQ did not hinder learning;
- battery life was a significant problem;
- students were not put off using the devices through difficulties in knowing how to use them;
- the perceived advantages of having a PDA outweighed the disadvantages of taking part in the trial.

The study was never intended to explore learning gains brought about by using mobile technology. However, the surveys clearly showed that although the technology had been useful to them, it had not transformed or greatly enhanced their learning. It would appear that the Learning Organiser was just another resource amongst many.

For some students, the PDA complemented their use of desktop computers, providing a convenient means of viewing course material. But there is no evidence that it replaced other communications or entertainment devices such as mobile phones and MP3 players. Though it entered the activity space of communication and entertainment, the PDA was neither as convenient nor as powerful as their other mobile technology.

Institutional aspects

The questionnaires highlighted issues relating to institutional support for the Learning Organiser and these were explored further in the final focus group. An important impediment was that the course information was not complete, nor was it updated throughout the year. Thus, instead of providing students with a definitive source of information, the Learning Organiser created a further source of uncertainty, to be reconciled with printed course material and the departmental website. Birmingham, like most UK universities, already supports an institutional Virtual Learning Environment (VLE). It is currently not possible to access this VLE from mobile devices. Even if it were possible, it is not clear how much of the content would need to be re-formatted for the small screen. The fact that some students read course materials on their iPAQs suggests that giving mobile access to current VLE content could be of benefit.

The Learning Organiser also created another activity system, with a new community of practice and modes of communication between the department and among the students. Some students were eager to enter this community, for example by using the instant messaging tool to discover whether other students were available, or to engage in more frequent e-mail communication. But for wider adoption to take place, the students indicated that it would be necessary to be given more training on using and extending the devices. In particular, concept-mapping should be taught as a skill before students could be expected to use the mapping tools.

This raises important issues for institutions concerning training and support. How should the institutions enter the space of informal technology-mediated communication? It would be tempting, for example, to use instant messaging to contact students. But would this just add another unreliable means of communication, would it be accepted by staff, and would it impinge on students' social space? Similarly, most universities already teach study skills to their students, but should these be extended to skills for studying on mobile technology? These questions can probably only be answered by trials to investigate the benefits and costs to the institution.

What next?

A trial is now underway with third-year undergraduate students using pen tablet computers. These devices fit a different activity space to PDAs, combining many of the properties of a laptop computer with the affordances of direct pen input. The focus of the research, supported by Microsoft, Toshiba and Viglen, is on the benefits of tablet technology for collaborative learning and mentoring. Student teams equipped with tablet computers are encouraged to explore new ways of recording their learning experiences and sharing these with each other and their mentors. They will use a range of tools including portals, Internet messaging and video conferencing.

References

Dundee University (2003) Mobile Communications Survey. On-line. Available HTTP http://www.dundee.ac.uk/elecengphysics/mobilesurvey_results.php (accessed 22 November 2004).

Engeström, Y., Miettinen, R. and Punamäki, R.-L. (eds) (1999) *Perspectives on Activity Theory*. Cambridge: Cambridge University Press.

Longmate, E. and Baber, C. (2002) A Comparison of Text Messaging and Email Support for Digital Communities: A Case Study, in X. Faulkner, J. Finlay and F. Detienne (eds) *People and Computers XVI – Memorable Yet Invisible. Proceedings of HCI 2002*. London: Springer-Verlag.

University of Leeds (2003) Student Computer Ownership Survey. On-line. Available HTTP http://www.leeds.ac.uk/iss/surveys/PC_hefce_report.pdf (accessed 22 November 2004).

Chapter 16

Tuning in to students' mobile learning needs

A Singapore interactive initiative

*Ian Weber, Kin Choong Yow and
Boon-Hee Soong*

Context and background

Singapore has invested more than $2 billion on integrating information technology into its national education programme. This investment forms a significant part of the nation state's ambitious transformation to a knowledge-based, information and communication technology hub in the Asia-Pacific region, which began in 1992 with the Vision of an Intelligent Island: IT 2000 Report. In 2003, Singapore embarked on its second, five-year Master Plan for IT in Education (mp2), which is designed to sustain the momentum of integrating IT and develop key areas, including shifting the emphasis from teacher-centred education to a learner-centric model (MOE 2003a, b). To achieve this aim, Singapore universities have begun blending mobile technologies into e-learning infrastructures to improve interactivity and connectivity for the user.

Singapore's Nanyang Technological University (NTU) has built its e-campus-wide learning environment around the Blackboard-driven edveNTUre delivery infrastructure. The website-based platform provides users with an access point to electronic materials such as lecture notes and tutorial questions or activities, assessment items such as quizzes, announcements and diary, bulletin board facilities and links to external websites. Within this e-learning environment, students have some degree of mobility and interactivity using laptops and Personal Digital Assistants (PDAs) connected to the wireless network infrastructure. However, instructors and students face the problem that wireless connectivity is only available on NTU's campus, thus limiting mobility, interactivity and flexibility within this e-learning environment. This problem is similar to wireless classroom projects conducted in the United States, which provided initially encouraging results, but faced limitations because of the restricted access to the Local Area Network (LAN) coverage (see University of Kentucky 1998; Evans *et al.* n.d.; Dominick 2002).

To address limitations of connectivity, mobility and flexibility, NTU implemented the NTUwireless and NTUmobile initiatives. NTUwireless provides campus-wide wireless LAN infrastructure that is accessible by staff and students anytime and anywhere. NTUmobile provides instructors and students with the ability to access the campus network by mobile devices such as PDAs and mobile phones using the Wireless Application Protocol (WAP).

Two projects launched in 2003 build into these initiatives. Hewlett Packard committed $250,000 to the development of the Wireless Mobile Learning Solution (WMLS) using Multimedia Messaging Service (MMS) and Internet Naming Service (iName) (Yow 2003). The second project integrates self-organising Mobile Ad hoc NETwork (MANET) technology and Collaborative Mobile Learning (CML) using location tracking information services. Both projects are designed to provide a communication environment that meets the university's philosophy of learning 'any time, any where, any pace and on any portable device'. To achieve this goal, the projects set out to:

- make wireless mobile interactive learning available to all NTU students both on and off campus without incurring the expense of costly hardware;
- provide mobile interactive learning capabilities in classrooms and off-campus to limit cultural and communication barriers between instructors and students through multimedia messaging and mobile phone services;
- extend the mobile learning opportunities in NTU to include the Wide Area Network (WAN) coverage provided by telephone companies using location tracking information services.

Rationale and problem statement

WMLS is specifically designed to address significant cultural and communication barriers (e.g. respect for authority, lack of language proficiency, or student anxiety associated with peer interactions) that contribute to low levels of student–instructor interaction within the Singapore classroom. In so doing, it harnesses the proliferation of mobile phone services among Singaporeans who send approximately 23 million text and multimedia messages each day. This technology provides immediate feedback to the instructor during classroom activities in a number of ways: 1) student polling; 2) real-time questions; 3) slide presentation synchronisation; and 4) remote access. Instructors can provide a pop quiz during class with students replying using MMS over the university's wireless local area network (WLAN). An application on the lecture console receives the messages, parses these responses and summarises them for the instructor who can then decide when to proceed to the next section of the lecture. Student messages to the instructor during the class can query a term, ask for further explanation or an example to illustrate a concept or slow the pace of delivery to increase comprehension. The instructor monitors the messages and decides if and when to respond, thus improving classroom management. A further advantage of MMS is that this interaction can be easily extended to students who are not physically present in the classroom setting, over a wide area network such as Hi Speed Circuit Switched Data (HSCSD) or General Packet Radio Service (GPRS).

Where the main focus of the WMLS is on classroom interaction (and mobility), the MANET initiative contributes to more mobility (and interactivity) in fieldwork situations. It is designed to address limitations associated with the use of current

CML platforms in an off-campus mode, which utilises communication infrastructures such as wireless LANs, WAP, or Short Message Service (SMS) or MMS. Limitations include: 1) CML service areas constrained by the 'reachability' of the infrastructures such as the locations of the access points and base stations and 2) the cost of public telecommunication services, which can be prohibitive to students. The MANET's network architecture exchanges multimedia information among instructors and students through multiple hops and does not need a communication infrastructure such as an access point. Its significant advantage lies in that a virtual class can be deployed anywhere, anytime and economically.

Such real-time multimedia applications provide a platform for new and varied educational activities that enhance teaching and learning. The wireless communication cultivates a more collaborative learning environment between instructors and students. By cooperatively completing shared tasks, students can generate ideas, explore concepts, share resources, and construct arguments to build deeper understandings of key concepts. The flexibility to customise this learning environment for diverse communities also offers more high-level student-to-instructor and peer-to-peer interactions. By combining with the emerging mobile and wireless communication technologies, a collaborative mobile learning environment, using devices such as laptops, Tablet PCs, PDAs and mobile phones, contributes to the development of a more effective instructional situation that meets the specific needs and challenges of the Singapore context. As education institutions continue to negotiate the blending of e-learning and traditional education approaches, these initiatives provide a mechanism to achieve benchmark service-based learning that is mobile, interactive and flexible for the specific needs of students via wireless technologies.

Technology and infrastructure

NTU created the world's largest wireless campus in 2000. The network covers 200 hectares of the campus at a cost of S$3.2 million. To support the wireless initiative, NTU lent 1,000 HP Jornada PDAs with WLAN cards to students who did not own laptop computers and another 1,000 wireless LAN 802.11b Personal Computer Memory Card International Association (PCMCIA) cards to students who owned laptops.

The WMLS, using Tablet PCs or PDAs, connects to the NTU LAN via wireless access points situated throughout the campus. It employs WAP, supporting either HSCSD or GPRS, with the potential to integrate easily into future technologies such as Enhanced Data rates for Global Evolution (EDGE) and Third Generation (3G). MMS-capable PDAs send messages through the MMS Centre to the WAN gateway. The MMS message goes through the iName server to determine the forwarding address of the instructor. iName translates a name query into network addresses such as IP address or mobile phone numbers. An application residing on the lecture console then picks up the MMS and displays it for the instructor for easy viewing.

When students move to an off-campus learning mode, by using PDAs enabled with e-learning and software, they can link to the MANET. The MANET nodes may be laptop PCs for network monitoring purposes and as a host system for the developed embedded software. These added facilities provide students with real-time video conferencing facilities and access to the wireless gateway using a GPRS connection to the internet.

Engaging with students

Student engagement with the NTUwireless initiative has been encouraging since the university launched its mobile and wireless initiatives in 2001. Results from NTU's Centre for IT Services (2003) 'Mobile Devices Survey' indicate that PDA ownership among the campus population was higher than expected with 14 per cent of undergraduate students owning a PDA. Consequently, PDA usage has increased dramatically across undergraduate students. From encouraging figures in the first year of the NTUwireless launch, the usage levels had risen 21 per cent in 2002 and 107 per cent in 2003. Figures for the first three months of 2004 are even higher with the number of log-ins registering more than twice the monthly average in 2003 (see Figure 16.1).

Riding on the back of increases in NTUwireless usage, the MANET provides a number of benefits to instructors and students. One clear benefit is the level of flexibility to conduct fieldwork and educational excursions. For example, instructors have the capability to establish a virtual on-site classroom for students within the field to investigate tidal life-forms. Instructors download documents from the internet using the wireless cellular GPRS and then exchange this information among students within the field. Another mobile fieldwork application is the ability for NTU students to survey a forest area for humidity, temperature

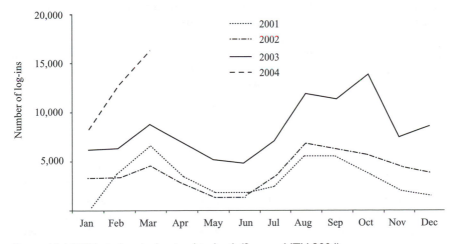

Figure 16.1 NTUwireless by log-ins (student) (Source: NTU 2004)

and sound using low cost sensor or measurement devices. Students obtain data, analyse it on their PDAs and share the results instantly across a dispersed group in the field. A future application of this interactive mobile technology is for location-based services, where geographically positioned exhibits are wireless enabled to broadcast and deliver audio or video clips to groups of moving students or tourists within educational facilities such as science or art museums.

When students move back to the NTU campus setting, the same instructors utilise the WMLS initiative to interact with students in different modes. Students who attend lectures can interact with the instructor using the PDA to ask questions, thus reducing the anxiety experienced in classroom interactions. However, students can also interact from their on-campus dorm rooms, within the library, or while commuting to NTU. In all these mobile situations, students listen to the voice of the instructor and send instant feedback.

Another important feature of this system is that it not only enhances instructor–student interaction but also encourages peer-to-peer interaction. Students in the classroom setting can compose an MMS query to be sent not to the instructor but to another student. From the pedagogical point of view, such peer-to-peer learning contributes as much, or even more, to the student's learning than queries directed to the instructor. If students lack confidence in interacting in class, a response from a fellow student may help them muster more courage and confidence to challenge ideas. This environment is designed to move learning from its current passive, instructor-centred focus (which plays into the cultural and communication barriers and inhibits current learning) to a more interactive, student-centred approach within this e-learning environment.

Evaluation and outcomes

Informal feedback from instructors and students on WMLS is generally encouraging. Both instructors and students felt that the technology improves the level of in-class interaction by minimising student embarrassment when 'asking simple questions', increasing confidence to 'query a lecturer's response even if it may be wrong' and building 'confidence to challenge the correctness of responses from fellow students'. Students, though, indicated that peer-to-peer interaction could become a distraction in class. They felt there was a need to monitor this interaction with 'some students abusing this feature by chatting amongst themselves throughout the lecture instead of listening'. However, instructors felt the benefits of improved interactivity and mobility outweighed the possibility of irresponsible use by students in the classroom setting.

The MANET technology has undergone extensive testing. Instructors and final year students measured the throughput and delay over several hops and evaluated the performance, with encouraging results (Ye *et al.* 2004). The technology has been exhibited locally in Singapore at the ICICS conference and internationally at the United States' IEEE Microwave Symposium. In both situations, the MANET received positive responses from e-learning professionals and educators. The project will be tested further in 2004 through a planned user behaviour study using log files and student responses to surveys and interviews.

Institutional aspects

Both MANET and WMLS offer an excellent fit with NTU's philosophy of learning 'any time, any where, any pace and on any portable device'. The next phase, upon completion of larger user studies throughout 2004, will see the university consider further deployment of both initiatives as part of its NTUmobile and NTUwireless plans. This development would enhance and extend existing services and applications that are to be deployed in the university's intranet.

Within the NTU structure, the existence of cooperation tools found in the MANET is especially useful in large and distributed lectures and fieldwork. At a broader institutional level, the frameworks and methodologies could be used in non-educational environments such as the military, industry and public community in Singapore and worldwide. Such applications are considered beneficial for battlefield communication, search and rescue, video conferencing and vehicle-to-vehicle communications.

The diffusion of the WMLS would see NTU equip its network, servers and lecture consoles with improved infrastructure and applications. Building on the current WLAN infrastructure, the key priority is to upgrade its servers to support the traffic generated from students' MMS responses. NTU also plans to train instructors in how to effectively utilise the technical capabilities and interactive educational functionality of the system to maximise its potential. This situation calls for a change in mindset as the teaching pace in the classroom will no longer be driven solely by the instructor, who will have to be more adept at maximising the interactivity of the learning environment while meeting the demands and expectations of a more empowered and mobile student body.

What next?

Following the implementation and evaluation of WMLS, further consideration will be given to adding features to the system. These improvements include:

- *Ongoing testing and technology deployment* – NTU researchers will complete student evaluations of both initiatives in the classroom and in off-campus situations to assess the viability, scalability, pedagogy and appropriateness of this new learning environment. Thereafter, WMLS and MANET will be gradually deployed to the larger campus population consisting of 20,000 students and instructors.
- *Active campus* – Extend the function of WLAN positioning technologies so students can call up a map of NTU on their mobile devices and display services such as library, bookshop, canteen and printing rooms. Students can also download updated laboratory manuals and course instructions.

- *Instructor training* – As the infrastructure and technology continues to be tested and gradually deployed, NTU will begin training instructors in how to effectively use the technical capabilities and pedagogical dimensions of these systems to provide a more interactive and mobile learning environment for NTU instructors and students.

Together, these initiatives offer NTU an opportunity to build a strong infrastructure that utilises a coordinated approach to improve the mobility and interactivity of its broader e-learning edveNTUre framework, using ubiquitous on- and off-campus instruction technologies. These initiatives support and drive NTU's philosophy of establishing learning 'any time, any where, any pace and on any portable device'.

References

Dominick, J. (2002) Ready or not – PDAs in the classroom. On-line. Available HTTP http://www.syllabus.com/article.asp?id=6705 (accessed 22 November 2004).

Evans, E., Morgan, M., Berger, M., Bilkey, B. and Wood, K. (n.d.) Wireless classroom. On-line. Available HTTP: http://ics.purdue.edu/rss/wireless.ppt (accessed 22 November 2004).

Ministry of Education (MOE), Singapore (2003a) Desired outcomes of education. On-line. Available HTTP http://www1.moe.edu.sg/desired.htm (accessed 22 November 2004).

Ministry of Education (MOE), Singapore (2003b) Thinking schools, learning nation. On-line. Available HTTP http://www.moe.gov.sg/corporate/sitemap.htm (accessed 22 November 2004).

NTU, Centre for IT Services (2003) Mobile devices survey: a survey of mobile device and PDA usage and trends in the university population, August 2003, Singapore: Nanyang Technological University.

NTU, Centre for IT Services (2004) Logins from Radius logs report, Singapore: Nanyang Technological University.

University of Kentucky (1998) Wireless classroom project. On-line. Available HTTP http://www.dcs.uky.edu/~wc/ (accessed 22 November 2004).

Ye, T.Z., Xiao W.D., Soong, B.H., Law, C.L. and Guan, Y.L. (2004) An integrated test bed for Mobile Ad hoc NETwork, *EEE Research Bulletin*, pp. 38–39.

Yow, K.C. (2003) Multimedia messaging over wireless LAN. Proceedings of the Hewlett Packard Worldwide Mobile Technology Conference 2003, HP Labs, Palo Alto, California, September 2003.

Chapter 17

University of South Dakota Palm Initiative

Kurt Hackemer and Doug Peterson

Context and background

As the result of an ambitious strategic planning effort that concluded in May 2000, the University of South Dakota consciously set out to reaffirm its status as the state's premier liberal arts university. With an eye towards its national reputation, the university also declared its intent to become the best, small, publicly funded institution of higher education in the United States. Technology, specifically handheld computing, was seen as one way for the university to distinguish itself.

Prior to the creation and implementation of the Palm Initiative during the 2001/2 academic year, the University of South Dakota had limited experience with handheld computing. Although faculty and staff had experimented with handheld technology on an individual basis, there was no specific institutional knowledge to draw upon. However, significant institutional experience did exist in terms of technology-enhanced pedagogy, infrastructure, and support staff. In creating the Palm Initiative, the central administration assumed that this general expertise would readily translate to handheld computing. Therefore, in the spring of 2001, the decision was made to require each of the 1,000 incoming freshmen and 100 first-year law students who would enter the university that fall to purchase (at a subsidized cost of US$125) a Palm m500 handheld valued at US$300. The university's 50 first-year medical students purchased Palm m505 handhelds, which had colour rather than monochrome screens. The university received a volume discount on the handhelds, with the difference between purchase price and subsidized price made up by the USD Foundation.

This project was overseen by the Palm Steering Committee, which contained representatives from the university's administration, academic community, information technology staff, finance office, and procurement staff. The committee contained relatively few teaching faculty, especially those who regularly taught freshman-level courses. As a result, the university did not pay enough attention to pedagogical issues when initially developing the Palm Initiative. The administrators who created the project made several key assumptions:

- handhelds would automatically make students more organized and therefore, by implication, better students;

- the educational software bundled with the handhelds could be readily applied in the classroom;
- because students generally understood how desktop computers worked, they would quickly understand and see the utility of handheld computers;
- the Palm Initiative would start in selected courses but would quickly spread throughout the curriculum as faculty and students became excited about the project.

The University's Center for Instructional Design and Delivery developed initial training materials. Students received their handhelds when they arrived for the fall semester and attended a one-hour training session explaining how to use them. Medical and law students were trained separately.

Technology and infrastructure

The majority of the infrastructure lies in the handheld units; however, the infrastructure for a handheld program extends far beyond the handheld computers themselves. Prior to distribution, all of the handhelds were unpacked, charged and pre-loaded with additional software for educational use. This preparation took considerable time but also uncovered any defective units. While handheld computers may appear to be standalone devices their functionality largely depends on synching to a personal computer or central server. Because the percentage of students without personal computers hovered around 40 per cent during the early stages of the program, a network solution needed to be found. This was solved through the placement of infrared (IR) network ports around campus where students could synch e-mail and AvantGo (http://www.avantgo.com) channels (one of the early application solutions for information delivery).

When it became apparent that students needed more than simple data distribution, the university reviewed several possible server solutions and ultimately settled upon XTNDConnect by Extended Systems (http://www.extended systems.com) because of its ability to distribute specific information to different user groups. Group folders were created on the central server. Any Palm-compatible files dropped into a folder would automatically synchronize with all registered members of that group when a synch was initiated through either a personal computer or one of the IR network ports. In addition, students without a PC could back up their handheld to the XTNDConnect server. The problem with this system was the complexity of the set-up for both the handheld and personal computer.

Entering the third year, it was apparent that the m500 model distributed in prior years was dated, so one of Palm's new models, the Zire71, was selected as the replacement. The Zire71 had more memory, a hi-resolution colour display, built-in digital camera and MP3 player. While the camera and MP3 player may have provided more appeal for students, they have also proven useful in academic endeavours. Expanded network connectivity was achieved in the third year through the use of Tribeam (http://www.tribeam.com) access points, which provided access to the internet and e-mail using an infrared connection. The Tribeam units also possess the ability to broadcast application or data files for distribution in the classroom.

A major obstacle during all three years of the Palm Initiative was the uncertainty regarding infrastructure needs and capabilities. Much of the infrastructure necessary for the initiative was in its infancy, particularly during the first year of the program. Another issue was that the University of South Dakota's vision for the implementation of hardware and software was often ahead of market-ready solutions. Further complicating the problem of preparing the necessary environment were the limited resources dedicated to exploring multiple possible solutions. There was also a tendency to 'wait and see' which technology was going to become the standard prior to adoption. This kind of strategy may make sound business sense but it is incompatible with staying on the leading edge of new technology. There are clear costs associated with being a technology leader, including a willingness to accept some risk in trying new approaches.

Engaging with students

During the first two years of the program, students were trained to use their handhelds right out of the box. Faculty with long-time Palm experience recommended that there be a gap between distribution and training to allow students to explore the technology at their own pace. That recommendation was not implemented until the third year of the program but seemed to be successful at that time. Students reported that they were able to figure out the handheld's basic software and use many of its built-in functions, partly because the initial start-up took the user through a well designed introduction and demonstration program.

While students were comfortable with the Palm's built-in functions, additional applications proved problematic. Individuals have developed most of the available handheld software or it has been done through open-source collaboration and it therefore lacks the formal usability assessment and support documentation that users are accustomed to in personal computer applications. Issues such as non-standard menu access in some applications and the use of unusual icons are common in Palm applications, most likely due to limited display space. These, however, do impact the usability of applications and may have contributed to the lack of student exploration on their own. Applications with a long history and from larger software publishers such as Documents-to-Go (http://www.dataviz.com) or Quizzler (http://www.quizzlerpro.com) were the exception. There is an obvious trade-off between usability and training required and this was certainly true in the University of South Dakota's experience. As a result, surprisingly few students seemed comfortable exploring applications in an effort to better understand their use and usefulness.

On the faculty side, a lack of knowledge regarding handheld capabilities severely limited class-specific implementations. However, there were some notable exceptions. For example, one faculty member discovered that Palm's web-clipping technology could be used to create standalone hypertext documents. Students received their syllabus in web-clipping format, including a glossary, lab guides, review guides and low-resolution images. Unfortunately this technology is no longer a part of PalmOS. Some faculty prepared review quizzes for major topic areas. An informal evaluation in a psychology course found that students who used the handheld-based review quizzes improved their exam scores on average by 10 points on a 100-point exam. Another successful application allowed students to complete peer evaluations of speeches on their handheld and beam the results to the speaker, who could view a summary of the evaluations. This application was developed in-house and in consultation with the faculty member using it.

Research projects generated from the initial Palm Initiative allowed faculty to explore the development of an internet-connected classroom using Bluetooth, and the development of educational assessment tools integrating the multimedia features of newer Palm models with data collection forms based on the handheld and synchronized with a central system. Faculty also began using handhelds for data collection in the field, including an anthropology project cataloguing the physical characteristics of local grave markers, a biological census of native wildflowers that linked descriptions of plants with Global Positioning System (GPS) data, and a psychology study that randomly queried participants over a two week period about their emotional state and use of alcohol and/or tobacco within a designated time frame.

Usage statistics indicated that very few students were synching their handhelds with the centralized XTNDConnect server. The same appears to be true of other network connectivity solutions such as the Tribeam. While students consistently suggest that additional training is necessary, the attendance at training sessions indicated that this training is not a priority. When the program employed a full-time graduate assistant during the third year to provide support this service was also not fully utilized.

The end benefit to the student appears to be directly related to the time invested in learning the use of the Palm. However, at the early stages of skill acquisition this learning curve appears difficult with no immediate reward, so few continue to the point where they understand the use and usefulness of handhelds. Those who do make the investment, although the minority, are quite vocal about the value of their handheld and several have upgraded to new models.

Evaluation and outcomes

During year one, all entering freshmen received a Palm handheld, but the device's use was limited to only a few classes, partly due to the fact that upper-level students did not have handhelds, partly because there were not enough Palms to allocate to all interested faculty, and partly because there was not enough time to integrate handhelds into all classes. (As it turned out, there was not enough time to integrate handhelds into *any* of these classes.)

During year two, the university again distributed Palms to all freshmen. This meant there were now two cohorts on campus with handhelds. The result was the development of 'Palm Only' and 'Palm Recommended' course sections. However, a registration process that could not exclude students without Palms and a disturbing number of students who chose not to retain their handhelds resulted in Palm Only courses where many students did not have a Palm handheld. Rather than drop these students, most faculty simply made the Palm component optional or dropped it completely.

Evaluation at the conclusion of year two primarily used focus groups and surveys. Faculty responses almost uniformly agreed that while they could envision how handheld technology could be beneficial in education they simply lacked the necessary experience and time to implement it. This was particularly true during the first year of the initiative, when very few faculty had handhelds. Most faculty who responded positively had previous experience with handhelds and already understood their capabilities and limitations.

The assumed benefits in time management were never formally assessed. Many students simply did not make the switch from paper planners to electronic organizers. They also failed to see the Palm's potential usefulness. One contributing factor might have been that the overwhelming majority of the undergraduate students who participated in the Palm Initiative were first-year college students. These students were adjusting not only to the increased rigors of college but also to entirely new living environments and an increased level of responsibility. In short, many were simply overwhelmed, and trying to learn how to use a new technology was an additional hassle they did not need. A limited number of handhelds were offered to upper-level students, most of whom realized their value immediately and utilized the devices to their fullest extent. To fully appreciate what a handheld computer can do, a student must have the requisite experience regarding college as well as an understanding of the technology's capabilities.

Additional student perception problems arose from the fact that students were required to purchase the device (at approximately 40 per cent of the market price) during the first two years of the program. Many students misinterpreted the university's publicity and assumed that the handhelds would be provided free of charge. Concern over cost was exacerbated by limited classroom use of the handhelds during the first year.

Focus groups were established to determine what the students' needs were. Those groups determined that the overwhelming majority of needs could already be accomplished using the existing models and software. Maintaining student awareness of a handheld's capability was and is an ongoing struggle. The number of students using handhelds in class remains relatively low, but appears to be driven more by personal experience than by any university-wide promotion.

Institutional aspects

From the outset, the Palm Initiative faced unnecessary faculty opposition. Most initial users were freshmen, so the administration decided that the project would best be implemented in key courses taken by students in their first year. Two courses were targeted: English Composition and Fundamentals of Speech. Unfortunately, academic departments and instructors were not consulted about this decision until after it was made, and then only to be told that it would be implemented in their classes. Instructors had only weeks between notification and the start of classes. They received their own handhelds, but the majority were graduate students rather than tenured or tenure-track faculty, which meant that relatively few regular faculty were actively involved. Needless to say, this created some resentment and hurt the process of faculty buy-in.

Those instructors with handhelds had little idea what to do with them. Before the Palm Initiative ever hit campus, the university and its faculty had invested a lot of time and resources in course-related technology. A significant percentage of faculty and instructors already had basic course materials prepared in electronic form. However, there was no concerted effort to show faculty how to move course materials that students might use to the Palm platform. Similarly, there was no concerted effort to identify additional PalmOS software that might be used for course-specific purposes.

One of the best campus resources available to the Palm Steering Committee was a faculty-based Palm user group, which consisted of faculty who had been experimenting with PalmOS technology before the Palm Initiative was created. By the second half of the initiative's first year, it was clear that things were not going as smoothly as planned, and the Palm Steering Committee asked the user group for its suggestions. The user group produced a report in March 2002 that recommended a more pragmatic approach to implementing handhelds in the curriculum and provided specific direction about how this might be done. The steering committee accepted the report, thanked the user group for its efforts, and then tabled most of its recommendations as the initiative entered its second year.

Early in the initiative's second year, the user group concluded that the program was fatally flawed, pointing out in a second report that the program was too big for the allocated levels of funding and staffing, that not enough faculty had handhelds, and that the initiative lacked the necessary dedicated technical support. Midway through the second year, the university agreed, turning over direction of the initiative to a subset of the user group. This group, known as the Palm Academic Committee, changed the focus of the program for its third year from the entire freshman class to 95 incoming honours students with the intent of exploring what worked and what did not in a more controlled environment. The revised initiative focused on programmatic rather than classroom issues and had dedicated technical support.

What next?

The University of South Dakota's experience suggests that the key to successfully implementing handhelds into the academic experience is informed and enthusiastic faculty who have the time and support to develop appropriate handheld materials and applications for their specific course needs. As a result, the university is altering the Palm Initiative for its fourth year and will no longer require students to own their own handhelds. Instead, it will deploy clusters of handhelds dedicated to an individual instructor or course. This approach offers three advantages:

- departments and faculty had to apply to receive a cluster of handhelds, specifying in their proposals what software would be used and in what context. Those who applied were genuinely interested in the concept and thought it would enhance their teaching;
- there have been enormous advances made in hardware since the first years of the Palm Initiative. Newer handhelds are capable of far more than the m500s deployed in the first and second years and faculty can see more possibilities for their use in the classroom and in the field;
- there have been enormous advances in software since the first years of the Palm Initiative. The latest iteration of the project will take advantage of the fact that more and more software with a variety of classroom and field applications is now available, making handhelds a potentially powerful learning tool in specific environments and for specific tasks.

One final goal of the Palm Academic Committee is to make the university a handheld-ready campus where any student with a handheld can find the necessary tools that would make them a better student and more informed campus citizen. Positive steps in that direction have been taken but more remains to be done.

In retrospect, the University of South Dakota may have been too far ahead of its time in terms of a mass deployment of handheld technology. Only now are some of the things that faculty dreamed of doing technically possible.

Bibliography

Carlson, S. (2002) Are Personal Digital Assistants the Next Must-Have Tool?, *Chronicle of Higher Education*, 11 October 2002. On-line. Available HTTP http://chronicle.com/prm/weekly/v49/i07/07a03301.htm (accessed 22 November 2004).

Fallon, M.A.C. (2002) Handheld Devices: Toward a More Mobile Campus, *Syllabus*, November 2002. On-line. Available HTTP http://www.syllabus.com/article.asp?id=6896 (accessed 22 November 2004).

Leibiger, C.A. (2002) Beyond the Organizer: A Manual of Educational Uses For the Handheld Computer. On-line. Available HTTP http://www.usd.edu/pda/downloads/Palmmaual.pdf (accessed 22 November 2004).

PalmOne (2001) College Orientation's New Twist – Palm Handhelds for New Students. PalmOne press release. On-line. Available HTTP http://www.palmone.com/us/company/pr/2001/090201a.html (accessed 22 November 2004).

Peterson, D. (2002) Implementing PDAs in a College Course: One Professor's Perspective, *Syllabus*, November 2002. On-line. Available HTTP http://www.syllabus.com/article.asp?id=6897 (accessed 22 November 2004).

Vahey, P. and Crawford, V. (2002) *Palm Education Pioneers Program Final Evaluation Report*. Menlo Park, CA: SRI International. On-line. Available HTTP http://ctl.sri.com/publications/displayPublication.jsp?ID=115 (accessed 22 November 2004).

Chapter 18

The future of learning at IBM

Empowering employees through mobile learning

Chris von Koschembahr and Steve Sagrott

Introduction

IBM defines itself as a learning organization. Investing more than $750 million per year to train its 300,000 plus employees, IBM stays on the cutting edge of learning technology, paradigms and offerings. In 2003, the company began extensive research into the 'future of learning,' an effort to identify what trends, technologies and demands would drive organizations to begin viewing learning as more than a one-time, separate-from-work event.

Through its research, IBM determined that learning is a critical competitive differentiator and vital tool for driving innovation and new revenue sources. IBM's recent survey of over 450 CEOs worldwide indicated that chief executives know they need to build new internal capabilities and skills while enabling their leaders to be change agents. They recognize the paramount importance of aligning learning initiatives to address market challenges. And finally, they see organizational responsiveness in meeting customer needs as critical to driving growth.

Consistent with those findings, companies are defining organizational value less by physical capital and more by an analysis of earning power derived from human capital (Moe 2000). Even manufacturing and production operations are becoming more knowledge intensive. In today's marketplace, knowledge – an intangible – is a key ingredient in the success of a tangible product (Oblinger and Verville 1998).

To make that knowledge relevant and valuable, IBM believes market forces will ultimately compel organizations to turn old paradigms on their heads – moving from a purely instructor-centric model to one that embeds learning into every day workflow and empowers the learner to control when, where and how he learns. And given the current and future marketplace, mobile learning is a key component of IBM's overall learning initiatives.

A business environment primed for mobile learning

Consider today's business environment and the technologies that support it. It is widely agreed upon that the changing demographics of the US workforce and evolving business needs are creating a need for learning programs, but those changes also point to a need to rethink the way learning is delivered.

Today, the most highly skilled or 'gold-collar workers,' are engaged in more specialized and high paying activities, while the tasks demanding less-rigorous training are being handed over to a growing body of 'paraprofessional' support workers whose roles in today's service/information world equate roughly to those carried out by skilled mechanics and quality control engineers in the Industrial Age (Goman 2000). And competition is only becoming fiercer. By the year 2010, the average 10-year-old will have access to more computational power than existed on the planet in 2001 (Harris 2003). And by 2010, the codified information base of the world is expected to double every 11 hours (Bontis 1999). Examining this phenomenon, the American Society of Training and Development (ASTD) has concluded that new knowledge is growing at a rate much faster than our ability to learn it.

This skills gap is largely being fueled by the educational demands of knowledge work. 'Eighty percent of the new jobs created since 1992 require some degree of post-secondary training or education,' says Emily Stover DeRocco, Assistant Secretary of the US Department of Labor's Employment and Training Administration. This dramatic acceleration in the educational demands of new jobs is 'driven largely by technology and the tremendous growth in knowledge workers who now account for a third of the U.S. workforce,' she notes (Taylor 2004).

As equally alarming is the workforce gap that will be left this decade as the Baby-Boomers retire. According to the Bureau of Labor and Statistics, Generation X is about half that size – with only 38 million people born in the United States between 1965 and 1975. As total employment is projected to increase by 21.3 million jobs, or 15 percent by 2012, the workforce will only grow by 17 percent (*The Monthly Labor Review* 2004).

This worker void will create a significant gating factor for growth across most industry sectors in the US economy. Moreover, the differences between Generation Y and today's workforce are significant. They have grown up on-line and in the 'global village.' They use instant messaging, have carried cellphones since high school (or earlier) and expect to access information on the go.

The changes in the workforce will create enough challenges for organizations, but they also must grapple with the implementation of talent supply-chains that enable increased productivity, transformation and innovation. In order to survive and thrive in an increasingly service-led and knowledge-driven economy, individuals and organizations must continually acquire and apply new skills and develop new ways of leveraging information and knowledge. And they need the ability to develop those skills in a work context, on demand.

In short, according to former Royal Dutch Shell Group Financial Director Arie De Geus, 'A company's success no longer depends on its ability to raise investment capital, but on the ability of its people to learn together and to produce new ideas.'

Indeed, employers have always asked for employees who can 'hit the ground running.' Capable employees bring usable skills and work-readiness into the organization. As organizations change, they need employees who are adaptable – individuals who can change, learn new skills and add to their knowledge. They also require employees who are capable of making decisions that can transform the organization and enhance its success.

To keep up with these changing demands, learners must have the ability to rapidly access relevant resources and leverage advanced skills to address new market opportunities and deliver customized solutions to clients – all with the speed of a keystroke.

The evolution of mobile learning at IBM

For more than five years, IBM has focused on making learning more accessible and consumable for its employees. In 1998, the company began exploring the concept of 'create content once and distribute it in many ways.' That initiative began with IBM's Web Lecture Services. This project became an effort to take presentations delivered in the classroom and make them available to a wider audience via the internet. Instead of signing up for a scheduled training course and then fitting it into an already busy agenda, IBM created a convenient alternative to learn materials necessary to stay up-to-date and meet rapidly changing job demands.

IBM created Web Lecture Services to deliver communications, information and training to large numbers of people regardless of their location. Using web lectures, it is possible to communicate strategic messages clearly and consistently, train sales and marketing teams on new products, reduce training costs and improve overall communication. Web lectures are an effective resource to teach applications for the first time, but they can also be used as an ongoing tool to keep the learner updated on developing news and information.

Bob Browdy, IBM consulting program manager, software group worldwide field enablement, was one of the first IBM managers to implement web lectures and more recently, mobile web lectures, in his group.

'We stumbled onto web lectures as a method of training because we'd failed in other areas,' Browdy explains.

> Five years ago, IBM Software Group was training employees through an event called e-business University every January. We made a promise that after a week at e-business University, employees would be better equipped to identify opportunities, deal with competition and close sales opportunities. It didn't work. We had a 30 percent satisfaction rate.

After the e-business University, employees reported back that, according to Browdy, 'We missed the mark.' Employees knew the products, but still did not know how to identify opportunities, nor did they know anything about competition or how to close deals. Given 90 days to fix the training problem and a small budget, Browdy started looking at how his team could leverage content that already existed.

Browdy heard about web lectures and had a 'eureka' moment for how he could use them to solve his problem. 'I realized I could deliver relevant content to anyone in the world any time they wanted it,' he said, recognizing web lectures as a unique learning tool because of their flexibility.

Once a web lecture is created it can be delivered many ways – in person, live at a seminar, at a learner's PC in his office, or to a group of people gathered around a projection screen. Therefore, the web lecture's flexibility made it a natural fit to go mobile. When IBM introduced web lectures in 1998, it quickly became a popular resource and the most broadly used learning program. Since the web lecture's inception, more than 158,800 users have benefitted, and more than 1,250,000 lectures have been consumed. So in 2002, web lectures evolved with the current technology movement and went mobile.

Learning's ace is already in employees' pockets

Consistent with IBM's vision to embed learning into everyday workflow, mobile web lectures allow employees to access important learning opportunities any time of the day, from any location with technology most Americans already carry.

More than 150 million Americans have a mobile phone. According to research firm IDC that number will grow to more than 180 million by 2007 (Slawsby 2004). Americans are trading in their landline phones for cost-effective wireless deals. And many carry smartphones that are alternatives to hand-held computers and Personal Digital Assistants (PDAs).

Overall, mobile devices are coming equipped with more advanced features – such as streaming video, color-touch screens, internet browsers and compatibility with desktop applications – that make mobile learning not only possible, but practical. Given such advances, Stamford, Connecticut-based research firm Gartner reported that by 2010, 80 percent of key business processes would involve the exchange of real-time information involving mobile workers (Clark 2004).

Moreover, market trends indicate a significant number of employees are already using their mobile devices to access e-mail, search the web, organize calendars, read the news or access documents during down time. Although manufacturers are building PDAs, cell phones and hand-held computers that deliver applications and content, the burden lies with employers to deliver the information and materials that keep employees engaged and competitive. IBM saw these changes as an opportunity to rethink how employees can use their hand-held devices to enhance productivity through 'just-in-time' learning.

Using mobile phones, hand-held computers or PDAs, the twenty-first century workforce can now turn to their mobile devices for the latest skills and news relevant to their industry. Perhaps more importantly, mobile devices are tools that individuals *want* to use to better perform their jobs. Regardless of whether the learner is stuck in a traffic jam, on his daily train commute, or in the airport terminal, a learning opportunity is available at his fingertips, taking advantage of down time and reducing training costs.

After accessing e-business University learning content through the intranet for about three or four years, Browdy's team said they were satisfied, but began indicating they wanted the ability to review content at the 'tip of the sword' – or at the time of need.

For many of these employees, this meant having access to learning in the field. They wanted content available while waiting to visit a client office or during the execution of their job.

These employees confirmed IBM's vision for learning – that learners wanted to take a more active role in the learning experience. In response, IBM recognized that learners are constrained for time and that by using mobile learning, they could access learning in shorter 'chunks.' IBM began breaking an hour-long web lecture into six ten-minute segments, finding that more people take advantage of easily digestible learning 'nuggets.' Sparing ten minutes here and there to download the latest web lecture is a lot more reasonable – and desirable – than finding an hour-long break.

As part of its learning-on-demand initiative, IBM sought to make vital information instantaneously accessible 24 hours a day. The company also strived to customize that content for the needs of the individual employee. Therefore, part of IBM's mobile web lecture solution lets employees customize a learner profile based on their individual needs in regards to their job function and line of business. This is called 'profiled notification.'

Profiled notification has a multi-faceted approach to matching an individual to appropriate content. First, it links to an organization's HR data, accessing information such as title, job role, business unit and management level. HR data provides a basic foundation of an individual's position and potential learning needs. Once that foundation is laid, the learner creates a self-prescribed profile, including qualifications such as geographic region, customer accounts, subject expertise, interests, preferred means of notification and job challenges. The self-created profile ensures that a learner only receives that information of greatest interest to her.

On the content side, profiled notification organizes and tags content so that it can be easily aligned with a learner's profile. Getting content organized involves a two-pronged approach – leveraging technology to crawl through and tag existing content in IBM's learning databases, and offering subject matter experts the opportunity to tag their content when they publish it.

The more organized the content, the more effective profiled notification. Once the content is organized and the individual is profiled, the learner is instantly notified, either through an e-mail or a Short Message Service (SMS) to their cellphone, when relevant content is available. If their device has the capabilities, learners can download the content immediately. For many employees, this 'just-in-time' information could be the difference between making a sale and losing a potential new customer.

If a salesperson only has a few minutes before meeting a client and just prior to going in receives a notification that a new product has just been released, the salesperson now has the opportunity to quickly access a ten-minute web lecture on the topic and adjust his selling points accordingly. Therefore, anytime a learner is sent a notification, he knows there is important information waiting for him – information tailored just for him.

The tools for a mobile learning program

In a business environment that welcomes wireless technology, it is no surprise that the learning industry has adopted the movement towards a convergence of enterprise applications and wireless devices that allows for a mobile learning opportunity. Mobile phones, hand-held computers and PDAs now have the capabilities, connectivity and features to support mobile learning. Simultaneously, employees are embracing the opportunity to learn what they want – through their customized profiled notifications; when they want – accessible 24 hours a day; and where they want – in a cab to a client meeting or at the local café on a coffee break.

To make a web lecture, IBM uses the Web Lecture Services Authoring and Management System to upload a previously created presentation. Then the lecturer uses a normal telephone to record an audio narrative for each slide of the presentation. Once in the management system, the lecture can be reviewed and updated as many times as necessary. With the lecture created and reviewed, the Learning Technologies product team takes the lecture and moves it to the delivery server, either the internet or intranet. Once created, the lecture is now accessible via a PC, laptop or mobile device.

A mobile learner needs a Pocket PC or a Symbian-based device that is equipped with an internet browser and a media player – a standard in 'smartphones' and most mobile devices. The internet browser is the only software needed to view the web lecture and the media player allows for audio and visual learning tools to accompany the written material of the web lecture. Other features that enhance the learning experience include: streaming video, color-touch screens, an 'Ask a Question' option and a choice of multiple language audio.

While IBM's Web Lecture Services made a smooth transition to mobile learning, one challenge did develop: the small resolution of downloaded lectures. A mobile device offers a much smaller screen than the average desktop, resulting in a smaller resolution. Therefore, when lecturers are building their presentations, they must be 'device aware' and alter the font, graphics and formatting. To address this challenge, IBM has provided its web lecturers with a 'preview mode' where they can see what their presentation would look like on a mobile device and make any necessary changes. IBM is committed to making the Web Lecture Service desirable for both its learners and its lecturers.

Early successes

Mobile learning is a new tool for IBM employees, and because it requires a somewhat robust mobile device, only a small percentage of employees have the capabilities to use mobile web lectures. About 10 percent of Browdy's team currently uses them, including Browdy.

Browdy carries a combination Pocket PC/cellphone to access his mobile learning programs.

> Mobile learning has literally bailed me out of tough situations. For example, I run a live class where I stand and deliver a presentation on IBM's 'Signature Selling Methodology.' A few months ago, I had an hour-and-a-half lecture to deliver and had not done my homework. But I knew I had four hours of travel time, so I went on-line and downloaded the web lectures I needed to know to deliver this piece and learned what I needed on the plane.

After implementing web lectures via the internet and then taking them mobile, Browdy needed to find a way to measure and assess the program's success. To meet those needs, employees were tested after completing a web lecture to assess their understanding and absorption of the content. As employees completed a web lecture and passed a test, they completed a skill acquisition level, from one to five. IBM also implemented surveys to garner employee satisfaction with the methodology.

Browdy's team has given the following test sample of feedback regarding mobile web lectures:

> The material presented is applicable to MY current job; short, sweet, to the point. I liked it. I like doing this on my time, so the web presentation was effective.

> I liked EVERYTHING about this [web lectures] method. This is a great sales aid for new Sales Reps. I am very pumped and excited to find and close new opportunities.

> I loved that I could learn anytime and at my own pace.

On the cost side, IBM's innovative implementation has allowed for web lectures to be inexpensive, quick and easy to create, and since going mobile – even easier to access. Thus, web lectures have become increasingly popular among learners and since most professionals are already equipped with the technology to view them via mobile devices, they welcome the opportunity to learn on the go instead of being restricted to an office or conference.

Once having transitioned the e-business University on-line, employee satisfaction rose from 30 percent to over 90 percent. Moreover, the mobile implementation of web lectures makes it an even more affordable learning medium. IBM Web Lecture Services cost only one dollar per person – which includes creating the lecture content and then delivering it in several ways.

However, it should also be noted that web lectures are not a substitute for in-person learning. IBM also found that employees were conflicted about how they best learn. They would prefer to learn in a live environment, as they tend to be human interactive oriented vs. system oriented; however, web lectures met the time requirements and 'on demand' needs of their job roles.

In addition, the asynchronous nature of web lectures does not lend itself to topics that require an ongoing stream of interaction between the student and the instructor. IBM made provisions for interaction between student and instructor through the use of an 'Ask the Author' button, but for those topics such as negotiation skills for example – where the only proof of knowledge or skill acquisition is observed behavior – the web lecture delivery technique will not work by itself. Though IBM has been pleased with the results of the program, there is an overall recognition that blending mobile learning with other learning paradigms remains important.

What's next?

Mobile web lectures are a small but wildly successful initiative within IBM. Looking beyond sales teams and towards mainstreaming such initiatives, IBM expects to create similar mobile learning capabilities for the multitude of IT professionals within the organization, including programmers, technicians and service consultants.

Moreover, advancements in mobile devices will mean mobile learning is more easily adopted by more employees. Many of today's mobile devices lack either the display or memory to handle web lectures. However, future mobile technology will make multimedia functions more ubiquitous and less expensive.

Finally, company learning executives expect to scale the initiatives over the next several years by intersecting with the overall IT strategy. As more robust mobile devices become available, employees will use them for far more than e-mail, internet browsing and learning. Mobile devices will not only bring learning into the field, but also Siebel and CRM that will even further enable the salesforce.

For IBM the future of learning is already here. Employees are empowered through mobile devices and flexible programs to control their learning experiences and are positively responding to the freedom such programs offer. But this is only the beginning. In a business environment that is constantly growing and changing, offering new innovations, advanced technology and different market conditions, IBM will continue to find new ways to respond rapidly to the needs of its customers and the marketplace. This means having an adequately educated workforce that will not only respond to evolving issues, but also even foresee upcoming trends and proactively pursue these arising challenges.

References

Bontis, N. (1999) Managing Organizational Knowledge by Harnessing Intellectual Capital, *International Journal of Technology Management*, 18 (5/6/7/8), Geneve: Inderscience Enterprises Limited.

Clark, W. (2004) *Enterprises Must Assess Impact of Mobile Applications*, Stamford: Gartner.

Goman, C.K. (2000) *The Forces of Change*, Link and Learn, Burlington: Linkage.

Harris, J. (2003) *The Learning Paradox*, Oxford: Capstone Books.

Moe, M. (2000) The Knowledge Web. On-line. Available HTTP http://www.internettime.com/itimegroup/MOE1.PDF (accessed 22 November 2004).

Oblinger, D.G. and Verville, A.-L. (1998) *What Business Wants from Higher Education*, Phoenix, AZ: Oryx Press.

Slawsby, A. (2004) *Worldwide Mobile Phone 2004–2008 Forecast and Analysis*, Framingham: IDC.

Taylor, C. (2004) Retention Leadership, *TandD Magazine*, 58(3), Alexandria: American Society for Training & Development, Inc.

The Monthly Labor Review (2004) Bureau of Labor and Statistics, Washington, DC: US Government Printing Office.

Chapter 19

Institutional issues
Embedding and supporting

John Traxler

Introduction

Embedding and supporting mobile learning within any organisation will require an understanding and evaluation of it that extends beyond pedagogic considerations and examines it alongside other forms of provision and delivery in terms of institutional expectations about a range of issues. These issues include:

- costs, funding and resourcing; scaling up and sustaining;
- quality assurance, fitness-for-purpose and validation;
- infrastructure and technical support;
- staffing issues and the management of change;
- monitoring and evaluation;
- legal and ethical expectations.

This chapter will explore this institutional dimension of mobile learning. It is probably the chapter with the greatest UK focus and context but the arguments have been framed with a global readership in mind and the globalisation of education means that the issues will have resonance around the world. The topics in question have been loosely grouped around the themes of financing, institutional missions, staffing, quality and the estate.

Financing

This section will look at issues around the costs, funding and resourcing of institutional mobile learning.

One of the most significant issues that institutional managers (and advocates of mobile learning) will have to address is that of resourcing mobile learning. It is useful to categorise the resource arguments that might be used to underpin a sustained mobile learning strategy within an organisation or institution:

- Social Inclusion and Social Capital – appropriate forms of mobile learning should be used where they enhance the progress and success of specific disadvantaged communities; it is sensible and ethical for society to bear the cost in these cases.

- Leveraging the Consumer – forms of mobile learning should be used that exploit the widespread ownership of mobile devices, especially increasingly powerful mobile phones, since this is highly cost-effective for the institution.
- Training Niches – mobile learning should be used where it can uniquely deliver or support specific subjects or courses, for example trainee teachers on placement in schools, ecology students on fieldwork, trainee nurses on hospital wards, highly mobile part-time students.
- Added-Value – mobile learning should be used to give full-cost courses added-value especially vis-à-vis competitor institutions, for example MBAs and other professional postgraduate provision.
- Institutional Cost-Effectiveness – mobile learning should be considered where it might increase recruitment, retention and progression and thus increase institutional performance and efficiency and where it might help students and staff function more effectively in a complex and novel environment.
- Raising or Maintaining the Institutional Profile – mobile learning should be considered for its capacity to capture public and informed attention, and to make or underline a statement about the institutional mission and style.
- Reducing Pressure on PCs and the Estate – mobile learning should be considered where it might reduce other aspects of institutional costs, perhaps the need for networked PCs and dedicated computer labs.

For any given institution, these arguments may not amount to a complete and rational case for institution-wide mobile learning. However, some institutions already consider there are sufficient grounds for taking the risk and making the necessary investment. This is certainly the case with our case studies from Singapore and South Dakota. There are other similar examples, for example the University of Twente in Holland with its Wireless Campus (http://www.utwente.nl/wireless-campus/en/).

A further insight into the decision-making process can be gained by looking at the reasons given by UK institutions (Jenkins 2001) for adopting an earlier institution-wide technology, namely Virtual Learning Environments (VLEs), in the early stages in VLE adoption (see Table 19.1). Some institutions gave several reasons. The last reason is a colloquialism for 'responding to peer pressure'.

Few, if any, of these reasons were based at the time (or subsequently) on credible objective or empirical evidence, and the last one merely acknowledges the institutional imperative not to be left behind.

It is worth bearing in mind, when looking at VLE take-up figures and thinking about institutional mobile learning, that there are ongoing differences between institutional take-up (meaning perhaps that technology is procured and installed by the institution) and individual engagement (meaning perhaps that individual teachers incorporate the technology in their work) (Jenkins *et al.* 2003; Social Informatics Research Unit 2003) – these differences are significant when we look later at the implications for institutional staffing.

Table 19.1 Reasons for VLE adoption (Jenkins 2001)

Improving teaching and learning	27%
Widening participation	21%
Distance learning	21%
Flexibility	19%
Cost-effective	16%
'Keeping up with the Jones!'	5%

The institutional mission

All educational institutions have mission statements that underpin their priorities, their strategies and their development. For UK institutions, these can focus on research, on learning and teaching, on social and economic issues or on a mixture of all three.

The focus on research is probably the least relevant to institutional mobile learning. However since much mobile learning is still in the development phase, it does raise the more general issue of the status of learning and teaching research against other traditional, established and recognised forms of research and of research in the use of technology within learning and teaching research. This uncertainty has hindered the development of mobile learning since the distribution of research resources is skewed away from learning and teaching research and towards more established research topics.

The focus on learning and teaching is directly relevant to the issue of institutional mobile learning and it is a technology that if exploited judiciously can enhance the quality of learning and teaching and increase its efficiency. This is, in fact, the case being made throughout this book.

Moreover, universities and colleges are faced with pressure to:

* widen participation, improve retention and increase access;
* reduce unit costs;
* recognise student difference, diversity and individuality.

Sophisticated mobile learning, particularly as it becomes more 'personalised', may finally enable educators and trainers to reconcile these previously mutually antagonistic goals.

The final focus, that on social and economic issues, may include:

* greater participation by under-represented cultural and ethnic minorities, by non-traditional entrants and by under-represented catchment areas;
* increased accessibility and inclusivity of provision;
* local and regional economic, cultural and social regeneration;
* knowledge transfer, income generation, consultancy and so on.

Many of these are, in fact, learning or teaching issues seen from a different viewpoint.

A growing though perhaps implicit component of the mission of many universities, colleges and trainers is the need to compete locally, nationally and internationally (mobile learning can increase their range and competitive advantage) and to generate income from increasingly diverse sources. Mobile technologies can underpin many of these activities either by supporting learning and training as described in this book or supporting teachers in the administration and management of their other responsibilities.

Institutional staffing

The possibility of institution-wide mobile learning raises several issues for institution staff, both academic and non-academic. The most immediate of these are concerned with introducing and managing a large-scale change that involves technology, people and organisations. A subsequent issue will be the changed nature of work across the institution.

Management of change

The success of an institutional strategy to introduce a substantial component of mobile learning to the institution will depend on the nature of the institution, on the strategy adopted and on the characteristics of mobile learning itself. There are several rather different areas of research that address this.

The first of these illuminates the relationships between institutional change and staff attitudes and comes from studies of universities in the last two decades. They did not, in general, address technical change. They did, however, specifically examine educational organisations. Trowler (1998) for example investigated the reactions of academics in a new UK university to a particular enforced change of institutional policy and found a variety of individual attitudes and behaviours in the academics confronting this change. He believed that two dimensions would account for them:

- content *or* discontent;
- working around/changing policy *or* accepting the status quo.

Combining these two dimensions gave four possible states (Figure 19.1):

- *swimming*, that is content *and* accepting status quo;
- *sinking*, that is discontent *and* accepting status quo;
- *using coping strategies*, that is discontent *and* working around/changing policy;
- *policy reconstruction*, that is content *and* working around/changing policy.

He then characterised each of these states as follows. Sinking was characterised by academics feeling:

- under increased workload;
- deskilled;
- subject to increased student numbers;
- the labour process was becoming degraded;
- disenfranchised;
- cut off from decision making.

Swimming was characterised by the attitude that:

- change is an unquestioned opportunity.

Using coping strategies was characterised by:

- working-to-rule;
- minimal engagement.

Policy reconstruction, the fourth and most complex category, was characterised by:

- reinterpretation of policy in the course of implementing;
- proactive and inventive, robust and creative attitudes;

and this was sub-divided into:

- reinterpretation of policy: that is the exploitation of gaps in top-down policy left by ambiguity, lack of detail, lack of certainty and lack of unanimity from

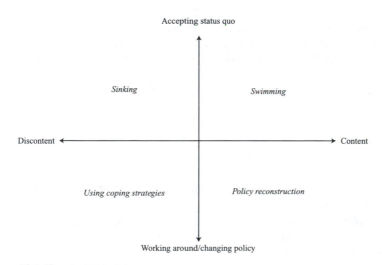

Figure 19.1 Trowler's Model

above; exploiting a lack of adequate oversight and supervision; selective implementation;
- policy manipulation: that is subverting policy; the letter but not the spirit of the law;
- reprofessionalisation: that is redefining, at a personal level, the nature of the profession;
- syllabus innovation and curriculum innovation.

Such a diversity of reactions has probably been evident in colleges and universities wherever institutional managements have driven the implementation of technology supported learning (for example, the introduction of institutional VLEs). This diversity should be anticipated once mobile learning becomes a possible institutional policy. However, the nuances, the presentation and the implementation of such a policy are significant factors when viewed in terms of Trowler's work. Any institutional mobile learning strategy must be ready for the diversity of possible reactions.

Trowler's ideas may be both generally true and relevant to institutional mobile learning strategies but an additional factor is likely to be the existence of different cultures within the institution. Different Schools, strictly speaking different disciplines (Becher 1998) in universities, are permeable, to a greater or lesser extent, to the culture of their corresponding bodies of professional practice in the outside world. This means that staff within universities acquire or absorb the values and standards of their professional counterparts working in industry, commerce, government or wherever. These bodies of professional practice may take the form of, for example:

- unified or homogeneous employers such as national healthcare provision, state schools;
- coherent regulated professions such as law, medicine and accountancy;
- industries with a fragmented and volatile culture such as marketing and IT;
- subjects with little or no outside practice such as history and philosophy.

Institutional strategies must recognise this diversity and provide room for different inflections across the different cultures present in a multi-disciplinary institution. In the case of institutional mobile learning, there is the added fact that these different bodies of outside practice will have adopted mobile devices to very different degrees, for example, IT and business with considerable enthusiasm, medicine less so.

Trowler also discusses attempts to classify institutional and departmental cultures within universities and colleges, drawing a distinction between 'managerial' and 'collegial' cultures. How any given institution and any given department is characterised in this respect will affect its responses to change and how that change can be best facilitated.

A related issue is the balance between the institution's central support departments (and their capacity to catalyse and implement institution-wide policy) and the individual schools, faculties and departments who deliver the teaching and research (and as a consequence of the income associated with students and funding bodies, may have considerable autonomy). This varies from institution to institution but can be a barrier to innovation and can fragment resources and enthusiasm.

Later work by Knight and Trowler (2001) further complicated the picture of change and management in higher education by investigating the way in which departmental structure and organisation mediate and interpret institutional change. Departmental managers clearly have their priorities, not always congruent and consistent with institutional managers and their intermediaries. These will affect how institutional policies are prioritised and instantiated within their departments. It has also been the case that subject specialists have argued, with varying amounts of cogency and conviction, that the introduction of new learning technologies, such as mobile learning, must be delayed, diluted or modified by the needs of their specific subject. These issues should influence the composition of any institutional mobile learning strategy.

The second area is the work on the diffusion of innovations associated with Everett Rogers, investigating how novel technical ideas travel through social systems. He published a major review of diffusion theory in 1962 and continues to research and publish. Rogers and Scott (1997) now list the reasons why some innovations spread more quickly than others as:

* relative advantage;
* compatibility;
* complexity;
* trialability;
* observability.

The relative advantage of the innovation is the perception by potential adopters that the innovation is, in some sense, 'better' than the current alternatives. This advantage might be seen in terms of economic advantage, social advantage, convenience or other criteria. Any policy to institutionalise mobile learning must obviously explore relative advantage in the broadest possible terms if it is to maximise its appeal. In terms of the other characteristics of the innovation, mobile technologies probably are likely to diffuse successfully. The technologies are simple, concrete and understandable; low-risk, small-scale pilots are easy to conduct and observe. Mobile learning is, however, not the same as mobile technologies and the success of the diffusion of mobile learning will also depend on whether mobile technologies are seen as capable of supporting the diverse conceptions of learning and teaching espoused by teachers and students.

Information about innovations is communicated through social systems such as organisations and groups through what Rogers and Scott describe as 'channels'. The diffusion literature discusses the nature and effectiveness of different channels of communication in promoting adoption. Broadly speaking, these channels can be divided into impersonal, such as broadcast mass media, and interpersonal, such as informal social contact and conversation. These perform rather different roles. The impersonal channels create some awareness and knowledge of innovations; the interpersonal channels change attitudes. The impersonal channels have a capacity to reach greater numbers of potential adopters and work best with low complexity innovations. The interpersonal channels work best with high complexity innovations but do not have the capacity to reach many potential adopters. So any strategy intended to institutionalise mobile learning must seek to change attitudes as well as understanding and must use local and informal media and structures to complement official and formal ones. The relative simplicity of standalone mobile devices argues for using informal channels though this dichotomy is of course an over-simplification.

The most widely known part of Rogers' work (1962) is his characterisation of the members of social systems where innovativeness is seen to be the extent to which a person or organisation adopts new ideas earlier than other members in their particular social system.

These categories or classifications are listed as:

- innovators;
- early adopters;
- early majority;
- late majority;
- laggards.

Rogers and his associates devote considerable effort to exploring the characteristics of each category and any strategy to institutionalise mobile learning must appeal to all of them, in the right ways at the right times. Perhaps the most problematic are innovators (who will always be moving onto the next innovation) and the laggards (who will not move at all).

Rogers also attempted to identify key individuals who he saw as opinion leaders within given social systems. These were those individuals who seemed able to influence others' attitudes and behaviour by informal means. This is an argument for implementation strategies that target certain individuals, opinion-formers for example. These are the people to issue with mobile devices when resources are limited.

Rogers also introduces the concept of 'critical mass' where sufficient individuals have adopted an innovation that its subsequent rate of adoption is self-sustaining.

This characterisation of the population within an organisation leads to the idea that innovation may become self-sustaining due to weight of opinion – it has reached 'critical mass'. Adoption and 'critical mass' will depend on the exact nature of the innovation – fax machines need other fax machines, whereas ballpoint pens do not need other ballpoint pens. This distinction may underpin a success differential in mobile learning: didactic mobile learning does not depend on a collective take-up in the same way that discursive mobile learning might do.

Within organisations themselves, Rogers suggested that various factors promote or inhibit innovation. Innovative organisations generally had:

- large size;
- complexity;
- interconnectedness;
- organisational slack (in terms of personnel, resources etc.);
- system openness.

Non-innovative organisations were characterised by:

- formalisation;
- centralisation.

The relative autonomy of schools, faculties and departments within some universities, colleges and corporates confuses this picture since these become organisations-within-organisations, in terms of resources, management culture and so on.

Introducing mobile learning into a large institution requires an institutional policy and strategy. Gilman (1991) exploits Rogers' work to define a practical programme that will give an innovation the best chance of acceptance. This ranges from pilot projects, publicity and incentives to regulation and coercion and is incorporated in our action plan.

Moore (1991), in his work on 'the Technology Adoption Life Cycle', has developed Rogers' original work by pointing to 'the chasm' that separates early adopters from the early majority and emphasising its significance when seeking to move a technological innovation into the mainstream. This chasm is explained by the different appeal of innovation for the different categories. The 'early adopters' are attracted by increased functionality and the power to do new things; the 'early majority' are attracted by just doing the same old things but more easily. This paradox represents the challenge facing advocates of mobile learning if it is to become established; presenting mobile learning as both revolutionary and conservative.

Following from this work, market analysts Gartner have proposed a 'Hype Cycle' in which unduly raised expectations, the 'Peak of Inflated Expectations', are followed by a slump in confidence, the 'Trough of Disillusionment'. Advocates of mobile learning might expect these before reaching the 'Slope of Enlightenment', that is the widespread critical understanding of mobile learning.

Apparently, the adoption of new technologies goes through three phases. First, adopters attempt what was previously too difficult. Second, they attempt what was previously impossible. Finally, they move on to attempting what was previously inconceivable. Mobile learning is generally working towards the end of the first stage though some work has already reached the second. Some of the confusion about the strengths and weaknesses of mobile learning may be due to the difficulties involved in discussing the impossible and the inconceivable! Perhaps also, early adopters are interested in addressing impossible or inconceivable tasks whilst the early majority are concerned with addressing difficult tasks.

A third exploration of change within educational institutions is that of Hall's *Concerns-Based Adoption Model* (Hall 1974). This takes a relatively individualistic view and sees the adoption of change or innovation as being determined by the concerns or worries of individual teachers and lecturers. When faced with change (the possible adoption of a new learning technology, for example), they go through a sequence of phases. It is a developmental model. They start with self-oriented questions or concerns about the impact of change on themselves, on their jobs or workload for example. Task-oriented questions or concerns about how to operate or use the innovation follow these. Finally when these issues are addressed and resolved, the concerns or questions are about the impact and value of the innovation for their students. This conceptualisation of technological change and innovation within educational organisations and institutions provides further input into any staff development process designed to support the wider introduction of mobile learning. It implies the need to recognise where each individual starts from, and not to rush to training that delivers know-how or rush to policy that specifies implementation before first addressing individual and personal concerns and questions.

We can to some extent draw together these different perspectives. They are saying in their different languages that any systemic institutional change requires willingness, sensitivity, flexibility, structures and resources. These must come in different forms from all the stakeholders, both in themselves and in their influence and interactions with the others. Furthermore, collecting these various perspectives together allows us to identify an action plan for institutional managers wishing to introduce mobile learning and training. As we have said, this is not merely a technical or a pedagogic issue; it is also a social and institutional issue. Within any institution, a range of tactics will optimise the long-term success and sustainability of a mobile learning strategy, including:

• short-term pilot projects that reward and support innovative teachers, gain and publicise valuable early insights and give mobile learning local visibility;
• exemplar content, lessons and courses across a range of disciplines that give teachers a sense of what they themselves could achieve; some 'quick-and-dirty' and hence not intimidating;
• high-level 'buy-in', managers seen to be using the technology and the methods.
• identification and discussion of the resource and financial aspects of mobile learning as fully as possible; developing a rich, multi-faceted advocacy and rationale for the policy;
• encouraging everyone to ask 'what's in it for me?' – and answering each such question;

- providing support staff to initiate content development or redevelopment;
- ensuring that mobile learning is represented in the staff recruitment, selection, appraisal and promotion cycle;
- easy access to a range of mobile devices, developing familiarity and confidence amongst teachers;
- reliable and robust technical support, infrastructure and hardware so lecturers can innovate without risk;
- the development and introduction of standards only as experience accumulates.
- regulation and coercion are the last resort and are only worth applying to staff who will never change, or who will undermine change;
- sustained, timely and accessible staff development that addresses all the teachers' pedagogic and technical worries; mixing staff development and support that is 'just-in-case' with some that is 'just-in-time';
- credible channels of feedback and communication between management and teachers so that teachers can influence and 'own' the institutional strategy as it evolves;
- institutional resources for additional non-pedagogic overheads;
- meaningful and acceptable ways of measuring the progress and success of the strategy.

The nature of work

In common with much technology supported learning, mobile learning raises staffing issues for institutional managers since technology will change the nature of teaching both qualitatively and quantitatively.

Traditional UK face-to-face teaching is still largely governed by contracts and conditions of service that stipulate workload in terms of hours of 'contact' with students. As institutions change to mobile learning or other forms of technology supported learning, there may be less face-to-face contact with students and the need for new conditions of service will become pressing. These must recognise the workload involved in supporting on-line, remote and asynchronous communities of learners at a distance, and the changes in the balance of the work as mobile devices facilitate some interactions with students and hinder others.

The part of teaching specifically related to developing content will also evolve (and possibly separate into an academic activity divorced from delivery, supervision and assessment) as institutions see learning objects as commercial entities, generated and marketed separately from the courses and lectures that may once have been their source. There is currently little data on the time or effort involved in developing computer-based teaching material. Marshall and his colleagues (1995) used industry data to validate one model and this was subsequently generalised (Traxler 2003), so the commercial viability of such schemes is largely untested. However, if these schemes are to be successful they will also require a re-examination of the intellectual property rights that govern the development of learning content and the balance of rewards between individual lecturers and the institutions that employ them.

The development of content for technology supported learning including mobile learning will need a wider skill set than that of today's lecturers. The evolution of 'para-academics' – staff skilled in learning materials, design, graphics, technologies and content – and team working will accelerate and will contribute to a redefinition of teaching.

Mobile learning will have other consequences for teaching staff. Extensive research (Bacsich *et al.* 1999) looking at the 'costs of networked learning' describes how lecturers find their working day being extended as networking enables them to work at home and find themselves committed to personal expenditure for hardware, consumables and line charges. Mobile learning will exacerbate these trends, enabling (or forcing) lecturers to work in transit and bringing pressure to buy and update mobile devices and software. These trends also seem to be altering institutions' views on the quality and extent of accommodation for staff.

Support staff and departments

Mobile learning will create a demand for support structures and its progress will be determined by the institutional capacity to provide this support.

One issue that will militate in the short-term against the rapid institutionalisation of handheld computers in universities and colleges is the perception amongst IT support staff that the whole area of handheld computers, their platforms and their applications is too personal, fluid and diverse to (regulate and) support at an institutional level in the way that PC provision is supported. As one university website says, 'The variety of such devices on the market and the constant model changes make it impractical for [name of support department] to offer comprehensive support'. This kind of attitude will inhibit experimentation and progress, and so will uncertainty about the basic platform – Personal Digital Asstistant (PDA) or smartphone – and connectivity – wireless or telephony.

Another IT support issue is interoperability and integration with existing institutional systems such as VLEs (PDAs can access Blackboard but not necessarily other VLEs), conferencing systems (FirstClass has a PDA conduit but other systems may not), library systems (some are Short Message Service (SMS)-enabled) and student records systems (again, some are SMS-enabled). This will not only affect the progress of mobile learning but also the extent to which it can blend or co-exist with other learning technologies. Mobile learning must eventually find an appropriate place, however small and inconsequential, within every course, subject and institution. The exact nature of this will depend on the students, the curriculum, the staff and the resources. There are currently few principled frameworks for developing courses that blend technologies, media and formats. There are early attempts that focus too closely on now-unused technologies (Reisner and Gagné 1983) and some later attempts that try to move beyond such constraints (Traxler 2002).

The estate

It is reasonable, though perhaps fairly speculative, to explore how a substantial commitment to mobile learning might lead an institution to reassess the nature and extent of its physical estate. Currently a significant part of many universities and colleges is dedicated to rooms full of fixed networked desktop PCs. They may lie idle for much of the institutional vacation and when they are used they are often used largely for word-processing, e-mail and web access. The size and layout of these rooms is usually inflexible and prescribes specific styles of teaching to specific sized groups of students. Maintaining, upgrading and replacing these PCs represents a sizeable commitment. Universities and colleges have tried to break this stranglehold on their finances by encouraging out-of-hours and off-campus access and by encouraging laptop ownership and loan, by, for example, networking student residences, creating short-term loan schemes and wireless-enabling their buildings. These efforts are only partially successful and as more powerful wireless-enabled PDAs become available, there is the possibility of introducing them into the equation. They will have to be financed in a rather different way to the rolling replacement programmes that underpin institutional PC systems.

Large-scale mobile learning also provokes some philosophical questions about the role of universities and colleges, about the nature of their core business and the nature of their role within their host communities. If universities and colleges are to deliver wider participation and lifelong learning, mobile learning provides models for taking learning beyond the campus, into the community. In doing so, mobile learning also poses implicit questions about the essence of learning: if mobile learning supports various conceptions of learning for diverse groups of students 'anytime, anywhere', then what is the function of academic buildings, what is the purpose of the library, what is the place of the lecture and the role of face-to-face teaching? How also do we reconcile this view of learning with the role of universities and colleges in social and personal development?

Quality assurance

Validation

Courses in universities and colleges usually undergo a process of 'validation' – the name and the details may differ – whereby they receive official recognition and status. Validation is the process of scrutiny to determine whether new courses or revised courses are 'fit for purpose' from a wider institutional perspective. Adopting new technologies for learning and teaching will usually trigger validation or revalidation and hence embedding mobile learning within an institutional context, whether course-by-course or on a more systematic basis, highlights a range of hitherto unconsidered issues.

In the UK, many institutions consider validation under six main heads derived from those used by the country's Quality Assurance Agency (QAA), namely:

- curriculum design, content and organisation;
- teaching, learning and assessment;
- student progression and achievement;
- student support and guidance;
- learning resources;
- quality management and enhancement.

These are clearly quite general headings and in practice the validation or revalidation of programmes involving the introduction of new learning technologies has often focussed on the following topics and questions:

- Equivalence and parity: are the proposed course and the student experience comparable to those of a face-to-face course?
- Equity: are the proposed course and its delivery mechanisms fair to all of its students or are some disadvantaged?
- Monitoring and evaluation: does the proposed course have robust and sensitive mechanisms that assess its quality and performance?
- Counselling and guidance: does the proposed course offer access to pastoral support comparable to that of a face-to-face course? This includes personal counselling, careers guidance, study skills and tutorial support.
- Student representation: does the proposed course offer its students mechanisms to articulate, discuss and present their views?
- Informal learning: does the proposed course offer its students adequate opportunities to learn to work together and learn from each other, and to learn to function in groups?
- Assessment regimes: specifically are the assessment procedures proposed using mobile learning technologies as rigorous, fair and objective as conventional techniques?

These issues will have a greater or lesser importance depending on the place and importance of mobile learning within the overall portfolio but it is important to consider them carefully if mobile learning is to become established.

Legal expectations

Accessibility is an aspect of inclusivity and is the recognition of diversity in staff and students. In many countries, including the UK, there are legal obligations (as well as the more obvious but ill-defined ethical ones) placed upon educational institutions to anticipate and accommodate this diversity. These obligations are having implications for all forms of technology supported learning, especially web-based learning, where the relationships between legal requirements and technical specifications are slowly becoming clearer (Sloan 2001; Phipps *et al.* 2002; Dunn 2003). Unfortunately, these relationships are currently less clear in the case of mobile learning. This is unfortunate since mobile devices have considerable assistive potential.

The requirements of confidentiality and data protection legislation are another legal aspect of mobile learning. This is most obvious in working with groups and synching a group of PDAs to one PC where some data is public and some is personal. Previous work in education recognised this as an ongoing issue:

> Although synchronization is integral to the utility of handhelds for professionals, off-the-shelf synchronization solutions created problems in classroom use. Traditional synchronization models assume that each user can synchronize with an individual computer—a situation that does not exist in the classroom. Problems often arose from asking many students to synchronize with a small number of computers. Many PEP project teachers had to administer the synchronization process themselves, but education-specific solutions are now available (http://goknow.com).
>
> (Tatar *et al.* 2003: 31)

Having recognised the nature of the problem, it is in fact not particularly difficult to set up the necessary procedures and protocols, and appropriate synching software is becoming available.

References

Bacsich, P., Ash, C. and Kaplan, L. (1999) *The Costs of Networked Learning*, Sheffield: Sheffield Hallam University.

Becher, T. (1998) *Academic Tribes and Territories*, Milton Keynes: Society for Research into Higher Education/Open University Press.

Dunn, S. (2003) Return to SENDA? Implementing Accessibility for Disabled Students in Virtual Learning Environments in UK Further and Higher Education. MSc dissertation. On-line. Available HTTP http://www.saradunn.net/VLEproject/index.html (accessed 16 April 2005).

Gilman, R. (1991) Reclaiming Politics – The Times are Changing and Our Approach to Politics May Need to Change as Well, *Context*, Fall/Winter (10). On-line. Available HTTP http://www.context.org/ICLIB/IC30/Gilman.htm (accessed 22 November 2004).

Hall, G.E. (1974) *The Concerns-Based Adoption Model: A Developmental Conceptualization of the Adoption Process Within Educational Institutions*, Chicago: ILL.

Jenkins, M. (2001) *Management and Implementation of Virtual Learning Environments within Universities and Colleges*, Cheltenham: UCISA Teaching and Learning Information Group.

Jenkins, M., Browne, T. and Armitage, S. (2003) Management and Implementation of Virtual Learning Environments – A UCISA funded survey, Cheltenham: UCISA.

Knight, P.T. and Trowler, P.R. (2001) *Departmental Leadership in Higher Education* (H. Eggins, ed.), Buckingham: Society for Research into Higher Education/Open University Press.

Marshall, I.M., Sampson, W.B. and Dugard, P.I. (1995) Predicting the Developmental Effort of Multimedia Courseware, *Information and Software Technology*, 36(5): 251–8.

Moore, G.A. (1991) *Crossing the Chasm: Marketing and Selling High-Tech Goods to Mainstream Customers*, New York: HarperBusiness.

Phipps, L., Sutherland, A. and Seale, J. (2002) Access All Areas: Disability, Technology and Learning. JISC TechDis and ALT. On-line. Available HTTP http://www.techdis. ac.uk/accessallareas/AAA.pdf (accessed 22 November 2004).

Reisner, R.A. and Gagné, R.M. (1983) *Selecting Media for Instruction*, Upper Saddle River, NJ: Prentice Hall International.

Rogers, E.M. (1962) *Diffusion of Innovations*, New York: Free Press.

Rogers, E.M. and Scott, K.L. (1997) The Diffusion of Innovations Model and Outreach from the National Network of Libraries of Medicine to Native American Communities. On-line. Available HTTP http://nnlm.gov/pnr/eval/rogers.html (accessed 22 November 2004).

Sloan, M. (2001) Web Accessibility and the DDA, *Journal of Information, Law and Technology*, 2001(2). On-line. Available HTTP http://elj.warwick.ac.uk/jilt/01–2/ sloan.html (accessed 22 November 2004).

Social Informatics Research Unit (2003) Managed Learning Environment Activity in Further and Higher Education in the UK, Brighton: University of Brighton. On-line. Available HTTP http://www.jisc.ac.uk/uploaded_documents/mle-study-final-report.pdf (accessed 22 November 2004).

Tatar, D., Roschelle, J., Vahey, P. and Penuel, W.R. (2003) Handhelds Go To School: Lessons Learned, *Computer*, 36(9): 30–7.

Traxler, J. (2002) Developing Web-based Education using Information Systems Methodologies, in J. Grunspenkis (ed.), *Information Systems Development: Advances in Methodologies, Components and Management*, New York: Kluwer Press.

Traxler, J. (2003) *m-learning – Evaluating the Effectiveness and the Cost*, MLEARN 2003, London: LSDA.

Trowler, P.R. (1998) *Academics Responding to Change*, Milton Keynes: Society for Research into Higher Education/Open University Press.

Chapter 20

Conclusions

Agnes Kukulska-Hulme

The paradox facing mobile learning today is that devices that were not designed for learning are being used for learning. How successful is this undertaking? How far can one 'bend' the features of existing mobile devices and services to fit educational goals? And do planned learning activities have to be revised so that they fit with mobile technologies? These questions resonate with researchers as well as those who are engaged in teaching and training. Ahonen *et al.* (2003) ask whether a device such as a PDA, originally designed as a digital organizer, can really assist learning. If it cannot, then, they suggest, one has either to redesign elements of a course to fit the device's parameters, or press for technologies that correspond to the expectations of mobile learners.

On the whole, current mobile learning practice as represented in this book does not set out to measure learning gains, although there is typically an expectation that some aspect of learning will be improved. Future projects ought to address learning gains more directly, to gather evidence of what can be learnt using these devices. Project aims are often expressed in terms of wishing to explore, investigate or assess the application of mobile technologies with respect to enhancing or enabling teaching and learning. This chapter briefly reviews reasons for using mobile technologies and the benefits and pitfalls identified through experience. It then summarizes what is revealed about patterns of usage and changes in practice, and gives some reflections on emerging themes for the future.

Reasons for using mobile technologies

The dozen case studies in this book reveal a wide range of reasons for trying out and implementing mobile learning. Several are driven by practical concerns such as needing to deliver teaching and learning in a particular situation, or wanting to identify the practical problems of using mobile devices. Occasionally there is an explicit intention to push, develop or take advantage of mobile technology. In most cases, mobile devices are being used by educators and trainers to achieve one or more of the following aims:

- *Improve access*
  - Enhance access to assessment and learning materials.

- Give portable access to learning resources (e.g. medical reference works on the internet).
- Increase flexibility of learning for students.
- Implement the requirements for compliance with special educational needs and disability legislation.
- Develop and evaluate solutions for knowledge access in distributed training.

- *Evaluate and enhance learning*
  - Evaluate to what extent a mobile device can help student learning.
  - Explore the potential of the technology for collaborative learning.
  - Develop a model of how learners collaborate and learn using mobile on-line devices.
  - Identify the learning processes in distributed training.
  - Identify students' needs for just-in-time knowledge in training situations.
  - Explore the potential of the technology for increasing students' appreciation of their own learning processes.
  - Enable each student to keep a learning diary to help consolidate learning.

- *Evaluate and enhance teaching*
  - See how mobile devices could be used to teach a particular subject.
  - Guide students to think critically and to see differently than they would have without the use of mobile devices.
  - Give student designers the opportunity to experience and understand the use of mobile technology for learning.
  - Reduce cultural and communication barriers between instructors and students.
  - Remotely monitor performance, to check that students have adequate opportunities to practise the skills they have been taught.

- *Explore learners' requirements and behaviours*
  - Explore whether students need a similar set of tools as employees (e.g. electronic diary, notebook, to do list) to help them manage their studies.
  - Monitor when mobile technologies are used by students and for what purposes.
  - Investigate how mobile technology alters patterns of study and communication activity among students.
  - Assess experienced technology users' attitudes towards the new technology.
  - Investigate interface and usability limitations within an educational context.

- *Align with institutional or business aims*
  - Conduct a viability study for future larger-scale implementations of mobile learning devices.

- Evaluate relevance to MLE (managed learning environment) and VLE (virtual learning environment) programmes.
- Blend mobile technologies into e-learning infrastructures to improve interactivity and connectivity for the learner.
- Make wireless mobile interactive learning available to all students without incurring the expense of costly hardware.
- Distinguish oneself from other education providers or competitors.
- Deliver communications, information and training to large numbers of people regardless of their location.
- Extend mobile learning to include location tracking information services.
- Harness the proliferation of mobile phone services and their many users.

By addressing these aims and through the experience of implementing and evaluating their projects, our case study contributors have confirmed or discovered a number of benefits and some potential pitfalls. These are summarized in the next section, in the context of issues reviewed in other chapters of the book.

Benefits and pitfalls

Mobile devices that are in current use were designed as personal tools and that aspect can bring certain benefits. One way in which a device is understood as being personal is when it is customized by users storing personal content and data and installing applications that correspond to their particular needs. Another way in which it becomes personal is when content is delivered to learners in a customized form, again based on the needs of individuals (e.g. IBM's 'profiled notification'). Mobile devices also offer enhanced opportunities for learners to carry out independent (personal) investigations, perhaps in the context of fieldwork or educational excursions. A mobile device can allow students to experience learning wherever they happen to be.

Other contributors to this book have made the point that mobile learning makes e-learning more easily available to a wider range of participants. Some noticed that learners wanted to take a more active role in the learning experience. Students were able to participate in discussion boards and undertake on-line activities such as surveys and quizzes. Computer-aided assessment on a portable device provided the benefits of formative assessment available 'on demand'. It was found in the application of PDAs to music composition that handheld tools were of real benefit when learners used them to think critically about working creatively within a given set of device and software constraints. The benefits in healthcare were identified as the potential for mobile and wireless technology to support many functions on the go, such as documentation, communication, sharing memos, and accessing appropriate medical references when needed.

Potential pitfalls should be considered at the same time as benefits. Contributors have stated that mobile devices should save time, not create additional work. In other words, a risk has been identified that the technology may cause more problems than it solves. It would be fair to comment that such a risk is not specific to mobile devices, since it is well known in relation to more commonplace technologies; however there is a hint here that mobile devices might be more difficult to support or may be prone to more problems. One case study puts forward the view that there are 'clear costs' associated with being a technology leader, and this includes a willingness to accept some risk when trying out new approaches.

The success of mobile learning may well depend on the pedagogical tasks that the devices are used for, and on the integration of tasks within a well defined pedagogical approach. Conceptions of teaching and styles of learning will also be important factors. It has been suggested that teachers should specify in their proposals for using mobile technology what software is to be used on the devices and in what context. Indeed, this might encourage them to consider the suitability of what they are planning in relation to target students; for example, in a first-year undergraduate course, students are likely to have less well developed independent learning skills and may find it hard to switch away from using pen and paper and taking notes in a lecture. New students could be adjusting to life at a new place of learning and some may feel overwhelmed when faced with using an unfamiliar technology.

Other contributors suggest that some e-learning tasks are particularly suited to mobile learning: for example, tasks that are 'content light' and that require reflection and communication might be well suited to the use of PDAs, in particular if the learning process is based on a period of reflection followed by a dialogue with other learners. The risk here would be directly transferring tasks that have worked in other settings to a mobile environment without any thought being given to whether they need to be redesigned. On the other hand, mobile technologies may encourage cost-effective practices in which content is created once and delivered in many ways. In that case, the precise ways in which the content is delivered and how it is used by learners may need to be adjusted. We are also reminded that those providing mobile technology or mobile learning need to be aware of the needs of disabled students and integrate accessibility into initial development.

Other potential pitfalls surrounding mobile devices are that learners will reject technologies and learning materials, finding them unusable. In striving toward improved usability, new factors specific to mobile learning, outlined in this book, have to be taken into account. Familiarity with a device makes it easier to use, which means that usability is also connected to the issue of device ownership. This comes back to the fact, mentioned earlier, that mobile devices are 'personal'. There is a view that a mobile device is unlikely to be used to its full potential if it is only loaned to a student – in that case, it is a *portable*, but not a *personal* device. Students may be reluctant to spend time inputting personal data if they know they have to return the handheld at the end of the year or the end of the project. They may also dislike having to carry more than one device, for example a personal mobile phone and another device loaned out to them for a specific project. It has also been pointed out that it can take time for mature professional learners to absorb a new technology into their culture and in those circumstances a sense of ownership is important. Consequently, a loaned device may not be appropriated by its user or integrated into daily patterns of activity.

Patterns of use and changes in practice

Examples in this book have described how learners use mobile devices in very different settings, ranging from formal learning situations to more informal ones, e.g. at home or while commuting. It has been shown that employees can take advantage of 'downtime', e.g. small amounts of time between meetings, to download some materials and get on with learning. Since many university and college students nowadays are also working part-time, the time available for study has been reduced, so there appears to be more demand for an electronic learning resource that can be used during spare moments.

A case study reported here suggests that learners will access resources at any time of the day if given the opportunity. We should be careful not to assume that they will also want to receive information or resources at any time of day. Patterns of access and use also concern the timing of when text messages are sent and received, which will include the preferred time of day to receive messages from course administrators and teachers, the intervals between them, how many messages arrive and how often they are repeated.

Although flexibility regarding when learners can access materials and messages is rather appealing, the capabilities of current devices are not always up to the study patterns and requirements of many learners. This is exacerbated when less powerful, cheaper devices are used. Whilst some students are working part-time, others may be at university or college for up to eight hours a day. Even if they are not using a mobile device for that whole period, it may remain switched on for various reasons, including carelessness. Short battery life, in some cases less than two hours, is a real hindrance, and use of mains power for battery recharging has some obvious limitations. What is more, we have seen in one case study how students left their devices disconnected from mains power for longer periods during their vacations, which resulted in them losing all their software and data that had not been synchronized with a PC. Anyone preparing to ask students to synch their handheld device with centralized computers or servers on a regular basis should be aware that in case studies reported in this book, students could not be relied upon to do this regularly.

It should also be noted that it takes time for learners to settle into a pattern of use. One study reports how, at first, some students used their mobile device for everything, before realizing that some tasks were better done on a normal PC; others were sceptical to start with, but later became regular users. After ten months, the students had got to know the capabilities of their mobile devices and settled into a personal pattern of use. Although people are increasingly using their mobile devices to access e-mail, search the web, organize their time, read the news or access documents, their personal use of a mobile device may need to evolve to accommodate new learning practices.

It has been suggested in this book that mobile learning has the capacity to challenge much of conventional practice, including the need for education and training to take place at fixed times and at fixed physical locations; however, in practice several instances of mobile technology use are taking place within quite traditional settings. It does appear that we have yet to exploit the full potential of portable, multifunctional devices and their distinct characteristics, but we can already see some changes in practice.

The use of a PDA can offer a new dimension to face-to-face teaching, for example by enabling learners to participate in a discussion board during a lecture, with the teacher pausing from time to time to review and answer questions. This seems to be well received by students but for some it can be difficult to participate in this process and still keep up with the lecture. Learners may have to adapt their current learning strategies which may be focused on taking notes or annotating slides. Similarly, adaptation is needed on the part of educators and trainers. Ingenuity is often required in the production of course materials, for example having to devise questions within a specific character limit for delivery on mobile phones, or selecting websites with the knowledge that many of them do not render well on the small screens of mobile devices. We have seen in one case study how lecturers needed to be 'device aware', considering what their presentation would look like on a mobile device, and making any necessary adjustments. It has also been noted that just as in e-learning more generally, lecturers will find their working day being extended as portable devices enable them to work at home and in many other locations.

Sometimes there is little motivation to use a mobile device when there is relatively easy access to PCs or when other technologies are already very well embedded. In this book, we have seen an example of how an instant messaging service and the use of PDAs could not compete with an existing effective communication infrastructure of pagers and telephones in a hospital environment.

Themes for the future

As mobile devices acquire more and more features, both teachers and learners will need to develop their understanding of what facilities are needed and how they will be used in education or training. The findings from case studies presented in this book suggest, for example, that a Bluetooth or an all-in-one unit might be preferable to an infrared connection between a user's phone and PDA. Yet cramming more features into a device can make it more difficult to use, and simultaneously it may divert effort away from making it easier to use. It has been suggested that a collection of separate, specialized devices that performed their intended tasks well and could communicate with each other might be preferable. Other contributors put their faith in the next generation of mobile devices that are likely to have integrated wireless communication, streaming video, compatibility with desktop applications, and removable memory cards that can be transferred to other devices. Multimedia functions are expected to become more ubiquitous and less expensive, and mobile devices will be used for far more than current practice indicates.

Multipurpose devices have the potential to enrich the lives of disadvantaged groups, although the sheer speed of development and the current trend to design increasingly smaller gadgets may hinder advancements in accessibility. An optimistic outlook is that inclusively designed devices will become more widespread and there will be more innovative technology solutions for accessibility problems, with greater control given to users enabling them to make changes to the user interface. Currently, most mobile devices are not fully inclusive and have features that present difficulties for learners with disabilities.

A vast range of technical, usability and accessibility issues have been reviewed or signalled in this book. There is no consensus as to whether mobile devices are reliable, probably because several factors may enter into the equation. Certainly, synching issues between mobile devices and PCs or servers, problems with software and with connectivity are quite commonly reported. In several projects, technical support was a key aspect. It is recognized that if mobile devices were to be deployed in larger numbers, training and support could be significant overheads. Widespread use is likely to require a change in support mechanisms, with a more sophisticated support structure. A shift towards more self-help documentation and developing a culture of peer support are recommended. In the opinion of key usability specialists such as Nielsen (2003) and Weiss (2002), the current generation of mobile devices still lacks key usability features required for mainstream use. In this situation, users and prospective users of mobile devices have an important role to play in shaping the usability of future devices. Educators and trainers have a crucial role in asking whether the device they are planning to use has been tested in educational contexts and what tasks it was found to support most successfully, not forgetting that it is not just individual tasks that need to be supported: helping learners link together different elements of study appears to be a good way forward. At the same time, more effort needs to go into encouraging technology designers to work with educators and trainers. Learning technologists have been identified as fulfilling a useful role by bridging the barrier between technology and education.

Most of the work described in the case study projects is likely to continue in some form. Aspects for possible further research and evaluation include the following:

- What the ideal mobile learning device would be like, and how many types are needed.
- How to specify mobile learner requirements and assess mobile usability from a pedagogical point of view.
- The use of mobile devices as communication tools in education and training.
- The benefits and constraints of mobile technology for collaborative learning and for mentoring.
- Understanding learners' reasons for selecting particular technologies.
- Why devices are most valued, e.g. be it for reference, audio notes or location specific information.
- The role of mobile learning in support of e-learning, e.g. on courses with dispersed learners.
- Patterns and contexts of mobile use.
- Differences between use patterns across disciplines and across pedagogical approaches.

- New ways of recording learning experiences, e.g. applications involving reflective logs and personal development profiles.
- The sharing of content and annotations between mobile users.
- Creating gateways between networks, integrating parts of existing institutional, social and technical resources, and making them available on mobile devices.
- The provision of campus synch stations.
- The provision and display of new services, and facilities for downloading of manuals and course instructions.
- Portable speech recognition and text-to-speech software.

As noted in an earlier chapter, the possibility of institution-wide mobile learning raises issues concerned with introducing and managing change that involves technology, people and the organization, and affects the nature of work and study. The introduction of new technology brings with it many social and cultural changes, and in the case of mobile technologies, this is happening at a time when e-learning has not yet matured or become fully embedded in educational practice. Donofrio (2004) believes that future innovations will be pervasive and will be noticed through subtle improvements experienced by users, such as not having to do anything to stay connected to the web. Weller (2002) explains that 'the course of the future' will provide learners with material that can be viewed on different platforms, such as PCs, e-book readers and PDAs. From this perspective, mobile learning can be seen as part of a larger enterprise of on-line and distributed learning that is set to stabilize over time.

Educators and trainers can put forward visions of the kinds of learning activities they would like learners to engage in and how mobile devices and services can support this. However, at the same time, it is vital to be kept informed about where technology developments are heading, so that plans are not made in isolation from knowledge about the next generation of devices. Those who are involved with technical developments must realize the growing importance of mobile learning and must do more to communicate with education experts in terms that they can understand.

References

Ahonen, M., Joyce, B., Leino, M. and Turunen, H. (2003) Mobile Learning – A Different Viewpoint, 29–39, in Kynäslahti, H. and Seppälä, P. (eds) *Mobile Learning*, Finland: Edita IT Press.
Donofrio, N. (2004) When Invention Turns to Innovation. Report by Jo Twist, BBC News, Science and Technology. On-line. Available HTTP http://news.bbc.co.uk/1/hi/technology/3965265.stm (accessed 10 November 2004).
Nielsen, J. (2003) Mobile Devices: One Generation from Useful. On-line. Available HTTP http://www.useit.com/alertbox/20030818.html (accessed 16 November 2004).
Weiss, S. (2002) *Handheld Usability*, Chichester: John Wiley & Sons.
Weller, M. (2002) *Delivering Learning on the Net: The Why, What and How of Online Education*, London: Kogan Page.

Glossary

Simon Rae

Terms in bold appear elsewhere in the glossary.

2G, 3G, 4G as in Second Generation, Third Generation etc. Method of categorising the facilities available on mobile phones/**wireless** internet devices. Successive generations are afforded more capabilities, e.g. higher data rate, by improved technologies and/or infrastructures. First Generation phones were early analogue voice systems succeeded by a Second Generation (2G portable/mobile phones) that took advantage of **GSM** capabilities. 2G mobile phones are capable of sending **SMS** text messages and photos and receiving **text alerts**. 2.5G is usually linked with **GPRS** functionality and is a halfway house towards 3G with 100 MB/sec speed, video and **location-awareness**. 4G is the next stage in the development.

Ambient Intelligence An encompassing electronic environment that is aware of and responsive to the presence of people within it. Sensor, mobile, and computer technology 'in the background' reacts and adapts to people's everyday activities. (See also **Ubiquitous**.)

Beam, Beaming Sending information or data from one **wireless device** to another device via an **infrared** or radio wave transmission, e.g. from a **PDA** to a desktop computer.

Bite-size Gobbets of information designed to be short enough to be readable on a **Pocket PC** or mobile phone, for example about 800 words plus a couple of pictures.

Bluetooth An open technology specification backed by several key mobile and networking players, for short-range radio transmission of data between **wireless devices**. Bluetooth works over a radio frequency (rather like a remote control model plane) that allows data transfer through obstacles over distances of ten metres (unlike **infrared beaming** which needs a clear line between devices). Bluetooth-enabled devices can communicate with each other when they come in range and, for example, can automatically update or synchronise address books, play lists and calendars.

Broadband A high-speed, multi-channel data transmission. The point at which the speed of data transmission deserves to be called broadband, as opposed to narrowband, is undefined but is commonly taken to be at least ten times faster than a simple 56K connection to the internet via a phone-line. Broadband connections to the internet via a home phone-line can be 'always on' and will not disable the use of the phone.

Cached   Information or data that has been stored somewhere that can be accessed more quickly or more easily than by going back to the source. Often used in terms of cached web pages stored in local, high-speed memory on a **PDA** that are quicker to access than connecting and **downloading** the pages again.

Connectivity   The ability to connect a device electronically with other devices, for example, a **PDA** with a printer or the internet. The connection can be achieved via electrical wires, **infrared**, phone lines or radio waves. Losing connectivity implies going **off-line**.

Coverage   The specific area in which a mobile phone or **wireless device** can make and receive calls or transmit and receive data.

Cradle   A device in which a **PDA** or **wireless device** is placed so that it can **sync** with a desktop computer. The cradle is connected to the desktop via a serial or **USB** cable and can also be used to recharge the device's batteries.

Download   To download something means to get a copy of it from another computer via a network, and save it on your own device, e.g. to download an **e-book** onto your **PDA**.

E-book, E-text   A digital or electronic version of a book or text, often formatted to make available better functionality (e.g. searching) on the **e-book reader** to which it is **downloaded**.

E-book reader   A device that enables an **e-book** to be read. Can be a dedicated device, i.e. reading e-books is all that it can facilitate, or an application on a PC or **handheld** device that facilitates the reading of e-books.

EMS   Enhanced Message Service, an evolution of **SMS**. EMS messages can include pictures, animations and sound effects as well as formatted text.

Flash/Compact Flash   Flash memory retains its data even when its power is removed. Removable Compact Flash cards can be used in devices for storage or to add modem, fax, or networking functionality.

Form Factor   The general size and shape of a **handheld** device.

GPRS   General Packet Radio Service is an enhancement to **GSM** that supports larger messages than **SMS** and faster data transfer rates and is a point between **2G** and **3G**. GPRS mobile phone users can effectively maintain a continuous connection to the internet but they only pay for the amount of data transferred. As the GPRS network works alongside the **GSM** network, users can handle voice calls without interrupting their GPRS internet session.

GPS   Global Positioning System, a satellite-based radio positioning system providing 24/7 out-of-doors location information. Controlled by the United States Department of Defence and freely available, GPS-enabled **wireless devices** 'know where they are' to within 30 metres.

Graffiti   Proprietary handwriting/character recognition software used by **PalmOS** that allows users to 'write' data into their **handheld** device using a **stylus** on a **touch screen**.

GSM Global System for Mobile communication is a 2G mobile phone network enabling a high quality and secure voice and data transfer service with **roaming** facilities. GSM also provides **SMS**. GSM was introduced in 1991 and is the dominant standard in Europe and Asia. GSM mobile phones depend on a **SIM** smart card that contains the user's account information.

Handheld A hand-sized computer that can be kept in a pocket and is easily used while being held, e.g. a **palmtop**, a pager, a mobile phone, a **PDA** etc.

Infrared Handheld devices can **beam** information or data to other devices via an infrared beam without being connected, similar to the way that some video/ TV controllers work. Unlike **Bluetooth**, data transmission between **infrared ports** requires a clear line-of-sight.

Infrared port With two infrared ports facing each other, data can be **beamed** from one **wireless device** to another via an **infrared** beam, e.g. between two mobile phones.

Location-aware A location-aware device knows where it is (see **GPS**) and can respond to the user's location, either spontaneously by reacting to transmitting devices in the local proximity or when initiated by the user's request for information. Such a device could provide local information (e.g. the nearest open garage) or connect to the nearest available **wireless device**.

Memory Stick A Sony proprietary **Flash** memory system used for temporary storage or for transferring data between devices such as **PDAs**, cameras and **MP3** players.

MMDS Multichannel Multipoint Distribution Service, facilitates two-way voice, data and **video streaming**. It facilitates **wireless, broadband** access and can provide internet **connectivity** or television. It requires a direct line of sight between the server and the client device. MMDS is often preferred when the laying of cables is not economically viable.

MMS Multimedia Messaging Service, a further evolutionary upgrade of **EMS** and **SMS** capable of handling pictures and text, sound and video. MMS-enabled mobile phones can take a picture and send it to anyone with internet **connectivity** or another MMS phone.

MP3 A standard for compressing, storing and transmitting music that has been converted to a digital format while preserving adequate sound quality. MP3 music files can be transmitted over the internet, downloaded and played back on an MP3 player.

On-line/Off-line Being connected/not being connected to a network, e.g. the internet via wires, **infrared**, phone lines or radio waves.

PalmOS PalmOS software is the proprietary operating system developed for Palm **handhelds** and licensed for used on many other third-party **PDAs**.

Palmtop A generic name for any small computer or **wireless device** that fits the palm of your hand, also known as a **PDA**, a **handheld** or a 'handy'. They usually include handwriting/character recognition software for data entry via a **touch screen** and **stylus** or they have a built-in keyboard. Functionality includes word processing, games, and **connectivity** with the internet affording e-mail and web browsing facilities. Palmtops are especially useful for certain functions e.g. address books, calendars and **PIMs**. They can usually **synch** with other devices e.g. a desktop computer via a **cradle**, a **USB** or an **infrared port**.

PDA   Personal Digital Assistant, a generic term that applies to a wide variety of **handheld** devices. PDA functionality usually includes **PIM**, a digital calendar, an address book, memo pad, note taking facilities and to-do lists with input via a keyboard or **touch screen** and **stylus**. PDAs are increasingly combining with mobile phone functionality and internet **connectivity**.

PIM   Personal Information Management, functionality for devices that organises personal information, such as addresses, dates, scheduling and task lists.

Pocket PC   A proprietary operating system for **handheld** devices developed by Microsoft, often licensed to run on third-party devices in competition with **PalmOS**. Facilitates internet **connectivity**, word processing, spreadsheet, handwriting recognition, and **e-book** reading.

Predictive Texting   A feature built into many mobile phones that enables the phone to 'guess' the next word of the text message from the first letters keyed in.

Roaming   Affords the ability to use a mobile phone outside its country of purchase. The phone will scan the available networks and connect to any that your **service provider** has a roaming agreement with.

Service Provider   A company that provides access to a network e.g. an Internet Service Provider (ISP) or a mobile phone network.

SIM Card   Subscriber Information Module, the small smart card that clicks into a mobile phone that contains the phone's unique ID, number, **service provider** details and directory etc.

Smartphone   A **palmtop** device combining the features of a mobile phone and a **PDA**.

SMS   Short Message Service, allows **GSM**-enabled mobile phone users to send and receive text messages up to 160 characters long; also known as **text messaging**. An unexpectedly popular method of sending and receiving individual messages: on New Year's Day 2005, 133 million text messages were sent in the UK. (See also **Text alerts**.)

Streaming, Video Streaming   A technique that allows a server to transfer data so that a client can process it continuously, i.e. with video streaming, the server begins sending the video data which the client can start to display before the entire transmission has finished.

Stylus   A small pen-like instrument for pointing or writing on a **handheld**'s **touch screen**.

Synch, Synching   The act of synchronising the data between two devices, usually between a **handheld** device and a laptop or desktop computer, e.g. to make sure that your calendar on your **PDA** and on your desktop computer are the same. Synching is usually done using a **cradle** to copy the data between the connected devices. The process can also be used to create a backup of any data on the **palmtop** on the desktop computer.

Tablet PC   A type of laptop computer that has a **touch screen** resting flat on top of the computer's main hardware components. Data is entered through the **touch screen**, although a keyboard, mouse or other accessories may be incorporated.

Text Alerts   Short text messages automatically sent out to subscribing mobile phones by information providers, e.g. the sports results as they happen or a regular feed of revision questions – with answers a day later.

Text Messaging, Texting   See **SMS**.

Touch Screen   Screens that are touch sensitive so that icons or symbols displayed on the screen may be touched or tapped with a **stylus** to invoke the action defined by the icon, e.g. tap the Address Book icon to display the list of contacts.

Ubiquitous   Ubiquitous computing looks to a time when our **wireless devices** will respond to information transmitted to them from countless devices embedded in the environment and generate dynamic models of the current situation, recall past situations and offer potential solutions to anticipated needs or problems.

USB   Universal Serial Bus, a way for **handheld** devices to connect with desktop computers via a USB cable. USB-enabled devices support plug-and-play and hot plugging, i.e. the computer automatically recognises when any USB device is plugged into it and can support a fast enough data transfer speed to be suitable for use with video.

VoiceXML   A Markup Language that allows developers to define and handle audio dialogues that feature synthesised speech, digitised audio and spoken input so enabling voice activated services. VoiceXML technology will allow users to interact with pre-recorded or computer-synthesised voice services via voice-recognition technology from a mobile phone.

WAP   Wireless Application Protocol, facilitates a cut-down, small-screen version of the internet that affords **connectivity** for mobile phones and **PDAs**. WAP is a standard that describes a display interface for **handheld** devices and affords Wireless Markup Language (**WML**), a reduced version of HTML, and WMLScript, a JavaScript-like language.

WAP push   WAP push functionality enables **SMS** messages containing embedded **WAP** links to be sent and received. It allows **text alerts** to direct readers to further information on a **WAP** page.

Web Clipping   Web clipping applications extract the relevant information from a web page so that it can be displayed on a **smartphone**, a **PDA** or other small **form factor** and **wireless** devices.

Wi-Fi   Wi-Fi, or Wireless Fidelity, is a set of standards for facilitating wireless networks in a local area and enables those with Wi-Fi enabled devices to connect to the internet when in range of an access point (often available in internet cafés, airports and libraries etc.).

Wireless Access   The ability to access networks (usually the internet) from a device without being connected via a wire or cable. (See also **Wi-Fi**.)

Wireless Device   A device that operates normally without being connected to anything else via a wire or cable, e.g. a mobile phone, **PDA**, **handheld** or **smartphone**.

WML   Wireless Markup Language is used to create **WAP** content.

XDA   A proprietary **wireless device** integrating the functionality of a mobile phone and a **PDA**, including internet **connectivity**, e-mail, word processing, voice-recorder and **MP3** player using the **Pocket PC** operating system via a **GPRS** connection. XDA II devices are **Bluetooth**-enabled and are marketed outside the UK under a variety of other names, for example Qtek 2020 and i-mate.

Index

Windows Journal application 51
Wireless Application Protocol (WAP) 32,
    150, 152
wireless-enabled public spaces 15;
    wireless campus 152, 174; wireless
    connectivity 150; Wireless Fidelity
    (Wi-Fi) 15
word searches 8

WordSmith 125
workplace learning 37

XDA 116–17
XTNDConnect 158

young adults 35